THE

REFERENCE

SHELF

IMMIGRATION TO THE U.S.

Edited by ROBERT EMMET LONG

THE REFERENCE SHELF

Volume 64, Number 4

THE H. W. WILSON COMPANY

New York   1992

THE REFERENCE SHELF

The books in this series contain reprints of articles, excerpts from books, and addresses on current issues and social trends in the United States and other countries. There are six separately bound numbers in each volume, all of which are generally published in the same calendar year. One number is a collection of recent speeches; each of the others is devoted to a single subject and gives background information and discussion from various points of view, concluding with a comprehensive bibliography that contains books and pamphlets and abstracts of additional articles on the subject. Books in the series may be purchased individually or on subscription.

Library of Congress Cataloging-in-Publication Data

Immigration to the U.S. / edited by Robert Emmet Long.
    p.   cm. — (The Reference shelf ; v. 64, no. 4)
    Includes bibliographical references.
    ISBN 0-8242-0828-5
    1. United States—Emigration and immigration.   2. United States—Emigration and immigration—Government policy. I. Long, Robert Emmet.   II. Title: Immigration to the US.   III. Series.
JV6455.I559   1992
325.73—dc20   92-28399
                                                                          CIP

Cover: A group of Haitian refugees, arriving by boat to a beach in Florida, await a bus that will take them to Miami.
Photo: AP/Wide World Photos/Mike Brown

Printed in the United States of America

CONTENTS

PREFACE

In recent years a tidal wave of immigration has been sweeping over many parts of the globe. In Europe, immigrants from the Balkans and other regions of Eastern Europe have poured into Germany in search of employment and a higher standard of living. The collapse of Communism in the Soviet Union has brought far-reaching changes, including a removal of restrictions on immigration for Soviet Jews, who have been coming to Israel and the United States in vastly increasing numbers. In addition to legal immigration, vast numbers of others—in Africa, the Far East, and Central America—now seek asylum as refugees. Living on the edge of starvation, in many cases, or in political repression, or both they make up something like fifteen million people. The goal of many of them is to be admitted to the United States, a situation that poses acute problems for the government's Immigration and Naturalization Service (INS).

Since only a fraction of those desiring to settle here can be accommodated, what should be the criteria for deciding who shall be admitted and who not? Should certain countries have preference over others? Should priority be given to immigrants wishing to be reunited with their family members already here, or should those with capital to invest in the country, or others with skills needed for science and industry, be put at the front of the line? All of these questions, together with many others relating to immigration, are examined in this collection of articles.

Section One concerns refugees and illegal aliens from the Caribbean and Central America who have been seeking asylum in the U.S. in large numbers. Often they are fleeing from regimes they feel threaten their safety, but as several of the articles point out, it is not easy to gauge whether they are truly at risk or are merely seeking a higher standard of living. Complicating matters further, the INS has favored the admission of refugees from certain countries at odds with the United States, such as Nicaragua, over those from other countries with which we have amicable relations, such as El Salvador, Guatemala, and Haiti. Critics charge that such preferential treatment is illogical and unjust. Two articles in this section focus on the passage to Miami of boat people from Cuba and Haiti; and two other articles consider the subject of friction between blacks and hispanics in Miami, and the transformation of the city into a center for companies doing business in Latin America.

Section Two treats the subject of illegal immigration from Mexico into the southwestern states, particularly California and Texas, over the past two decades. The articles dispel the notions that the illegals damage the social system, deprive native workers of their jobs, and are a drain on the economy, but also present first-hand narratives of the often brutal conditions that illegals encounter when they cross the border and enter detention camps of the Rio Grande Valley. Also considered are the implications of the free-trade pact now being negotiated between Mexico and the U.S., particularly as it bears on immigration.

Section Three covers refugees and other immigrants from Southeast Asia. The articles generally agree that these newcomers have much to offer the country. A final article notes the manner in which immigration from Asia has affected life in the city of Los Angeles, making it a trading center with the Far East.

The final section of this compilation illuminates the debate over immigration policy in general. One of the pieces expresses some doubt that the new immigrants can be assimilated by American society as effectively as the immigrants who came here at the turn of the twentieth century, but other articles take a decidedly positive view of the new immigration, arguing that the newcomers offer youth, vitality, and a drive toward upward mobility that will be needed as the country's overall population ages and as a larger labor force is required to maintain the nation's competitive edge in the international market place. Despite opposition to immigrants by some, particularly in a period of recession, the articles in this section offer confidence that the melting pot concept still works and brings immeasurable benefits.

The editor is indebted to the authors and publishers who have granted permission to reprint the materials in this collection. Special thanks are due to Joyce Cook and the Fulton (N.Y.) Public Library staff, and to the staff of Penfield Library, State University of New York College at Oswego.

ROBERT EMMET LONG

June 1992

I. REFUGEES FROM THE CARIBBEAN AND CENTRAL AMERICA

EDITOR'S INTRODUCTION

The opening section of this compilation focuses upon the influx into America, particularly Florida and the southwestern states, of immigrants from the Caribbean and Central America. This large-scale migratory movement has stirred controversy and put a strain on schools, hospitals, and social services. Moreover, the problem, has been compounded by the fact that many of these newcomers are illegal aliens many of whom are sent back to the countries from which they came, but others of whom are permitted to remain on a temporary basis that may stretch out for a period of years. The first article in this section, by Antonio Fins in *Business Week,* indicates the scope of such immigration: over 200,000 Haitians have arrived in Miami as illegals, while half a million Salvadorans live in Texas and California.

In the second article, reprinted from *The Progressive,* Jane Juffer discusses the Immigration and Naturalization Service's containment of refugees and illegals in the Rio Grande Valley. Because local governments have objected to the presence of illegals, the INS has established a large detention center where illegals, who have been denied asylum and lack bond money, are likely to spend long periods of time behind bars. The third article, by Jill Smolowe writing in *Time,* discusses the plight of the Haitian boat people, over 10,000 of whom have been held in a detention camp in the U.S. naval base at Guantánamo, Cuba, and now face deportation to Port-au-Prince. Next, an article by Howard W. French, from *The New York Times,* sheds light on immigration from the Caribbean countries, which export more of its people in terms of percentage than any other place in the world.

The increasing volume of boat people from Cuba is the subject of the next article, from *Newsweek* and written by Spencer Reiss. With the collapse of Communism in the Soviet Union, Cuba without Soviet economic aid has been particularly hard-pressed.

Thousands of Cubans have been attempting the 90-mile journey to Key West on inner-tube rafts and homemade boats.

In an article in *Time,* Alex Prud'homme reports on one of the consequences of the sharp increase in the number of Hispanics in Miami—namely, the friction that has developed between them and blacks. Blacks charge that they have been discriminated against by Miami's dominant Hispanics. The city of Miami is the focus of the final article in this section, by Gail De George writing in *Business Week.* De George points out that Hispanics—including not only Cubans but also Nicaraguans, Colombians, and Venezuelans—now make up nearly half of Miami's metropolitan population. This ethnic composition has had the effort of reshaping the business life of the city and attracting a large number of companies who do business in Central and South America.

THE BATTERING RAM AT
THE GOLDEN DOOR

The sound of gunfire, said Pedro Antonio Garcia, made him feel as if he were back home in Managua. In reality, the 39-year-old, his wife, daughter, and 250 other Nicaraguans were huddled in a Miami baseball stadium set up as temporary housing. Within earshot, angry Miamians were pelting riot police with rocks and burning cars and buildings in the city's black Overtown section. "It's not what I expected," Garcia allowed, "but I still feel lucky to be here."

A former traveling salesman and jack-of-all-trades in economically strapped Nicaragua, Garcia claims that he was beaten there by state-sponsored paramilitary troops. He is among growing numbers of people all over the world who are seeking safe harbor in the U.S. as victims or likely targets of political persecution. Thousands of emigrés from Central America and the Caribbean are making their way here first, and then seeking political asylum. They are overwhelming the cities to which they flock—

Article by Antonio Fins, staff writer, from *Business Week* 52–3+ F 6 '89. Copyright © 1989 by McGraw-Hill, Inc. Reprinted with permission.

nowhere more than Miami, "*la capital del exilio,*" where blacks already frustrated by Hispanic political power now see themselves competing with new arrivals for scarce jobs, housing, and resources.

Work Permits

Yet most of these newcomers will be refused asylum—and their plight shows up the failures and inconsistencies of U.S. immigration policy. In theory, the U.S. opens its doors to all those fleeing state repression, a goal strongly linked to American idealism. In practice, though, quotas are set for every national group, and rarely evenhandedly: Those fleeing governments the U.S. opposes are often more warmly embraced than are those who suffer at the hands of this nation's friends.

The refugee problem stems in part from attempts to control illegal immigrants. The Immigration Reform & Control Act of 1986 placed stiff sanctions on employers who hire illegal aliens. But whether that has done much to reduce new arrivals from Central America is a matter of controversy. Repression in the region is escalating. Many simply turn to the refugee laws instead. Indeed, after the 1986 law was passed, applications for political asylum by Salvadorans rose tenfold. One reason: Asylum application brings a work permit, valid as long as the case is tied up, and appeals can last years. "The word all over Central America is to get to the U.S. any way you can," says U.S. Representative Dante B. Fascell, who heads the House Foreign Affairs Committee.

Many illegal aliens, of course, are afraid to apply for asylum, some believing they have no case. Some 20,000 Haitians in Miami are trying their luck as illegals. So are at least half a million Salvadorans in Texas and California. But more than 70,000 new asylum cases are pending. The foreigners continue to come and apply even though the INS, under Commissioner Alan C. Nelson, eventually turns down nearly all of them.

Rickety boats crammed with Haitians are interdicted on the high seas. Those who get through and apply for asylum are held in an INS prison camp on the edge of the Florida Everglades, reviewed, refused, and deported. Salvadorans, too, face almost certain deportation at the end of the appeals process, which can last for years.

Thousands of Nicaraguans also are fleeing their war-torn country. Despite the U.S. anti-Sandinista crusade, there has been

no heroes' welcome. They remain in immigration limbo while
their applications are processed. But Nicaraguans, unlike Haitians and Salvadorans, have made friends in high places. Nicaraguan groups have been challenging INS and State Department
policies—and their lobbying may soon pay off. . . .

Three Strikes

Political considerations certainly shape refugee policy. One of
[President Ronald] Reagan's last Presidential acts was to transfer
7,000 slots marked for refugees from Vietnam, Thailand, Cambodia, and Laos next year to Soviet Jewish emigrés. Contrast that
to the treatment of refugees from Haiti, where wholesale human-
rights violations have been documented by the Congressional Research Service and human-rights groups. "Haitians have three
strikes against them," notes a cynical [Fritz] Longchamp [of the
Haitian Refugee Center in Washington]. "Their government is
friendly to the U.S. They are poor. And they are black."

While diplomacy is on the side of the Nicaraguans, they have
further learned the art of political maneuvering. The Nicaraguan
American Bankers Association, mostly U.S.-educated business
leaders who left Nicaragua after the 1979 Sandinista triumph,
have taken their compatriots' case to top-level Republicans. They
backed George Bush's Presidential bid with money and volun-
teers—passing out flyers and Florida oranges in New Hampshire.
INS Miami district director Perry Rivkind is an advocate. In 1987
he arbitrarily stopped deporting Nicaraguans—claiming he
lacked manpower.

Critics of such maneuvering cite the 1980 Refugee Act. It
mandates that asylum rulings be independent of U.S. approval of
the foreign government in question. They argued that adhering
to the act would actually reduce immigration, by excluding those
who, though coming from dictatorial states, are in fact economic
refugees.

Meanwhile, an out-of-date INS infrastructure is overwhelmed
by the sheer numbers. Immigration lawyers in Miami throw up
their hands at having to report to regional offices in Dallas. "What
does anyone in Dallas know about what's going on here?" asks
Miami immigration attorney Michael A. Bander. Arthur Helton,
a director of the Lawyers Committee for Human Rights, wants
political asylum cases handled by a new office. "It would separate

duties," he says. "State could care for foreign policy, and INS could go back to law enforcement."

Ultimately, the U.S. must face the issue of just how many refugees it can take. Warren R. Leiden, executive director of the American Immigration Lawyers Association, says the U.S. should "look to our neighbors to get them to shoulder some of the burden. After all, these people are walking through several other countries to get here."

For cities on the asylum route, the burden can be huge. In Dallas, some 50,000 Salvadorans are straining the resources of food banks and shelters. Los Angeles is coping with as many as half a million Salvadoran illegals. Last year [1988], the federal government provided $347 million to aid 64,000 official refugees.

Housing Crunch

Nowhere have the ramifications been more dramatic than in Miami's melting pot, where tempers are boiling. Refugees from Asia and Eastern Europe, often sponsored by voluntary organizations before they arrive, are resettled into homes and jobs across the U.S. But most Hispanic and Caribbean Basin refugees head for south Florida. In mid-January [1989], hundreds of Nicaraguans cruised into Miami on Greyhound buses offering special one-way fares from Brownsville, Tex. Miami already was trying to find housing for homeless Nicaraguans and clear the streets in time for the Super Bowl.

Private groups in Miami are helping with emergency housing, but hundreds of refugees are homeless—in addition to the thousands of street people who flock to southern Florida each winter. Affordable housing is in short supply, new school buildings are overenrolled before they open, and day-care services and hospitals are taxed beyond the limit.

"It's a totally unfair burden," says Monsignor Bryan Walsh of the Catholic Archdiocese of Miami, which is providing apartments for some 140 Nicaraguan emigrés. Struggling with its social problems, Miami is caught in the crossfire of a refugee policy that has been incoherent and unenforceable. "Our country has been very generous," says Fascell. "But we can't handle everybody's excess, everybody's overflow." The hard question is where to draw the line.

ROUNDUP ON THE RIO GRANDE

It has never been easy for a Central American entering the United States in southern Texas to pursue a claim to political asylum. But as of February 21 [1989], the task became impossible—unless the claim is pursued from behind the barbed-wire fences of the Immigration and Naturalization Service detention center.

All Central Americans who file "invalid claims" for asylum are now immediately arrested and detained. Previously, many were allowed to initiate paperwork in the Rio Grande Valley, then join families and support systems elsewhere in the United States to await their hearings.

The new policy is intended to be a "strong signal" to people who file "frivolous asylum claims" with the idea of staying in the United States, INS [Immigration and Naturalization Service] Commissioner Alan C. Nelson said.

But such signals won't work so long as U.S.-funded wars continue to destroy economies and lives in Central America. Proof of that is the failure of the vaunted 1986 Immigration Reform and Control Act, which was intended to cut off the flow of "illegal aliens" by fining employers who hired them. The INS crowed about the Act's success in 1987, when the number of Border Patrol arrests fell, but now, in the midst of increasing refugee entries, hardly a word is heard about that law.

Refugee advocates in the Valley doubt that the latest warning sent South will be any more effective. "It's an extremely inhumane policy which is not going to discourage people from fleeing Central America and coming to the United States," says Jonathan Moore, who works with Proyecto Libertad, the only nonprofit refugee legal-aid group in the Valley. "It's only going to discour-

Article by Jane Juffer, an associate editor of Pacific News Service, from *The Progressive* 53:32–3 Ap '89. Copyright © 1989 by *The Progressive*. Reprinted with permission.

age people from presenting themselves to the immigration service."

The new policy sends a soothing message to local residents, who in the past four months have been increasingly resentful of INS policies. For three years, the INS has been using the entire lower Rio Grande Valley as a de-facto detention center for refugees apprehended but released on their own recognizance and not allowed to travel outside the Valley. Gradually, the number of homeless refugees awaiting INS decisions on their cases has increased, and in December, when the agency forced yet another group of refugees to remain in the Valley, the numbers grew to the thousands. Local governments could not ignore the fact that INS policy was turning the Valley into a holding pen and demanded that the INS take responsibility for getting the refugees off the streets and out of the abandoned homes and hotels.

Under the new asylum procedure, refugees must submit their claims to an INS adjudicator and await the decision. Those denied asylum are immediately incarcerated and held for deportation. All this happens in one day at the INS detention center, twenty-five miles from the nearest Valley city of any size.

Refugees who want to enter their asylum claims must walk or hitchhike through isolated countryside to arrive at the detention center. They may even be arrested by the Border Patrol on their way to turn themselves in, but upon denial of their claim they are arrested anyway. Virtually all claims will be denied. On the first day of the new policy, 233 claims were heard and only two refugees, both Nicaraguans, received asylum. The rest were detained on bonds of at least $4,000.

Refugees whose claims are denied may bring them before an immigration judge in a courtroom, but unless they can raise the bond money they are likely to spend months—perhaps years—behind bars. Before the policy was enacted, refugees seeking asylum entered their claim at the INS office in Harlingen and often received permission to travel. That made it much easier for them to pursue asylum in court, and though many claims were eventually denied, the refugees gained a one- or two-year reprieve from the war zone and perhaps earned some wages.

The prospect of months in prison will cause more refugees to accept deportation orders, says E. J. Flynn, one of two lawyers with Proyecto Libertad [Project Liberty]. "They are forcing people with strong [asylum] claims into an unwinnable dilemma."

Who are these people whose claims are being deemed invalid

by the INS? According to Proyecto paralegals who interviewed some of the refugees on the first day of the new policy, those denied on the spot included:

• A Salvadoran man whose brother was dragged from their home by a group of armed men. The men, whom the Salvadoran believes to have been guerrillas, threatened him before killing the brother, cutting off his head, and mounting it on a stake outside the house.

• A Guatemalan Indian from the violence-ridden region of Quiche. One of his brothers disappeared last year and another in 1981.

• A Honduran woman whose brother was an activist in a union of electrical workers. Her brother has been forced to go into hiding because DNI, the Honduran investigative police, came to their house looking for him. The woman saw DNI shoot a young man and plant a gun on him. Also, DNI tortured a friend of the woman with electric shock.

While Proyecto lawyers will represent these individuals and others at their eventual asylum hearings in court, many more will go unrepresented. With the new policy, the INS has received funding to increase detention-center capacity from about 500 to 3,000. The INS claims it could hold up to 5,000, using contracted facilities, county jails, and other detention centers in the Southwest. Aside from Proyecto, only a handful of Valley attorneys provide legal assistance to refugees; probono aid is extremely rare.

Word travels fast in refugee circles. In the first week of the new policy, the number of applications dropped from 233 the first day to about eighty the next three days combined. Of all those, only three—all Nicaraguans—received asylum. Escape from the Valley has been made more difficult with the addition of 269 Border Patrol officers, almost doubling the previous force.

Local residents are pleased that the "eyesore" has been moved from the streets to the scrubland. Previously, refugees applied for asylum at an office building in Harlingen. In recent months, hundreds of refugees camped out around the building in an effort to obtain the interviews that would, at least, result in permission to travel. Harlingen city officials finally evicted the INS for violating sanitation regulations.

Traditionally, local officials have worked hand-in-hand with Border Patrol and INS officials to control the "illegal alien" problem. For the last three years, local governments have virtually

ignored the fact that INS policy has stranded up to 5,000 refugees at a time in the Valley, the poorest area in the whole country.
If refugees were arrested when the detention center was full, the
INS released them on their own recognizance but prohibited
them from leaving the seven-county Valley unless they could post
a $3,000 bond. Now these people, too, will be removed from the
streets.

The new policy is another step toward the complete isolation
of the Rio Grande Valley. With the Gulf of Mexico to the east and
the Mexican border running diagonally to the west, the Valley is
cut off from the rest of the United States like a slice of pie. Only
two highways lead north, and both are heavily guarded by Border
Patrol agents. At the top of the Valley sits the huge King Ranch,
its miles of rough terrain a formidable deterrent to anyone who
tries to skirt Border Patrol checkpoints on foot.

Until recently, the Valley has also been shielded from the national news media. The unwelcome publicity that erupted at the
height of the winter tourist season, combined with the local resentment of INS policies and pressure from refugee advocates,
raised the possibility that the INS might be forced to stop treating
the Valley as its private testing ground. For the past decade, the
INS has taken advantage of the isolation to enforce such policies
as these:

• In the early 1980s, the Valley INS office responded to the
rising number of asylum applications by virtually shutting down
its office for those claimants. Central Americans who tried to
apply for asylum were either shooed away or arrested and
detained.

• In 1985, the INS began to restrict those refugees released
on their own recognizance; within about a year, these refugees
could not leave the Valley without paying a $1,000 bond; within
two years, the bond had risen to $3,000. Harlingen is the only
INS district in the country to have had such a policy.

• In the fall of 1987, the Harlingen INS began to accept
affirmative asylums—but only because then-Attorney General
Edwin Meese had issued a public directive urging INS offices to
give special treatment to Nicaraguans fleeing the "communist
regime." The resulting high rate of asylum approval for Nicaraguans (84 per cent in 1987, 53 per cent in 1988) contributed as
much to the influx from that country as the deteriorating Nicaraguan economy.

• Finally, in the spring of 1988, the office also began to accept non-Nicaraguan claims. Having ignored this population of asylum seekers for years, the INS office was unprepared for the flood of applicants—28,000 between May 30 and December 15. The influx is understandable, given the troubles in Central America, but it does not warrant increased militarization of the border.

Faced with the flood of applications, the INS decided last December that its policy of allowing refuges to travel after filing a claim was acting as a drawing card, so it prohibited these refugees from leaving the Valley. Limited refugee-shelter space quickly filled up; thousands of refugees were forced onto the streets, into makeshift tents and abandoned hotels. Some Valley residents tried to provide food and clothing; local officials petitioned the Federal Government for assistance.

Refugee advocates sued to allow the refugees to travel, and Federal District Judge Filemon Vela granted a temporary restraining order on the INS policy which allowed refugees to travel until February 20, when the INS would again be able to restrict refugees to the Valley. By then the INS was ready with a policy that mollified local residents and gave it the excuse to shut its doors again on refugees who wish to report to its office to seek asylum.

"The new policy is a total gutting of our respect for the asylum process and international law," says Flynn, the Proyecto attorney. "The United States had two options. It could have conceded that people were coming here for good reason and given them refuge, or it could have slammed the door in people's faces. It chose the latter option."

SHOWING THEM THE WAY HOME

By the hundreds, Haitian boat people in search of asylum in the U.S. were delivered by Coast Guard cutters back to Port-au-Prince. Each was fingerprinted and photographed by local immi-

Article by Jill Smolowe, staff writer, from *Time* 44 F 17 '92. Copyright © 1992 by The Time Inc. Magazine Company. Reprinted with permission.

gration officers. Just routine procedure, police assured scores of foreign journalists. But the swiftness with which the returnees melted into the population suggested that these Haitians were more than a little skeptical—perhaps with good cause.

Three days after his repatriation from the detention camp at the Guantánamo Bay naval base in Cuba, a youth who identified himself only as Marcelin spoke briefly with *Time* [Magazine]. He said that last Monday, within hours of returning to his family in Carrefour on the southern fringes of the Haitian capital, a soldier and a man in civilian clothes appeared at this door. Addressing him by name, they asked where he had been for the past two months. "Cap Haitien," Marcelin answered, referring to a city in north Haiti. "You were over there in Guantánamo, not Cap Haitien," one of the men responded. "O.K., we'll come for you. We'll come and kill you." Soon after that, Marcelin boarded a bus back to Port-au-Prince and went into hiding.

Such accounts by frightened returnees have done nothing to move the Bush Administration to reconsider its plan to ship home more than 10,000 Haitian boat people from Guantánamo. The dilemma for Washington remains acute: Are these people merely looking for a better life, or genuinely in danger of persecution?

Those in danger are supposed to be admitted to the U.S.—but proving they face reprisals, even death, back home is rarely easy. Those seeking a better life pose one of the more painful questions for a nation philosophically committed to an open door. While Administration officials acknowledge that the political climate in Haiti has worsened since the Sept. 30 coup that deposed democratically elected President Jean-Bertrand Aristide, they maintain that most of the boat people are economic migrants whose free-floating fears of persecution are not grounds enough for asylum. Backed by a Jan. 31 Supreme Court decision, little can now deter the Administration's plan to empty the detention camps, save a public outcry.

On Capitol Hill, a House Judiciary subcommittee approved a bill halting the exodus until violence in Haiti is sufficiently reduced so that no returnee faces "persecution or politically motivated violence." But with Congress in recess until Feb. 18, the Administration has time to return thousands more Haitians before the bill can be put to both houses for a vote.

Human-rights activists are waging a loud campaign to halt the repatriations, backed by groups ranging from the N.A.A.C.P. and

AFL-CIO to the American Jewish Committee and the U.S. Catholic
Conference. But it is uncertain how long Americans will listen.
"The White House is banking on the fact that people won't care,"
says a disillusioned Republican congressional staffer. "Politics, not
principle, is the overriding consideration."

With the presidential race under way, the White House has
apparently not forgotten the drubbing Jimmy Carter took in
1980 from Florida voters after the Mariel boat lift, which settled
some 125,000 Cubans in the U.S., mostly in Miami. The state,
which already houses 80% of the 1,402 Haitians who have been
let in to make their case for political asylum, can expect to be hard
hit by further waves of refugees. Yet last week the repatriations
drew fire from Florida politicians, including Senator Connie
Mack, a conservative Republican, who charged that the policy
was "based on crisis management instead of the principle of
freedom."

Meanwhile, the Administration strove to create the impression that it was taking humanitarian steps to alleviate Haitians'
suffering. Officials spoke of "redirecting" the economic embargo
imposed by the Organization of American States, to relieve pressure on ordinary Haitians and target the assets of individuals
connected with the coup. Yet in the four months since the trade
ban was imposed Bush has taken no steps to implement such a
"scalpel embargo," giving coup sympathizers time to clear their
assets out of the U.S. An official acknowledged that the Administration had bowed to domestic business interests after complaints that the embargo had shut down U.S.-operated assembly
plants in Haiti, putting 40,000 locals out of work and costing U.S.
jobs.

Washington's decision emboldened Haiti's army officers to
stall the docking of two U.S. ships carrying 508 boat people. "The
military believes it can get the U.S. to soften up the embargo even
more," says a leading Haitian businessman. Last week, as the commander of the country's armed forces elevated to a top post a
former police chief who was fired by Aristide, the prospect of the
deposed President's return seemed more remote than ever.

Washington still has many untested weapons at its disposal. It
could grant the boat people temporary protection, spearhead an
oil blockade or try to rally support for an international peace-
keeping mission that would guard against human-rights violations. But as last week closed, it was hard to shake the sense that

the Bush Administration was giving up on Haitians—and their democratic aspirations—for good.

'THE ONLY DREAM LEFT IS TO GET OUT'

You can bask for hours in the calm blue water off Playa Santa María, one of the dozens of wide white beaches that stretch along the Caribbean east of Havana. A few miles away gleaming new sports facilities for the Pan American Games rise into the azure sky. Thanks to a cutback in Soviet aid and Fidel Castro's antique Marxist economics, food is scarce; in the countryside, Cubans are being asked to use oxen instead of tractors to till the fields. Yet Castro has spent an estimated $150 million on the Games, giving foreign and Cuban TV viewers alike a cheerful picture of crowded beaches and world-class athletics. To many Cubans, that sporting paradise—complete with bowling alleys imported from Japan to avoid the U.S. trade embargo—is a Potemkin village. In the weeks leading up to the Games, authorities released stock-piled food and fuel to take the edge off real hardship. "Remember the end of the Roman Empire—bread and circuses?" says a young graduate of the University of Havana. "That's the *Panamericanos*. Only soon even the *pan* [bread] will be gone."

Dreams of escape from Fidel's decaying bastion occupy the thoughts of Cubans by the tens of thousands. Two young musicians idling at Playa Santa María speak openly of their desire to leave Castro's world. "No future, no future, nothing," one says angrily. "Saturn, Jupiter, Mars—the only dream left is to get out." At that, his friend raises a finger toward Key West, 90 miles to the north. Over the last year almost 20,000 have made their way to the United States. Some came legally, but more than 14,000 simply overstayed their visitor visas issued by the U.S. interests section in Havana after Cuba lowered the minimum age for an exit permit to 35 for men and 30 for women. That is the largest

Article by Spencer Reiss, staff writer, from *Newsweek* 118:38–39 Ag 12 '91. Copyright © 1991 by Newsweek, Inc. Reprinted with permission.

migration since the 1980 Mariel boatlift, in which some 125,000 Cubans swamped U.S. shores in five months.

Officials in Washington and Florida are concerned the exodus could become unmanageable. "We're looking at an influx of 40,000 this calendar year," Miami official Joaquin Avino told The New York Times. Last week the State Department suspended applications for visitor visas from Cubans until it can sift a backlog of more than 28,000 requests. Privately, U.S. officials say their decision was motivated by cries for relief from south Florida; exiled politicians have also been complaining that Cuba profiteers by charging as much as $1,000 per person for exit permits, air tickets and other fees. Says Arturo Cuenca, a painter who arrived in Miami earlier this year: "Too many people have been staying. The visas were turning into a safe bridge out."

Tricky Currents

Unsafe ways remain popular as well. Record numbers of Cubans who don't qualify for visas have been trying to make the trip north on inner-tube rafts and ramshackle homemade boats, in spite of Coast Guard estimates that as many as half will not survive the sharks and tricky currents of the Straits of Florida. So far this year more than 1,400 such *balseros* have made it to the United States—triple the total of all last year. In addition to the rafters, a steady flow of artists and athletes have defected to the West, largely because of a clampdown on cultural expression. They include a boxer, a radio personality, a writer and her TV-cameraman husband, a historian, a television anchorman, and, on July 10, one of the Cuban national baseball team's ace pitchers, René Arocha. Last week Victor Cuéllar Pulido, 46, a Ministry of Culture official, defected in Mexico, calling life in Cuba "like being in a coffin. You can't speak or move."

Politically embarrassing though it may be, the U.S.-bound travel has benefits for a Cuban government bent on survival. It's more than just the millions in exit fees. Those Cubans who do return home bring tens of millions of dollars' worth of consumer goods, satisfying a demand the Cuban economy can't meet. The permanent departures constitute a political safety valve: unhappy Cubans focused on getting out—or actually gone—are less of a threat than they would be stuck making trouble at home. The U.S. decision to suspend visa applications gives the Cubans an opportunity to score points in their rhetorical contest with *Yanqui* imperialism. "After years of saying Cuba doesn't even allow people to leave," says one official, "the shoe is on the other foot— it's Washington that will be forcing them into the rafts." Cuban officials say the minimum age for exit will soon be dropped to 18 or even eliminated entirely, which will only sharpen the dilemma of Washington and Miami's Cuban exiles. Says one leading exile politician, "Many of us would like to jam a stopper in the kettle, and hope that it will explode." Nevertheless, says a senior U.S. official, "We want to encourage contacts that could lead to peaceful change, not violent overthrow."

For now, the Cuban people, distracted by the lure of the United States and intimidated by Castro's internal-security apparatus, seem unlikely to effect change, peaceful or otherwise. Despite rumblings from the Communist Party grass roots during elections for delegates to the Party Congress, Fidel has quashed any questioning of the country's top leadership from within the ranks. The heavy foreign presence during the Pan Am Games might have served as a kind of umbrella for would-be protesters, but that seems to have been pre-empted by a heavy deployment of police in an and around Havana, backed by new neighborhood militias called "rapid-action detachments." To offset grumbling over the cost of the Games, the government is sponsoring weekend parties in the parks, featuring cheap beer poured from buckets into quartsize brown paper cups.

'Tourism Apartheid'

Such dreary bacchanals only seem to accentuate the prevailing apathy and depression. Says dissident Elizardo Sánchez, released in May after serving nearly two years in prison for criticizing Castro's policies to foreign reporters: "There is a vacuum, a loss of values and a terrible consumerism, especially among the young." To many Cubans, the most galling byproduct of the government's drive for foreign tourist dollars is "tourism apartheid," the system that bars Cubans from dollars-only hotels, restaurants and nightclubs for foreigners. One exception seems to be prostitutes, servicing visitors despite Cuba's claims to have abolished capitalist vices. The only people more numerous than policemen after midnight along stretches of Havana's fashionable Fifth Avenue are miniskirted women beckoning to passing cars. Says one wide-eyed Cuban, taking in the scene at the Spanish-owned disco of the Commodore Hotel, "The women are all Cuban and the men are all foreign."

Ask people strolling along Havana's quiet, crumbling streets or waiting in two-hour lines for an ice-cream cone why so many want out, and they reply with either a blank look or a sarcastic laugh that seems to say: why not? As one 25-year-old artist puts it: "We've run out of theories. We've run out of ideas . . . like we've run out of gasoline and everything else. All there is everywhere is Fidel, Fidel, Fidel."

CARIBBEAN EXODUS: U.S. IS CONSTANT MAGNET

Santo Domingo, Dominican Republic—Before dawn on many days, in a ritual repeated across the Caribbean, long lines of people anxious to build new lives in the United States begin forming outside the high white walls of the American Consulate here.

Inevitably, many fail to clear the barrier before the building's sprawling courtyard is filled and no new applicants are admitted. But for those turned away, there are touts outside buzzing like eager ticket scalpers, offering illicit passage aboard small boats to Puerto Rico, the perilous first stop for many on the way to New York or Miami.

"You'll never get the visa," said a recruiter who identified himself as A. A., explaining that he had adopted the initials of American Airlines to help drum up business. "Don't be an idiot. Ride with us and your chances are much better."

Scenes like this occur daily throughout the Caribbean, a place affected perhaps more than any other by the gravitational pull of the United States.

Hit by hard economic times and seduced more than ever by influences like mass tourism and satellite television, this region of 15 independent countries and a smattering of dependencies of the United States and European countries, with a total population

Article by Howard W. French, from *The New York Times* A1+ My 6 '92. Copyright © 1992 by The New York Times Company. Reprinted with permission.

of only about 33 million, has been consistently exporting more of its people in percentage terms than any other area of the world.

While populous countries scattered widely around the globe, from Mexico to Thailand, often lead in one United States immigration category or another, a handful of Caribbean nations sit at or near the top of virtually every ranking.

"In some of these smaller countries, if you measure emigration as a portion of their total population, the numbers you come up with are just incredible," said David Simcox, executive director of the Center for Immigration Studies, a Washington-based group. "Tiny states like St. Kitts and Nevis, Grenada and Belize are sending 1 percent to 2 percent of their citizens to the United States every year, meaning they are basically exporting all of their population growth to us."

Between 1981 and 1990, the four Caribbean nations that supply the largest number of immigrants together accounted for nearly 12 percent of all legal immigrant admissions to the United States, according to Immigration and Naturalization Service data. The Dominican Republic sent 251,803 people to the United States, Jamaica 213,805, Haiti 140,163, and Guyana, a South American country that considers itself Caribbean in its economic and social structure, 95,374.

In 1990, 111,000 citizens of those countries already living in the United States applied to become legal residents. For Mexico, by far the largest supplier of illegal immigrants, that number stood at about 2,200,000. Mexico is not included among Caribbean nations, although it has some Caribbean coastline.

Debates rage over how much immigration the United States can support and which regions of the world should be given preference. The effect of the growing Caribbean presence, meanwhile, can be seen in most large American cities, especially on the East Coast, where people from the region have often created new communities or revitalized old ones in places like New York, Boston, Miami and Baltimore.

Islands Are a First Stop

Much attention has been focused on the surge of Haitians fleeing the violence in their country and the effects of an economic embargo imposed after a military coup there last September. But experts say the thousands who line up patiently each day at consulates around this region and the hundreds more who attempt clandestine trips each week constitute a far more formidable wave.

In the tiny English-speaking countries of the Leeward Islands, with their depressed banana economies, those who cannot get visas now steadily make their way to the United States Virgin Islands, where a third of the population is composed of people from elsewhere in the region. For many of the newly arrived, the relatively prosperous islands are merely a stopover on the way north.

In Guyana, desperate citizens who strike out on the visa line or cannot afford plane tickets often head north island by island, stopping awhile for short-term jobs, leapfrogging their way up the long, arching Caribbean archipelago to the economic promised land.

In Communist Cuba, those fed up with their own bureaucracy or the interminable wait at the backlogged United States consular office escape aboard small boats and even makeshift rafts, hoping to hit the Florida Keys. So far this year, more than 2,000 Cubans have gone to the United States in this fashion; American law allows them to become legal residents almost immediately upon arrival.

Experts explaining the region's disproportionate weight among United States immigrants say that in addition to the classic factors of economic opportunity and proximity, long-established West Indian communities in American cities have served as a magnet and facilitator, providing family ties, money, legal help and even hiding places to an extent that immigrants of few other regions can match.

On top of their large, officially recorded contributions to the United States' immigration, each of the larger Caribbean islands provides substantial numbers of illegal immigrants. The Immigration and Naturalization Service declines to provide data on the number of illegal immigrants from individual countries, saying that in any case such estimates are highly imprecise.

For Caribbean countries, the phenomenon brings both problems, including 'brain drains' of educated and trained people, and benefits, like the large amounts of money earned by émigrés and sent to relatives back home.

Jamaica, a relatively large Caribbean nation of 2.54 million people, saw 213,805 people, a number that is nearly 9 percent of its present population, emigrate to the United States in the 1980's, a higher percentage than any other country in the world. The island furnished nearly 3 percent of all United States immigration in that period, according to Immigration and Naturalization Service data.

Alarmed by the loss of so many of its people, including many of the country's most ambitious and best-trained young adults, the Jamaican Government commissioned a study of emigration that concluded that the island, with an annual per capita income of only slightly more than $1,000, was in effect providing foreign aid to its vastly richer neighbor.

"The Jamaicans concluded they were training all of these people, nurses, teachers, doctors and then watching them go off to the U.S.," said Anthony P. Maingot, a Trinidad-born sociologist at Florida International University in Miami. "In exchange, they complained they were getting a paltry $41 million in aid."

On the other side of the ledger is the amount of money sent back to relatives in the island nations by people living and working in the United States.

"You are losing good people, of course," Mr. Maingot said. "But those are the kind of people who can send back money, who can lobby for you. There is really a synergism at work there."

John F. May, a demographer with the Population Reference Bureau in Washington who focuses on the Caribbean, said: "Remittances have completely changed the structure of income distribution in some places. In Haiti, there was a boom in the construction sector that began in the 1970's, which mostly came as a result of this money. People may send only $20 or $25 a month, but you are talking about tens of thousands of people, and the total has a very big impact."

The Dominican Republic, Haiti and Jamaica are among the five nations that have lost the largest percentages of their populations to United States immigration in the last decade, according to the Immigration and Naturalization Service. Laos and El Salvador are the two other leaders.

American immigration officials say that in recent years Santo Domingo, the capital of this country of seven million people, has had either the second or third busiest American consulate in the world. These days it issues more visas to immigrants than any other office in the region, and the second most in the world after Manila.

Seemingly undeterred by an overall rejection rate of about 70 percent, crowds of Dominicans show up here daily in hopes of becoming one of the 300 to 350 who will be interviewed and, if truly lucky, gain legal entry to the United States.

"It has become like a game, the wheel of fortune or the national lottery," said Harry Edward Jones, the American Consul General in Santo Domingo. "People leave their kids with relatives. They will leave anything behind for a chance at a job in the United States."

In Santo Domingo, officials say that part of the "game" increasingly includes elaborate attempts to reinvent one's past, pose as a legitimate student, forge documents or claim fictional, well-to-do relatives, preferably already living in the United States, to increase the chances of being granted a visa.

For many Dominicans, like others in the Caribbean, the small odds of obtaining a visa, or the risks of trying to enter the United States illegally, seem worth taking because of limited opportunities at home coupled with the powerfully seductive images of life in America.

"The elites of this country have always sent their children to be educated in the United States, and when they have returned, it has always been a triumphant return, looking good and speaking English," said a Dominican newspaper editor who asked not to be identified. "The message for the rest of us has been so well received it has assumed an almost demonic force. If you stay here like good Dominicans, you will be left behind."

American officials say that more than 30,000 Dominicans travel illegally by boat each year to Puerto Rico, where they may travel freely to the continental United States. By comparison, the number of Haitians who have been intercepted at sea since September stands at 20,000.

Of those trying to enter Puerto Rico by boat, only 3,500 or so are caught each year, but untold hundreds more die when their boats capsize, officials say.

Asked why they wished to leave their country, Dominicans of a wide range of backgrounds who lined up for visa interviews echoed the residents of other Caribbean islands who complain that their nations have few opportunities for them and their children.

"The work here is no good," said Dionys Piguero, a 27-year-old shoe factory worker who accompanied her mother to the consulate, where she hoped to get a visa to join her son, a naturalized American who lives in Rhode Island. "I work from 7 A.M. till 5 P.M. and only get paid 180 pesos a week. When you stay here you are wasting your life away." At the official conversion rate, 180 pesos is a little more than $14.

Several young professionals said that despite their better than average earnings, they worry that high inflation and steep real estate prices will prevent them from ever owning a home or raising their children in a desirable manner, which for them includes private schools and music lessons.

Many third world intellectuals have long inveighed against the ravages of the "brain drain," but in much of the Caribbean a more subtle view of the costs and benefits of this large-scale emigration is emerging.

"Being so close to the United States, what we have developed is a kind of circular movement of people," said Frank Moya-Pons, a Dominican historian and economic development consultant. "Dominicans work there, stay for some years and come back. Even when they don't come back definitively, people travel often, bringing goods, money, merchandise, but, most importantly, new values."

BROWNS VS. BLACKS

Bitter divisions are breaking out between the nation's two largest minorities. Once solidly united in the drive for equality, blacks and Hispanics are now often at odds over such issues as jobs, immigration and political empowerment. At the root of the quarrels is a seismic demographic change: early in the next century, Hispanics will outnumber African Americans for the first time.

Though the differences were long submerged, they burst into the open [in 1990] just before the annual awards dinner of the Leadership Conference on Civil Rights in Washington. Instead of easy talk between old friends, an angry argument erupted. Contending that immigration laws discriminate against Latino workers, Hispanics asked the group to support repeal of the legislation. At first blacks refused, charging that Latino immigrants take jobs away from poor blacks. Furious, Hispanics threatened to storm out in protest. Only eleventh-hour diplomacy by Benjamin

Article by Alex Prud'homme, staff writer, from *Time* 138:15–6 Jl 29 '91. Copyright © 1991 by The Time Inc. Magazine Company. Reprinted with permission.

L. Hooks, executive director of the National Association for the Advancement of Colored People, coaxed the Latinos back to the table.

As their numbers have grown, Hispanics have become more strident in their demands for a larger slice of the economic and political pie. Blacks, long accustomed to being the senior partner in the minority coalition, fear that those gains will come at their expense. Meanwhile, demagogues on both sides have pitted black against brown in a bid for short-term political advantage. Says Arthur Fletcher, chairman of the U.S. Commission on Civil Rights: "On a scale of 1 to 10, I would put Latino-black relations on the negative side of 5."

Increasingly, these long-simmering tensions are flaring into violence, especially in cities where one of the groups has a monopoly on political power. [In May 1991], Hispanics in black-controlled Washington went on a two-day rampage after a Latino man was wounded by a black police officer. [In early July 1991] in Cuban-dominated Miami . . . blacks briefly rioted following the overturn of the conviction of a Hispanic police officer for killing two black motorcyclists. It was the sixth such disturbance in 10 years.

Underlying the disputes is a growing divergence of the interests of the two groups, reinforced by mutual suspicion. Black and Hispanic leaders, says Alejandro Portes, a sociologist at Johns Hopkins University, "see everything as a zero-sum game. If blacks get something, Latinos lose something, and vice versa." Many African Americans believe that Latinos are benefiting from civil rights victories won by blacks with little help from Hispanics. Says Fletcher: "During the height of the civil rights movement, Hispanics were conspicuous by their absence. They kept asking, 'What about us?' But rather than joining us in fighting the system, Hispanics were fighting us for the crumbs. And that in large part is still what's going on."

For their part, some Hispanics complain that blacks are unwilling to treat them as equals in the fight for equal rights. "We sometimes have assumed that because blacks have fought civil rights battles, they are more sensitive to our struggle," says Raul Yzaguirre, president of the National Council of La Raza, a federation of 140 Hispanic organizations. "That's not always the case. Blacks say to us, 'You're whiter than us. You're immigrants, and we've seen people like you get ahead of us. So we're going to be very suspicious of you.'" The major points of contention:

Immigration

In Miami the roots of Latino-black antipathy date back to the arrival of thousands of refugees from Castro's Cuba during the 1960s. Many of the newcomers benefited from U.S. government programs that provided $1 billion worth of refugee-assistance payments and small-business loans. Even worse, the immigrants soon began taking most of the menial jobs in the tourist-hotel industry, the city's largest-source of employment.

Relations have frayed even more because of U.S. immigration policy. Washington's hostility to Castro's regime means that nearly all Cuban immigrants are treated as political refugees and allowed to remain in the U.S. But almost all the would-be immigrants from Haiti are classified as economic refugees and sent back to their homeland. The disparity in treatment was vividly illustrated in early July, when a Coast Guard cutter intercepted a fishing boat carrying 161 Haitians and two Cubans they had plucked from a raft in the Caribbean. Both Cubans were permitted to stay in the U.S. All but nine of the Haitians were sent home.

Politics

Although black and Hispanics voters have often united behind candidates from one group or the other, attempts to weld long-lasting political coalitions in most large cities have been difficult to sustain. A case in point: the Latino-black alliance that helped elect Harold Washington as Chicago's first black mayor in 1983. Nearly 7 out of 10 Hispanics voted for Washington and gained a voice in local politics they had never had before. Acknowledging the importance of the Hispanic vote, Washington appointed Latinos to several key positions.

But cracks appeared in the coalition after it became known that blacks were being hired for patronage jobs at a much higher rate than Hispanics. When Washington suddenly died in 1987 just a few months into his second term, a succession battle split the city. Two years later, 75% of Hispanics deserted the black candidate, city alderman Timothy Evans, and cast their ballots for the winner, Richard M. Daley, son of the late Chicago boss. Explains alderman Luis Gutierrez: "Rich Daley sent a message—'I'll build a coalition with Hispanics, and my government will respond to you.' "

Jobs

Many blacks fear that Hispanic immigrants, who are often willing to work for less than the legal minimum wage, are supplanting them in even the lowliest positions. "Young black males stand on the street corner every day," says James H. Johnson, director of UCLA's Center for the Study of Urban Poverty. "Hispanic males stand on the street corner too. But somebody comes by and takes them to work. Nobody picks up black males but the police. Blacks look at Hispanics as the problem."

Hispanics say that blacks resist any attempts to increase Latino employment. In Los Angeles County, for example, blacks, who make up 10% of the population, hold 30% of the county jobs. Hispanics, who constitute 33% of the population, hold only 18% of the jobs. "Blacks think we want to take jobs away from them, so they're fighting us tooth and nail," says Raul Nunez, president of the Los Angeles County Chicano Employees Association. "They are doing the same thing to us that whites did to them."

What leaders in both camps fear most is that some white politicians will try to exploit their divisions by playing off the two groups against each other. Before George Bush selected black Appeals Court Judge Clarence Thomas to fill the Supreme Court seat vacated by Thurgood Marshall, the White House let it be known that a Hispanic jurist, Emilio Garza, was also being considered. Some Latinos believe that the information was leaked mainly to lure Hispanics to the Republican banner.

Some Hispanics and blacks are working to heal the rift between them. Last July, African-American and Latino scholars and politicians met at Harvard University to air their grievances. "We are seeing that it is time for society to pay attention to Hispanics' much delayed political maturation," says Christopher Edley, a black Harvard Law School professor. "The jury is still out on how the black community will respond: Will we welcome the growing strength of a longtime ally, or will we respond by feeling threatened or displaced?"

Events in Los Angeles could provide a model for how the two groups can work together. Last year Hispanic activists won a major victory when a federal judge ruled that the Los Angeles County board of supervisors had gerrymandered election districts to prevent Latino candidates from winning a seat on the powerful governing body, and ordered the lines to be redrawn. The case had been brought under the Voting Rights Act, one of the major fruits of the black civil rights struggle, and it resulted in the election last February of Gloria Molina, the first Hispanic supervisor since 1875.

From the start, lawyers for the Hispanic plaintiffs consulted with blacks to ensure that their voting strength was not diluted by the redistricting. "We shared our plans with them, they shared their plans with us, and we came up with a plan that didn't step on anybody's toes," says Richard P. Fajardo, an attorney for the Mexican-American Legal Defense and Educational Fund.

If current trends in immigration and birth rates continue, minorities will outnumber white Americans midway through the 21st century. Under those circumstances, blacks and Hispanics have no choice but to collaborate. They have far more to gain from pooling their strengths than from bickering with each other.

LATIN AMERICA'S NEWEST CAPITAL CITY: MIAMI

The image of Miami as the cocaine-snorting, Uzi-toting Gomorrah of America is a well-traveled one. When Thomas Ferguson, former president of the Beacon Council, an economic development body, was in South Korea thumping Miami business not long ago, he flipped on his hotel television set. There, clad in his trademark pastels, was Don Johnson blasting through a *Miami Vice* episode—and speaking dubbed Korean. The next morning, Ferguson learned that a Korean manufacturer of cigarette lighters had bypassed Miami when he had scouted plant locations in Florida. Why? "Oh, *Miami Vice, Miami Vice*, not safe, not safe," the manufacturer said.

maybe that was Miami's image in the 1980s. But like the popular TV show, that view is no longer prime time. Miami still has its unique set of problems. Arms and drugs are still pillars of its underground economy. And its battered image received a new blow recently with a highly publicized shooting of two British tourists. But such flaws aren't preventing the emergence of a

Article by Gail De George, staff writer, from *Business Week* 120–2 S 30 '91. Copyright © 1991 by McGraw-Hill, Inc. Reprinted with permission.

thriving and sophisticated mecca for international trade. Building on its deep Hispanic roots and proximity to promising markets in Mexico, the Caribbean, and South America, Miami is attracting a surprising new wave of blue-chip investors and traders from the U.S., Europe, and Asia.

Polyglot Paradise

When ground is broken for the 40-story Bristol Tower condominium overlooking Biscayne Bay this fall, about one-third of its 147 units will be owned by Germans, French, and Italians. One reason is that companies ranging from France's Aerospatiale to Italy's sewing machine maker Rimoldi are opening operations in Miami. Edward Bolden, president of the U.S. unit of French aerospace company Sextant Avionique, dined at Café Des Arts in Miami Beach last January and heard a different language at each table. "It was like having a mini-U.N. there," he says.

What also marks Miami's emergence as more than a hub for drugs, guns, and fast money is the arrival of big American companies. Both American Telephone & Telegraph Co. and Texaco Inc. are expanding their Miami offices, gearing up for new opportunities in the telephone and oil industries of Latin America. General Motors Corp. recently decided to relocate its Latin American strategists from São Paulo to Miami, and Eastman Kodak Co. is moving its Latin American headquarters to Miami from Rochester, N.Y. Hewlett-Packard Co. relocated its Latin American headquarters to Miami from Mexico City because it offered a more diverse Spanish-speaking labor pool and better telephone and airline connections throughout the region.

As a result of its expanding international links, economist Manuel Lasaga estimates that at least 25% of Miami's economy is directly tied to international commerce and tourism. Only New York's John F. Kennedy International Airport today moves more foreign passengers and cargo than Miami International Airport. Miami's and a few neighboring ports move more containerized cargo to Latin America than any other U.S. harbor.

Looking North

Several watershed events underlie Miami's new international reach. Latin America is rapidly shedding its anti-*Yanqui* policies and learning how to manage its pile of debt. One by one, countries such as Brazil, Argentina, and Venezuela are turning away from state-run economies, looking north for partners and capital. By virtue of its location and deep trade links southward, Miami is the headquarters of choice for big-league Americans, Asians, and Europeans eager to crack this long-dormant market. "Some say you can learn more about Buenos Aires or São Paulo in Miami because everyone's there," says Peter K. Kresl, an economist at Bucknell University.

What's more, expectations are high these days that Fidel Castro will soon fall from power in Cuba. The ongoing turmoil in the Soviet Union means dwindling support for the island nation. Only a 30-minute airplane ride away and full of expatriate Cubans eager to reestablish ties, Miami will be first to reap the rewards of a reopened Cuba.

And as Mexico negotiates a bold new free-trade agreement with the U.S., north-south business along the entire southern border of the U.S. is percolating. Miami is not attracting manufacturing investment as much as it is emerging as the administrative and managerial hub, a point of access where companies are moving decision-making for the region. Trade is also building between Miami and Caribbean islands as well as Central American countries that have preferential trade rights with the U.S.

Indeed, as trade winds blow in from all directions, Miami is securing its status as what urban experts call a "gateway" city, going beyond its role as a purely Latin hub. In much the same way, Buffalo is a center for Canada-U.S. trade, and Seattle and Los Angeles serve the Pacific Rim. Cities need the global economy as much as they need the domestic economy to develop these days, says Panayotis Soldatos, who studies international cities at the University of Montreal.

The old local economy, meanwhile, is a shambles. The city watched helplessly as its largest corporation, Eastern Air Lines Inc., died a slow death. Its biggest bank, Southeast Banking Corp., is now on the ropes. The largest savings and loan, CenTrust Bank, flamed out along with its free-spending chairman, David Paul. Since the 1980s, as many as 10 federally chartered international bank offices and 15 state-chartered agencies in Miami have closed. A construction bust and a glut of office space compound local economic woes, as high unemployment, at nearly 9%, fuels racial tensions and crime. With its key industries gone belly-up, Miami's gamble on international trade to generate jobs and growth is beginning to pay off just in time. Says Soldatos: "To compete with such major players as Charlotte, Tampa, and Atlanta, Miami needs international alliances. That in turn will enhance its domestic position."

Outdoor Cafes

Miami's growing international flavor is also drawing back tourists who steered clear of the bad old city in the early 1980s. Now, Europeans in particular are charmed by the 1930s Art Deco district in Miami Beach. The strip of freshly painted pastel hotels, restaurants, and clubs lures the European jet set. A once-small enclave of photographers and artists is growing into a lively fashion and advertising industry, using the blue, pink, and lime-green buildings as backdrops. Devastated by Walt Disney World and other Orlando-area theme parks, which siphoned off American tourists beginning in the 1970s, Miami is rebounding.

More Europeans also are living in Miami either on assignment for their companies or for U.S. companies. There are now 70 French companies in the Miami area, double the number five years ago. They range from Aerospatiale, which purchased a local instrumentation repair company that services Airbus and other planes, to shipbuilder GEC Alsthom International Inc. As a result, the French population in the city tripled in the 1980s, to 10,000.

With some natural affinity, Spaniards are coming in droves. There are more Spanish banks than any other foreign group. MAPFRE, a Madrid-based insurance company operating in 26 countries, chose Miami as its U.S. base for its Hispanic flavor and entrepreneurial spirit. Iberia Air Lines, the Spanish carrier, just won rights to service four flights to Mexico and South America from Miami. Even Aeroflot, the Soviet airline, is bypassing Havana and switching its refueling center for the Latin America area to Miami.

Asians, too—mostly Taiwanese, Hong Kong Chinese, and South Koreans—are arriving in greater numbers, drawn to the markets in the Caribbean and southward. Taiwanese computer maker Acer Inc. decided to locate in Coral Gables. Its chief competitor, Taiwan-based DTK Computer Inc., set up shop in Miami in 1988 to tap Latin America, particularly Venezuela. Now, DTK has opened one of two U.S. computer assembly lines in Miami, where thousands of machines will be made for sale in the U.S. and Latin America.

The Japanese have long been reticent to expand their stakes in Miami, partly because of its swashbuckling image. But there are signs that they, too, are nibbling. One company is Mitsui & Co., the big Japanese trader, half-owner of Caribbean Cutting Services, employer of 200 people in Miami. Taking advantage of trade preference laws, the company buys U.S. cloth, cuts it in Miami, and ships it to Haiti, where it is sewn into children's clothes that are returned to Miami for sale in the U.S.

Mosaic

Miami's strong Latin character has for so long been determined by its large Cuban population that few realize how many other groups call the city home. Even among Hispanics, the demographics are changing. Since 1970, the Hispanic population has tripled, and in 1990, it accounted for nearly half of the metropolitan area's population of 1.9 million. Cubans make up two-thirds of the Hispanics, but the numbers of Nicaraguans, Colombians, and Venezuelans are growing at a faster rate. Brazilian shopkeepers are moving into downtown Flagler Street stores. More than 150 Brazilian restaurants, shops, and trading houses are now part of Miami's mosaic.

Indeed, Latin culture is now in the very fiber of the city. Spanish isn't heard just in the kitchens or barbershops but in banks and boardrooms. It's also read in newspapers, billboards, and junk mail. Bilingual phone messages and business cards are commonplace. And visitors to corporate and law offices are offered a choice of coffee—*Americano* or *Cubano*, the thick dark concoction from Cuba.

Miami's dramatic demographic changes haven't suited everyone. As the Hispanic population grew, the white population dropped 20% in the 1980s. Although the city's internationalization provides opportunities for some people, the administrative and managerial jobs it creates do little to help Miami's large working class.

And Miami in 1991 is still very much a segregated community. Without Spanish, language can be a barrier to employment. Black attorney Gary Siplin says blacks are shut out of the work force—particularly in tourism—by the Spanish-speaking majority. Complains Siplin: "Why do you need to speak Spanish to make a bed, park a car, or wash dishes?" That brand of discrimination necessarily creates friction—and the friction occasionally erupts in violent outbursts.

Miami has its share of other chronic big-city troubles as well. Sunny skies and blue water aside, schools are crowded, and traffic snarls are common. Worried about Los Angeles-like smog, Dade County, which encompasses Miami and neighboring cities, is getting tough with auto-exhaust pollution. Future supplies of drinking water are threatened by periodic droughts and continued population growth on the fringes of the Everglades. And the woes will be exacerbated if another huge wave of Cuban refugees arrives. So far this year, nearly 1,200 Cubans have landed in Miami, almost triple the total last year.

But the opportunities seem to outweigh these worries, at least in the eyes of the business world. AT&T has added 70 people to its Miami office over the past two years. Last fall, the same office landed 60% of a fiber-optics contract, valued at $330 million, to upgrade Mexico's telecommunications infrastructure.

Further solidifying Miami's role as a communications hub, AT&T also has laid the first undersea fiber-optic cable to South America, connecting southern Florida to Puerto Rico, Jamaica, the Dominican Republic, and Colombia. And it's working with Spain, Italy, and Mexico to build another fiber-optic link between those countries, the Caribbean, and Florida. "People think all business in Miami is focused exclusively on Latin America, but that's not true," says AT&T regional spokesman Vincent Salas. "A lot of our customers are getting data-transmission and other services that are going to Europe and Canada."

Likewise, Texaco's Miami office, which is responsible for Latin America and the Caribbean, has increased its staff by 33%, to 240 employees, since 1987, to pursue new ventures in Colombia and Venezuela. Hewlett-Packard moved regional administrative functions to Miami from Mexico this past March, largely because of Miami's broader connections. "Miami provides a more Latin American environment than Mexico because it has people from other countries," explains Rui Da Costa, regional general manager for HP.

Springboard

Conversely, some Latin American companies are using Miami as a springboard to the U.S. With a trade agreement on the horizon, Mexican steelmaker Alceros Galpin has set up a U.S. office in

Miami to purchase cheaper and better quality U.S. steel. The free-trade deal could eliminate 15% in duties the company pays to import U.S. steel into Mexico and eliminate border delays, says manager Vita Samuels. She has also talked with a German steel company in Miami about importing both steel and technology into Mexico.

Miami will always be a unique place, seedy yet elegant, with a penchant for flash. Great dramas play out in the sun-baked city, from the tragedy of fleeing Haitians washing up on its shores to the farce of Panama strongman Manuel Noriega on trial. It may never lose all of its *Miami Vice* notoriety, but Miamians no longer feel the need to apologize for their city. And now there's the Florida Marlins, one of two new major league baseball teams. The city's social ills notwithstanding, a new population mix and set of business connections are turning Miami into one of North America's most dynamic cities for business.

II. THE FLOW OF IMMIGRATION FROM MEXICO

EDITOR'S INTRODUCTION

Aliens entering the country from Mexico have long been part of the public consciousness of the immigration issue. In the first article, George Vernez and David Ronfeldt, writing in *Science,* separate fact from fiction in their survey of Mexican immigration during the past two decades. Although the popular conception of the Mexican immigrant is apt to be of a single male, uneducated, working in agriculture, and living in the United States only temporarily, in fact a large number remain here and are accompanied by their families. Studies find no evidence that these immigrants have affected native workers' job opportunities adversely. In fact, many low-wage industries in which aliens are often employed have expanded while their counterparts nationwide contracted in the face of foreign competition.

The story of illegal immigrant traffic from Mexico to the southwestern U.S. is a grim one that is related in the next two articles. In an article reprinted from *The New Yorker,* Bill Barich recounts the conditions that prevail along a strip of scrubby desert that runs for fifteen miles between the U.S. and Mexico, "the most heavily travelled border in the world." Illegals who cross the border must elude not only the Border Patrol but also bandits who prey on them, robbing them of their grubstakes. In a companion article from *Harper's,* Earl Shorris describes the many forms of brutality that await aliens crossing into the U.S. along the Texas border. Robbed by bandits and hunted by *cholos* (young hoodlums), the illegals may suffer heavy casualties in their attempt to cross over. Many are Central Americans who have fled first to Mexico and are rounded up and interned for months at INS camps.

In a final article from *Newsweek,* S. C. Gwynne reports on another aspect of the border relationship between the U.S. and Mexico—the negotiation of a free-trade pact that could create a $6 trillion market. The pact is favored by the Bush administration, which believes that with the elimination of trade barriers investment will be stimulated that will result in hundreds of thousands of jobs on both sides of the border. Greater prosperity for Mexico would in turn relieve the flow of immigration northward.

THE CURRENT SITUATION IN MEXICAN IMMIGRATION

Mexican immigration to the United States has grown steadily during this century and has accelerated rapidly since the 1950s. Further, in the last 20 years, the number and proportion of undocumented Mexican immigrants have increased sharply. These phenomena create complex political, social, and economic issues for federal, state, and local governments, with profound policy implications.

Public response and policy debate are influenced by several popular misconceptions about Mexican immigrants: their numbers through time, their status as temporary workers, their socioeconomic characteristics, their integration into U.S. society, their effects on the economy, and their demand for public services. We review what is known about these aspects of Mexican immigration and the meaning for policy considerations.

How and Why Mexican Immigration Has Grown

Legal immigration. There have been three distinct phases of legal Mexican immigration to the United States during this century. The first phase began in the early 1900s with a steady increase of Mexican immigrants while aggregate immigration from other countries was declining. By the 1920s, Mexican immigration represented 11 percent of total legal immigration.

The second phase began after a temporary slowdown during the Depression of the 1930s. As the U.S. economy recovered in the early 1940s, Mexican immigration increased. It was spurred by a 1942 U.S.–Mexican treaty providing for the importation of an unlimited number of temporary workers (Braceros) in response to war-induced labor shortages in the agricultural indus-

Article by George Vernez and David Ronfeldt, from *Science* 251:1189–93 Mr 8 '91. Copyright © 1991 by the AAAS. Reprinted with permission.

try. By the Bracero program's end in 1964, more than 4.5 million Mexicans had come to work temporarily in the United States, exceeding the number of permanent legal immigrants eightfold. This phenomenon has left a lasting impression, on both sides of the border: that Mexican immigrants are temporary, going back and forth and that "their ultimate destination usually lies at the point of origin in Mexico, not somewhere in the United States."

The third phase began with the lapse of the Bracero program and the passage of the Immigration Reform Act of 1965. Although the latter placed the first ceiling on immigration from the Western Hemisphere, including Mexico, permanent Mexican legal immigration continued to increase steadily, and more rapidly than total legal immigration, until the late 1970s.

Further increases in legal Mexican immigration were checked by a 1976 amendment to the 1965 Act. That amendment imposed a maximum annual immigrant quota of 20,000 persons per country (already in place for the Eastern Hemisphere) in the Western Hemisphere, excluding immediate relatives (spouses, parents, and unmarried minor children) of U.S. citizens. Since then, the number of Mexican legal immigrants has stabilized at a yearly average of about 66,000, whereas total legal immigration itself continued to grow at a constant rate of about 30 percent per decade.

Undocumented immigration. . . . legal immigration (temporary and permanent) has been accompanied by continuous flows of undocumented Mexican immigrants. These flows have historically dominated the debate on Mexican immigration, triggering occasional U.S. enforcement crackdowns—when the volume peaked, and apparently became "intolerable." The Immigration and Naturalization Service conducted its first reported crackdown in 1929, when an estimated 100,000 or more undocumented immigrants were crossing the border yearly. After World War II, undocumented immigration resumed, and competition with the Bracero program led to another crackdown in the 1950s. As a result, more than 1 million undocumented immigrants were deported in 1954.

Following a 20-year hiatus, undocumented immigration became an issue once again when net undocumented immigrants into the United States increased from an estimated 23,000 annually by 1970 to 112,000 annually by 1980. By the early 1980s, an estimated 55 percent of all undocumented immigrants came from Mexico, and they accounted for an estimated two-thirds of all Mexican immigration.

Various scholars have associated three major factors with the most recent wave of Mexican immigration: (i) widening disparity between Mexican and U.S. earnings, (ii) decreasing job opportunities in Mexico for a population that has grown more than 3 percent per year since 1960, and (iii) self-reinforcing development of Mexican migrant networks between places of origin in Mexico and destinations in the United States, which lower the cost of migration through various kinds of housing, job search, social, and economic support.

This time, concern over illegal immigration led to the Immigration Reform and Control Act of 1986 (IRCA), which seeks to reduce illegal immigration to the United States by three means: (i) prohibiting employers from hiring undocumented workers, (ii) providing graduated civil and criminal fines for noncompliance, and (iii) increasing border-patrol enforcement across the 2000-mile U.S.–Mexican border. Under its two amnesty programs, IRCA also provided some 2.3 million undocumented Mexican immigrants the opportunity to become legal permanent U.S. residents.

Growth in the Mexican-origin population. During the past two decades, the increasing Mexican immigration has resulted in an equally rapid increase in both native Mexican-Americans and Mexican-born immigrants residing in the country. As counted by the Census Bureau, the number of Mexican immigrants in the United States quintupled between 1970 and 1988 to 4.1 million. During the same period, the Mexican-origin population tripled, reflecting both immigration and a fertility rate that is some 40 percent higher among Mexican-origin women than among white, non-Hispanic women. Nearly 45 percent of the increase resulted from immigration, the remainder from natural growth. Today, the Mexican-ancestry population residing in the United States trails only the English, German, Irish, and Italian in size, and is larger than the French, Polish, and Scottish.

Characterizing Mexican Immigrants

Given its growing size, the characteristics of this population have critical social, economic, and political implications, both here and in Mexico. In considering those characteristics, it is important to separate image from reality. The popular and scholarly image of the Mexican immigrant is one of a young, single male, uneducated and working in agriculture, residing temporarily in the United States in a predominantly Spanish-speaking residential enclave, and supporting a family that remains behind in Mexico. But what are the demographic and socioeconomic facts?

Increasing permanence and concentration in the United States. Mexican immigration to the United States can no longer be characterized by the persistent image of the Mexican immigrant as a temporary worker staying here for a short period of time and leaving his or her family behind, if it ever could be so characterized. Although we lack longitudinal data on the mobility of individual immigrants, many aggregate indicators suggest that Mexican immigrants come here to stay.

To illustrate this point, more than two-thirds of the 1.7 million undocumented immigrants legalized under the pre-1982 provisions of IRCA are Mexican. This proportion is 30 percent greater than was projected by census and INS estimates and confounded concerns that the 5-year continuous residency requirement would work against undocumented Mexican immigrants—the presumed "cyclical sojourners." Indeed, nearly two-thirds of the newly legalized immigrants residing in California have been in the country for 10 years or more, and four-fifths live with their spouses in the United States. Overall, the 1980 census indicates that more than two-thirds of Mexican immigrants in the United States live here with immediate family members.

In addition to size and permanency, Mexican immigration is made all the more visible by its geographical concentration. Today more than half of the Mexican-origin population is residing in the western United States (primarily in California), and this regional concentration is increasing. The relative concentration of the Mexican-born population in this region increased from 52 percent in 1960 to 64 percent in 1980. No other foreign-origin population is nearly as concentrated in one region, including Asians. Also, this population is further highly concentrated within selected county and city jurisdictions. Within the western region, in 1980, 87 percent of the Mexican-born population and nearly 80 percent of the Mexican-origin population lived in metropolitan areas, including Los Angeles, San Diego, Fresno, San Jose, San Antonio, Houston, and Phoenix. At current relative rates of growth, it will soon constitute a majority population in an increasing number of jurisdictions, most particularly in California.

Socioeconomic characteristics. ...Mexican immigrants are younger and more likely to be male and married than members of other immigrant groups and the native-born population. Although recent Mexican immigrants are generally more educated than those who came earlier, their schooling has increased at a slower rate than the schooling of other immigrants and those who are native born. Consequently, the educational gap between Mexican-born and other immigrants and the native-born population has widened over time. In 1960, 82 percent of Mexican immigrants had 8 years of schooling or less compared to 32 percent for native born, a ratio of 2.5 to 1. By 1980, this ratio had increased to 4.8 to 1, that is, 63 versus 13 percent, respectively.

In part because of less education, Mexican immigrants have lower earnings, experience higher unemployment rates, and are twice as likely to be working in the crafts and laborers categories than other immigrants and natives are. But, during the last two decades their participation in the agricultural industry has been halved to 15 percent of all native-born Mexicans in the labor force, whereas their role in the manufacturing industry has increased nearly twofold.

Female Mexican immigrants are playing a growing role in the labor force that has yet to be fully recognized. Although females have represented from 45 to 50 percent of Mexican immigrants, relatively few used to join the labor force. This is changing rapidly. In the last 20 years their labor force participation rate increased by 69 percent, compared with 50 percent for native females. Furthermore, the gap in hourly wages between Mexican females and their native counterparts is smaller than it is for males, having narrowed slightly over time. Reasons for this pattern remain to be identified.

Three Areas of Particular National Concern

The size of this population, its concentration, and its characteristics shape the effects that Mexican immigration has on U.S. society and on the immigrants themselves.

Sociocultural integration. Many people in the United States claim that Mexican immigrants are not acquiring English language skills and adjusting to U.S. political culture as rapidly as other immigrants. Reasons often given are their large numbers and concentration, lower education, and physical proximity to country of origin.

Addressing these issues fully requires looking at immigrants, their children, and grandchildren separately—that is, across generations. Using 1980 census data, McCarthy and Valdez showed that only about 25 percent of Mexican immigrants have a high school degree; 25 percent speak no English at all; only about 40 percent have a working knowledge of English. By the second generation, there is a dramatic improvement in high school completion and in English proficiency. Nearly 90 percent have a working knowledge of English and only a residual 4 percent remain monolingual in Spanish. Although the children of Mexican immigrants catch up rapidly in high school completion, they continue to lag behind other adults in educational achievement. At the post-secondary level, the second and third generations of Mexican immigrants reach about half the level of other adults: 12 versus 24 percent hold a post-secondary degree.

Immigrants' eventual participation in the U.S. political process is a symbolically important dimension of integration in the United States. For immigrants, a step that must be preceded by becoming a U.S. citizen. Overall, fewer Mexican than other immigrants become citizens and, when they do, they taken an average of four more years to do so (11 versus 7 years). This is also true of immigrants from Canada, which shares a border with the United States. The longer Mexican immigrants stay here, however, the more likely they are to become citizens. By 1980, only 21 percent of Mexican immigrants who entered in the 1960s were naturalized, compared to 56 percent of those who entered before 1950.

Later immigrants' lower propensity to become citizens also reflects the rising proportion of undocumented entrants. The latter must first convert to legal immigration status before they can even apply to become citizens. However, a random survey of the recently legalized population in California indicates the high naturalization intent of that population, as well as the diversity of immigration status among members of given families. Fifty percent of the IRCA legalized population had at least one family member who already is a U.S. citizen, and four out of five indicated that they intended to apply for citizenship.

Once immigrants of Mexican origin are U.S. citizens, available evidence suggests they behave like other groups of eligible voters. After accounting for educational differences, registration rates and voting patterns of Mexican-origin and Hispanics, more generally, do not differ significantly from those of blacks or whites. Hence, the main reason Hispanics have not fully translated their increasing numbers into proportional increases in political representation and power is because most are not eligible to vote because of either age or lack of citizenship. As more Hispanics reach voting age and more immigrants acquire citizenship, particularly among the recently legalized populations, their voting strength will potentially increase accordingly.

Growth and distributional effects. Many investigators have attempted to identify and quantify how immigrants affect economic growth, in general, and distribution of wealth among the native-born, in particular. The general consensus is that immigrants in the United States (legal or undocumented) have little effect on earnings and employment opportunities of native-born people but significantly affect earnings and employment opportunities of earlier immigrants. For example, a 10-percent increase in the number of all immigrants decreases the wage of the foreign-born individual by at least 2 percent.

Although these generalizations hold for the nation and for immigrants as a whole, they may not hold for smaller geographical areas that experience a large and sustained influx of low-skilled immigrants. Looking at the California experience, two recent studies documented that growth in Mexican immigration in the 1970s and 1980s coincided both with the more rapid growth of the California, and in particular the Los Angeles economies, and with slower earnings growth for all workers. These studies argue that heavy immigration into California, which accounted for 65 percent of the population growth between 1970 and 1980, let many low-wage industries continue expanding while their counterparts nationwide were contracting in the fact of foreign competition. This is most evident in manufacturing, which grew five times the national average whereas wages grew 12 percent more slowly in the state, and 15 percent more slowly in Los Angeles.

The studies found no evidence that this influx of immigrants affected native workers' job opportunities adversely. However, it appears that they may have slowed the growth-rate of native workers' earnings, with a disproportionate effect on low-skill occupations. Blacks as a group were not more affected than whites and, consistent with the national pattern, immigration had the largest wage-dampening effects on immigrants themselves. Their wage rates grew twice as slowly as other workers' rates.

However, other factors may enter into the equation, under-cutting generalization from these findings. Muller and Es-penshade noted that, during the 1970 to 1983 study period, there was a sharp decline in migrants from other parts of the country, especially low-skill migrants, with whom Mexican immigrants pri-marily compete for jobs. There was a net loss of 134,000 low-skill workers to other states, whereas there was a net gain of 205,000 white-collar workers. The extent and nature of this dynamic in-terregional adjustment process are yet to be analyzed.

Demand for public services. A frequent question is whether im-migrants "pay their way" (through taxes) for the public services they consume. That question cannot be precisely answered. There is no information available on the service use and tax pay-ments of individual immigrants and their families over time and disaggregated by level of government. Again, indirect ap-proaches provide a partial answer to this question.

Among public services, education has been the most affected by Mexican immigration, both legal and undocumented. Al-though undocumented immigrants are ineligible to receive cer-tain federal public assistance benefits (including Aid to Families with Dependent Children and foodstamps), they are eligible to receive state-funded public assistance benefits, where available, and their children have full access under law to public education. Because Mexican immigrants tend to be young and have large families, they consume more educational services than native-born families do. For example, in 1980, Mexican immigrant households enrolled 2.25 more children in Los Angeles elemen-tary and secondary schools than the average for Los Angeles households. In the 1980s, the number of students of limited En-glish proficiency doubled in that district. Statewide, more than one out of six of today's Californians speaks a language other than English at home.

Mainly because of this disproportionate demand on educa-tional services and the lower earnings of Mexican immigrants, they probably get more in educational and other federal, state, and local services than they pay. However, this kind of static ac-counting fails to consider the longer term effects of immigration on public outlays. Education, in particular, is both a consumption good and an investment in human capital.

Another concern over immigration, generally, and Mexican immigration, particularly, is the extent to which immigrants become dependent on income-transfer programs such as welfare and medical care. In 1980, immigrant households were only slightly more likely than native households to receive welfare, 9 percent versus 8 percent, respectively. However, Mexican immigrants were nearly twice (12 percent) as likely as the native-born and other immigrants to receive welfare. This reflects, in part, their lower education and, thus, their earning potential. Immigrants' use of welfare and other income-transfer programs also appear to increase with length of stay and achievement of legal status. One study suggests that, with legalization, use of services can be expected to more than double over time.

Conclusions and Implications

Our review of the current situation in Mexican immigration leads to several conclusions.

1) Mexican immigration to the United States has changed in character. In growing numbers, Mexican immigrants come here to stay, not to work awhile and return home. There are numerous indications of this shift to permanence besides the number of newly legalized who have been in this country for more than 10 years: for example, the high percentage living with families and with naturalized citizens, the rise in school enrollment for children of Mexican immigrants, and the number who intend to naturalize.

2) This population is highly concentrated in certain areas and is growing. That concentration tends to be self-perpetuating and to promote further immigration.

3) Until 1980, evidence suggests that intergenerational integration of Mexican immigrants was proceeding well. However, the process may be slowing for newer immigrants. There are indications that the educational gap of Mexican immigrants is increasing and their earnings growth is being slowed by relatively low educational levels and the large size of newer immigrant cohorts.

4) Among public services, education is affected most, and most immediately, by the growth in Mexican immigration.

Our review also suggests several implications for policy of the recent legalization of over 2 million undocumented Mexican immigrants. First, the sheer size of the newly legalized population will affect not only the speed and nature of their assimilation but that of their children, of other immigrant groups, and of future immigrants. Their economic progress will have a major effect on the nation's economic future, which will, in turn, depend on public and private investments that will be made in their education. Second, the legalized population will increase its demand for public services—including adult education—over time, as the 5-year ineligibility period for some service programs expires in 1992. The only uncertainty is by how much. Most affected will be California, Texas, Florida, and the large urban areas in these states where legalized immigrants are concentrated. Third, together, the newly legalized immigrants, naturalized Mexicans, and native Mexican-Americans will exert an increasing political influence on local and national affairs. At the national level, the Mexican-American community will probably be increasingly involved in formulation of U.S. policy toward Mexico and Central and Latin America.

LA FRONTERA

The most heavily travelled border in the world is a strip of scrubby California desert that runs for fifteen miles between the United States and Mexico, starting at the Pacific Ocean and ending at a thriving yet isolated spot called Otay Mesa. A chain-link fence follows the border for much of its course, but it is torn in many places and trampled in many others, and in some places it has fallen down. Where the fence is still standing, you find litter on both sides of it which illegal aliens have left behind—beer and soda cans, cigarette packs, diapers, syringes, candy wrappers, and even comic-book *novelas* that feature cautionary tales about the perils of a trip to *El Norte*. These *novelas* tell of dishonest employers, horrible living conditions, and the corruptive power of

Article by Bill Barich, free-lance writer, from *The New Yorker* 66:72–9+ D 17 '90. Copyright © 1990 by *The New Yorker*. Reprinted with permission.

American dollars. In their most dramatic stores, families come apart, brothers murder brothers, and lovers' hearts are broken beyond mending. The stories offer a liberal blend of truth and fiction, but that is an accurate reflection of the border, where nothing is ever absolute.

Between the ocean and the mesa, the only town of any size is San Ysidro, California, just across from Tijuana. About forty-three million people pass through its legal port of entry every year, in vehicles, on bicycles, and on foot, but nobody knows for certain how many undocumented migrants slip illegally over *la frontera.* An educated guess would be about five thousand every day. They come primarily from Mexico and Central America, and they carry their most precious belongings with them in knapsacks or plastic supermarket bags. The Border Patrol, in its San Diego Sector—a territory roughly as big as Connecticut—apprehends about a third of them, logging almost fifteen hundred arrests every twenty-four hours, but the others drift on to Los Angeles or San Francisco or Sacramento, or to farms in the great Central Valley, staying with relatives and friends while they look for work. If they fail to be hired anywhere, they go farther north, to Oregon and Washington, ready to pick fruit or to gut salmon in a packinghouse, willing to do anything to earn their keep.

Like many border towns, San Ysidro is conducive to paranoia. Set in the midst of sagebrush and dry, brown mountains covered with chaparral, it has the harmless look of an ordinary suburb, but this is deceptive and does not hold up under close inspection. For instance, there is a blood bank on the edge of its largest mall, and all day you can watch donors come out the door with balls of cotton pressed to their forearms, bound for a shopping spree at a nearby K mart before going home to Tijuana. The sky above San Ysidro is often full of ravens and buzzards, and skulls of small animals turn up in its playgrounds. Its population is mostly Hispanic, but more and more Anglos—retired people, and people who commute to San Diego—are buying property in the tile-roofed housing tracts that are devouring the last farms and ranches, and they get very angry the first time some illegal aliens dash through their back yards, trampling the shrubbery and pausing to drink from garden hoses.

The Border Patrol is the uniformed arm of the Immigration and Naturalization Service, and it is supposed to control the flow of uninvited foreigners into the States. In California, as in Texas, its stations are understaffed and underfunded, and are asked to perform a nearly impossible task. In the San Diego Sector, agents must police all of San Diego County, as well as substantial parts of Orange and Riverside Counties, scouring not only the canyons and the backwoods but also the teeming barrios in cities, where aliens frequently seek shelter. Although the sector captures more illegal aliens than any other sector in the country—more than four hundred and seventy thousand in fiscal year 1990, almost half the United States total—this record does little for the morale of the agents, since there is no real penalty imposed on those who are apprehended, unless they have some contraband or resist arrest. Mexicans are given a brief interview, then returned to Tijuana, sometimes so quickly that they get caught crossing again on the same night.

The law isn't the only obstacle that the Border Patrol faces in dispatching its duty. It used to be easy for agents to spot new arrivals because they dressed like field hands and looked dirty and frightened, but now the aliens disguise themselves in clothes fresh off the rack, relying on such items as bluejeans, Reeboks, and L.A. Dodgers caps for protective coloration. The business of providing goods and services to migrants has grown enormously, forming a closed economy worth millions, and they have an elaborate network of support, which often involves extended families and functions in the manner of an underground railroad. Then, too, illegal aliens are always testing agents by devising new tricks for sneaking into California. On a hot summer day, they like to put on bathing suits and wander up the coast, or they dive from a boat and swim to shore. They wade through raw sewage in the Tijuana River and slip into Imperial Beach, just north of San Ysidro. They jam themselves into car trunks and into boxcars, and they ride across the border spread-eagled on top of freight trains. The boldest ones merely sprint through the backed-up traffic at the port of entry, defying the Border Patrol to chase them.

Once illegal aliens get by this first line of defense, they can relax and blend into the crowd of legal Hispanics in San Ysidro. They treat the town as a sort of flea market, making connections and buying Stateside necessities, usually on the sly. If they require fake documents—anything from birth certificates to green cards—they seek out a dealer in such papers and begin negotiations. A high-quality document might cost more than a thousand dollars. Only an expert can detect that it's a forgery, while a so-called "fifty-footer" looks bad even at that distance and can be bought without much haggling. If migrants have some pesos to be laundered, they speak to the fellows hanging around the pay phones by the United States Customs gate. Those phones, supplied by half a dozen different companies, are the conduit through which a fortune in drug profits—from the sale of cocaine, marijuana, and methamphetamines—is annually rerouted. The men who smuggle in aliens used the phones, too, arranging transportation for their customers. The smugglers are known as *coyotes*, on account of their predatory habits, and they flourish on the border, where expediency is the rule of thumb.

In San Ysidro, there are also safe houses, where, for a price, a migrant can hole up for a while. The safe houses look like the houses around them, but everybody on a given block can point them out. As it happens, secrecy tends to play a very limited role in illegal immigration. Anyone who wants to see how openly aliens cross the border, even in broad daylight, can take a drive on Dairy Mart Road, which winds from the outskirts of town through beanfields, pastures, and fallow land scattered with junked farm machinery. On any morning or afternoon, in any season, you'll have to brake to a halt as people streak by in front of your car, speeding from one hiding place to another. For the most part, they are young men in their late teens and early twenties, and they never seem the slightest bit afraid. They emerge from arroyos, from stands of bamboo and pampas grass, from copses of trees, and from vacant buildings. One morning as I cruised on Dairy Mart Road, I counted twenty-two people in a two-hour period.

The action at night is even more spectacular, and it occurs on a much larger scale. At dusk, you start hearing sirens and whistles all over San Ysidro, as if several robberies were in progress, and then comes the chopping sound of helicopter blades slashing up the clouds. Step outside your motel room and you notice beams from above shining down on a Carl's, Jr., restaurant, on kids in baseball uniforms and elderly folks out for an evening stroll. Sometimes a beam illuminates a drainage ditch, and a human form scampers away, like a rabbit rousted from its burrow. It's disconcerting to find normal life going on in what appears to be a suburban war zone. If you walk to a weedy field near the blood bank, you can look toward the concrete levee of the Tijuana River, where, in the glare of I.N.S. floodlights and in full view of the Border Patrol, more than five hundred people will be congregated in little bands, waiting for an opportune moment to begin their journey to the United States.

All around Tijuana, there are settlements that cater to the

needs of people about to cross, and La Libertad, in Canyon Zapata, is one of them. Its most famous entrepreneur is a big, good-natured woman who goes by the name of Manuela. Manuela's friends like to joke that she is a witch, whose supernatural business acumen has permitted her to become well-to-do, at least by the diminished standards of rural Mexico. She has built up a profitable café trade by feeding meals to those who leave for San Ysidro from the base of the canyon, where the ground is so perfectly level that the migrants call it "the soccer field." Hundreds of footpaths are worn into it, fanning out in all directions, and every crack and crevice is stuffed with garbage, which scrawny dogs keep pawing through. Rusty, windowless cars and trucks dot the horizon, because occasionally migrants try driving to the States instead of walking, and they abandon their vehicles if they're foiled by the Border Patrol or by the many potholes, gulleys, and ravines on the way to California.

Manuela is about thirty-five years old. She has bright brown eyes in a handsome, peasant face. Her body is compact and fleshy, and she enjoys gossip and has an earthy sense of humor that makes men want to pinch her. Manuela does not actively discourage the men. Sometimes when she cooks she wears a T-shirt that says, in English, "Poverty Sucks," but she hasn't been poor since she started her business, ten years ago. There were no houses in La Libertad then, but now Manuela owns one on the canyon rim, sharing it with eighteen others, including her nine children, her husband, her two brothers, and an assortment of cousins. The house isn't fancy. It's constructed of plywood and concrete blocks, and has a plastic tarp over a leaky roof. In winter, when a cold wind blows in from the ocean, Manuela's youngest boy, Javier, who is eight, collects cardboard to cram into the walls for insulation.

For Manuela, the working day begins at noon, when she and a few designated children haul her cooking equipment from the house to the canyon. Pots, pans, bottles of peanut oil, tortillas wrapped in paper, tomatoes and onions for salsa, pickled jalapeños, strips of marinated beef—the whole cargo gets carried down in arms and on backs, along with some firewood and some cases of soda and beer. Manuela always sets up in the same place, where she has a wooden picnic table and a blackened oil drum. She starts a fire in the drum and puts an equally blackened grill on top of it. She uses this to roast chickens, to make quesadillas, to heat beans and tortillas, and to sear the beef for *carne asada*. In addition to food she sells cigarettes, mostly black-market Raleighs. Manuela keeps painstaking records in her account books, and they show that she earns about two hundred dollars a month—as much, she says proudly, as a documented maid in San Diego, or the girls at the *maquiladoras*, or twin plants, on Otay Mesa.

Other food venders operate stands in the canyon, but they don't have Manuela's expertise, or her reputation for cleanliness. She does things skillfully, exploiting every opportunity. This is also true of her attitude toward border life. She approaches it as if it were a contest meant to challenge her intelligence, and she takes pleasure in her victories. Like many other Mexican women without documents, she has managed to be in California "accidentally" while she was nine months pregnant, and two of her boys were born in San Diego County and became instant Americans. (Any Mexican can request a border-crossing card that allows day trips to the States. It costs the United States about a hundred and eighty-five dollars to process each one.) Her husband, a plumber, has papers and often works in San Ysidro, but he and Manuela would never think of living in the States, even if they could afford it. They have no desire to become Americans—they just want a little piece of America's wealth.

About three hours before dark, people start assembling on the soccer field, arriving singly or in pairs, in family groups or in loose-knit associations formed on the road. There are always more men than women. Sometimes there are children—infants, toddlers, newborns in pink and blue blankets, nursing at a mother's breast. Almost everyone is neatly dressed, and those who aren't spruce themselves up by buying shirts and trousers from two women who have piles of clothing heaped on folding tables. Many of the migrants have crossed the border before. They speak a bit of English, have the confident air of seasoned travellers, and impart tips to the less experienced. The younger men may have their hair cut in the slick, youth-gang style of East L.A.—flat on the top and long at the sides, or clipped close to the skull with a tiny pigtail at the back. Hip young women have tight pants and spiral perms, and may be wearing heels and makeup.

In the crowd, too, there will be a few criminals, who are concealing small packets of cocaine or black-tar heroin on their persons. (Large shipments of drugs go through the port of entry in tricks—hidden, say, in a load of sawdust or broken glass.) The criminals may have knives strapped to their legs, or revolvers tucked into the waistbands of their trousers, but in spite of their presence the atmosphere in the canyon is casual. Children kick balls around and play tag while adults eat tacos and sometimes polish off shots of tequila at a tequila vender's stand. Roosters crow, and chickens scratch at the dirt. Snippets of recorded music may filter out from a shack above—accordions, drums, guitars, trumpets. The feeling in the canyon is communal, much like that at a county fair, with crossing the border the ultimate game of chance.

The only people who appear to be anxious are the Central Americans. They have already crossed the border *into* Mexico illegally, and they are fearful that the Mexican border patrol may sweep through La Libertad and toss them into a Tijuana jail, where they are often beaten up before being sent home. The Central Americans are also tired and are probably suffering from some minor illness. They have travelled a great distance to reach the soccer field (in many instances, more than two thousand miles, through jungles, swamps, and highlands), escaping some- times from war and oppression but more frequently from out- moded agricultural practices that have stripped their homelands bare and made subsistence farming impossible. Nicaraguans, Guatemalans, Salvadorans, Hondurans—they worry that some- one is out to harm them, while they simultaneously cast about, in a shy way, for help.

Because of their uncertainty, Central Americans generally employ a *coyote*. They pay between five hundred and seven hun- dred dollars to be smuggled into the United States, whereas a Mexican seldom pays more than three hundred dollars. The money is paid half in advance and half on completion of the journey, so that the customers will have a slight measure of con- trol over their guides, whose unscrupulousness is legendary. *Coyotes* will lead a migrant across, store him in a safe house, and then refuse to release him until his relatives in the United States cough up a ransom. This could be construed as kidnapping, but *coyotes* think of themselves as above the law. In their book of etiquette, the health and safety of their *pollitos,* or chicks, comes last. They'll desert them under pressure from the Border Patrol, perhaps leaving them locked inside a van, where, sick from the stench of sweat and urine, the chicks run the risk of suffocation. In the hierarchy of illegal immigration, *coyotes* occupy an odd niche between the vaguely heroic and the decidedly villainous, and this gives them a mythic stature on which they capitalize, outfitting themselves in fancy sweatshirts and high-top sneakers in the Air Jordan mode.

As an alternative to hiring a *coyote*, it is possible to latch onto a border veteran who'll take pity on you and let you tag along, charging a reasonable fee. One afternoon at La Libertad, I met a young Mexican man, Omar, who regularly makes a little ready cash this way. He was about to return to the United States with five new friends, having completed a girl-chasing expedition to Tijuana. At the age of twenty-one, Omar knew the border intimately. He had crossed if for the first time at fourteen, going to Yakima, Washington, to join his parents, who worked the orchards there. He had hoped for a factory job, but he wound up picking apples, and he was still picking them every summer. In his Hard Rock Café sweatshirt, sipping from a cold Tecate, he looked supremely undaunted by the mission ahead and might have been preparing himself for a trip to the corner store. His car was parked on a street in San Ysidro. It had California plates, and so, he felt, was not likely to be stopped by inquisitive agents.

The route Omar planned to follow zigzagged up and down hills, traversing rough country that offered ideal habitat for scorpions, lizards, tarantulas, and rattlesnakes. If you hiked it by day, it wasn't too intimidating, Omar said, but after dark you could get lost, or take a fall, or trip on a root or over a boulder and sprain your ankle. On summer nights, the heat could be horrendous, and people became dehydrated and suffered from exhaustion. There were also bandits who ambushed migrants, knocking them over the head with a stick and stealing their grubstake. (Illegal aliens often have lots of money with them, since they deal strictly with cash.) If the Border Patrol wasn't out in force, it took about half an hour to reach San Ysidro, but if agents were in the canyon you could get pinned down for a long time, curled under a bush in a fetal ball. This didn't happen much, though, because the canyon was hard duty, and agents preferred to avoid it if they could.

For people who don't have the stamina for such a crossing, there are places on the border where success depends on other factors—cunning, bravado, even speed of foot. To cross from the Tijuana River levee, for example, an alien needs only good timing and a little luck. San Ysidro is about five hundred yards away, and though the Border Patrol tries to clog the buffer zone with agents in jeeps and on all-terrain motorcycles, the men can't grab everyone running past. Instead, it's a matter of random selection. At

the levee, illegal immigration has the look of a futuristic sporting
event that might have been dreamed up for a cable TV network.
Many Tijuanans drop by just to entertain themselves and be part
of the scene. There is always a hint of danger, mainly because of
all the drug dealers and junkies. Teen-agers in heavy-metal T-
shirts, high from sniffing glue, strut around listening to old Led
Zep tapes on their boom boxes, and every now and then one of
them takes off for the States in a goofy glide.

If you walk west from the levee for about a mile, you come to
a wooded hillside where migrants also meet. It is a much more
tranquil place, except on chilly evenings, when people uproot and
burn the surrounding vegetation to keep warm. Technically,
they're on American soil when they do this, having crawled
through holes in the border fence, but if agents make a move
toward them they jump back into Mexico. A fellow called Miguel
told me this one evening while he was eating his dinner, a ham
sandwich he'd bought from a vender. The vender, too, was talk-
ative. He reminisced about his years in Santa Ana, California,
where he had worked in construction until he got strung out on
cocaine. His life was much simpler now, he said. Some weeks, he
made as much as seventy dollars selling his wares on and around
the levee, keeping the sandwiches and drinks in an Igloo cooler
that his wife toted around, even though she was pregnant and
had already suffered two miscarriages.

Miguel was slender and sensitive. He had a gap between his
front teeth, and he fretted that, at thirty-seven, he was beginning
to lose his looks. A roofer by trade, he had hooked up with two
Guatemalans from Cobán, first-timers, and was taking them
across, planning to leave that night at eleven o'clock, when the
Border Patrol changed shifts and everyone was distracted. Miguel
spoke English with a German accent. An American Army colonel
from Wisconsin—an archeology buff who'd stopped in Miguel's
village to study the ruins—had taught it to him long ago. The
colonel had urged Miguel to visit him in the Midwest, but Miguel
was too busy exploring the United States, living in Los Angeles,
Palmdale, Chicago, Phoenix, Tucson, and Houston. He had been
caught only once, in New Orleans. It was his dream, he said, to
make it to San Francisco someday.

In Canyon Zapata, there are usually about a hundred people
on the soccer field at twilight. This is the time when Manuela
begins to put away her supplies and utensils. She is concerned
that somebody might try to rob her, and often she lingers at her
table until one of her brothers comes to escort her out. While she

douses her fire and scrapes her grill, the *coyotes* brief their customers, sketching maps on the ground and sending scouts to check on the whereabouts of agents. As night approaches, people move tentatively forward—ten steps, a pause, then ten more steps. They move as if they were inching themselves into a body of water. In a few minutes, they will have vanished from sight, and Manuela will be back in her house, cooking dinner for her family. The next day will be the same for her. Every day is the same for Manuela—except Sunday, when she observes the Sabbath by staying at home and attending to her Bible studies.

One of the busiest Border Patrol stations in the San Diego Sector has been Brown Field, on Otay Mesa. Named for an airport nearby, the station is plain and resembles a small-town firehouse in need of paint and refurbishing. The agents assigned to Brown Field frequently have the demeanor of firemen, in fact, because their work is routine, with long, dull periods during which they perform a repetitive chore—apprehending illegal aliens and returning them to Mexico. Their ranks are composed of Army vets, former cops, wanna-be cops, and many ordinary guys who are athletic, don't mind wearing a uniform, and enjoy working outdoors. When agents complain, it isn't about government policy but, rather, about how badly they're paid and how their wives must struggle to make ends meet. Boredom is their worst enemy, and sometimes they combat it by competing to see who can bring in the most aliens in a day, a week, or a month.

From Brown Field Station an agent can look across a highway to the part of Otay Mesa that drops off to the southwest, toward Tijuana. The mesa is huge, and most of it is still raw desert, but it won't be for long. Its history follows a common pattern of land and water grabs in Southern California, where the model for real-estate transactions appears to be the deal that John Huston pulled off in "Chinatown"—diverting the rivers of the West to L.A. Just before the turn of the century, the mesa had a saloon and a racetrack, but they died a natural death, and some settlers from Germany began dry-farming barley. Irrigation water became available in the Otay area around 1950, and the farmers diversified and put in vegetable crops and citrus orchards, like those in Imperial Valley, to the north. They couldn't beat the prices of Mexican growers, though, and the mesa languished until the late nineteen-sixties, when a combine of speculators bought up property very cheap and then lobbied to have the local zoning changed from agricultural to industrial and commercial.

The obvious appeal of the mesa was its strategic position,

directly across the border from what American business interests have always liked to refer to as Mexico's "inexhaustible pool of cheap labor." It was such thinking that helped to create an agreement in 1942 that, as a war-emergency measure, allowed farm workers to enter the States legally, so they could harvest crops that might otherwise have rotted in the fields. The agreement saved California farmers from terrible losses, but it also had the effect of reinforcing a notion already prevalent among rural Mexicans that there would always be work up north. (So many Mexicans came in as braceros that in 1954 the government, in an initiative called Operation Wetback, ordered them to leave the country or face being deported. According to government records, more than a million illegal Mexicans left, but who can say how many sneaked right back in?) California agriculture still depends on "cheap labor," and so do the *maquiladoras* springing up on Otay Mesa—one plant in Tijuana, for tedious piecework, and one in the United States, for the final assembly of products, and for corporate offices.

Among corporations that operate *maquiladoras*, the underlying assumption is that poor Mexicans will be delighted with humdrum jobs that pay them a fraction of what an American worker would earn for doing the same thing, but this hasn't proved to be true. The turnover rate at most plants is very high, and so is the rate of absenteeism, with employees often going home for the weekend and not returning until the following Wednesday. Industry journals address these problems in an oblique way, suggesting, for instance, that "task oriented" Americans have trouble understanding "relationship oriented" Hispanics, but it is more usual for the advice columns to provide cross-cultural tips, such as when to give a co-worker *el abrazo*, the friendly Latin hug—on holidays, of course, but also at funerals and at "any other moment of happiness or sadness." The journals are not as forthcoming about the environmental impact of *maquiladoras*, although *Twin Plant News* did report in a recent issue that American corporations had been caught dumping about half a million tons of toxic waste at "clandestine 'toxic cemeteries'" all along the border.

It can be instructive to visit both sides of Otay Mesa. On the American side, you see bright new industrial parks bearing triumphant corporate logos—Sony, Sanyo, Hughes Aircraft. The Golden Arches are in place. Truckloads of desert-hardy trees and shrubs go by, destined to form the instant landscaping on Ma-

quiladora Street or Pacific Rim Boulevard. Everything's clean.
Drive through the Otay Mesa port of entry, and you're in another
world. (The port, which opened in 1985, purportedly to ease the
traffic at San Ysidro, has been a tremendous boon to development.) The buildings in the Zona Industrial are drab, the roads
are miserably paved, and the air reeks of chemicals and diesel
fumes. Most *maquila* workers are young women from the interior,
and on their lunch break they leave the plants to eat at carts and
flirt with men. This appears to be a moment of happiness, but it
fades as soon as the women, whose wages, of fifty dollars a week,
barely cover their housing and transportation costs, must go back
inside.

The *maquiladoras* pose no difficulties for the Border Patrol.
They have stringent hiring policies, and almost all the employees
live in and around Tijuana. At Brown Field Station, the foremost
duty of agents remains the capture of aliens sneaking across the
mesa at night. They use a variety of high-tech gear to assist them,
and it adds a considerable amount of money to the annual budget
of the I.N.S. There are electronic sensors buried on the border,
and whenever anybody passes by one a blip flashes on a computer
screen at headquarters. There is an infrared telescope that rests
on a pickup truck, and it is deployed at a different spot each
night, somewhere between San Ysidro and the mesa. When you
look through it, you can pick out people moving in the dark.
They're an eerie green against the dull-red glow of fields and
earth. The agent manning the scope pinpoints the location of
migrants on a grid and relays it, and then a copter may be called
in to throw a search beam on the spot.

In spite of the high-tech equipment, most Border Patrol
tracking is done on foot or in a vehicle, often a Chevy Blazer
painted a sort of grayish camouflage color. The Blazers are sometimes so dented that they look as if they'd been driven off a cliff,
and some of them actually have been, because agents seldom
pursue migrants over established roads. Instead, they have to
motor through mud, marshes, sand, and loose gravel. As for the
mesa, it is as hard as a cast-iron skillet, even after a rain, and a ride
across it at top speed is a serious challenge to the human spine.
The shock absorbers in most of the Border Patrol's vehicles are
ancient, and you bounce around so vigorously that you may bang
your head on the roof. Agents also sustain injuries while they're
running, jumping fences, and wrestling with aliens. *Coyotes* do
them damage by pitching rocks and chunks of concrete at them

from fleeing vans. One agent got hit in an ear and went deaf. Another agent took such a solid crack to his forehead that it exposed the frontal lobe of his brain.

These "rockings" are a major nuisance. In the San Diego Sector, the Border Patrol spends about forty thousand dollars a year replacing its vehicles' windshields and side windows. At the same time, however, agents are spared other types of violence, which is a bit strange, given the potentially explosive climate on the border. There are theories to explain this. One theory has it that most illegal aliens are simple folk, who wouldn't know which end of a weapon to hold if you stuck it in their hands. Another theory has it that the criminals who do have weapons control their impulse toward violence, because they don't want to incur the wrath of the United States government and upset the subtle balances of a system that works so beautifully to their advantage.

Joe Nunez is assigned to Brown Field Station, and in his eleven years as an agent he has been involved in only one threatening incident—when a migrant pulled a knife and tried to stab Nunez' partner. Nunez gets excited when he tells about battling for the knife (which, it turned out, was made of wood), but he is really an easygoing type, who likes a beer and a barbecue and doesn't let himself become hung up on the most salient metaphysical issue of this job—that is, whether or not the chaos at the border is intentional. Sometimes it troubles him that the job isn't more stimulating, and he thinks about transferring to an investigative unit in L.A., because the thrills at Brown Field are few and far between. Nunez caught some Chinese illegals once, and once he caught some Yugoslavs, but then O.T.M.s (illegal aliens who are Other Than Mexican) are common in the San Diego Sector: in fiscal year 1988, its agents arrested (among others) three hundred and forty-seven Colombians, two hundred and sixty-six Brazilians, fifty-three South Koreans, twenty Indians, sixteen Turks, eleven Filipinos, seven Canadians, three Israelis, and one person apiece from Nigeria, Somalia, Gambia, Algeria, and France.

One night, when the moon was almost full, Nunez let me ride with him on patrol. Only minutes after we left the station, he noticed five people at the edge of the highway, moving stealthily forward. He shut off the Blazer's headlights, downshifted into first, and crept up on them. They were so preoccupied with the speeding cars and the unfamiliar turf that they didn't see him until he was about ten yards away. Then one of them shouted, and they all spun on their heels and ran, but when Nunez ordered them to halt they complied, slumping to their knees and putting their hands on their heads, as if they had practiced for the drill. There were three migrant men, a migrant woman, and a *coyote*, all in their early twenties. Nunez called for a Border Patrol van to collect them. Then he frisked everyone and found a handkerchief tied to one man's leg, hidden under his trousers. The man reacted as if the handkerchief held precious gems. In it were ten crumpled dollars bills.

The mood of the aliens was sombre. They seemed to be kicking themselves for getting caught. When hundreds were crossing the mesa, why had fate selected them to be pulled aside? Nunez made small talk with them, speaking in Spanish. This was always an awkward time—the dead time before a van arrived—and during it all pretense fell away, and the weirdness of the situation became manifest. Some agents joked about it, while others scolded their captives for breaking the law. Some agents knew what it was like to be poor and so were sympathetic, while others concealed their emotions behind the symbols of office. There were agents who were inquisitive, and there were agents who were rude and made racist remarks. As for Nunez, he was gentle, polite, and perhaps a bit embarrassed, since everybody knew that the arrest was just a momentary hitch—an inconvenience on the order of a traffic ticket—in a journey that would soon continue.

"Where are you from?" Nunez asked.

The oldest-looking man answered. He kept glancing menacingly at the *coyote*, as if he wanted to strangle him. "Oaxaca," he said. Oaxaca is home to Mixtec and Zapotec Indians. It is sixteen hundred miles to the south, and its hills are so eroded that a corn crop, which has always been a staple of the Indians, can scarcely be grown there anymore.

"Why are you crossing?"

The man shrugged. "To work," he said.

Trabajar—to work. All night, whenever Nunez asked "Why are you crossing?" the word was repeated. People wanted to work, and they didn't care what the work was like. They would do stoop labor, wrecking their backs and their knees picking strawberries or artichokes, and they would prune vineyards and orchards that had been sprayed with pesticides. They would swab floors, bathe infants, scrub pots and pans, and breathe in formaldehyde vapors in factories where particleboard was made. They would sell bags of oranges from traffic islands in Santa Monica, and they would hammer dents from bumpers at auto-body shops in Glendale. Contractors would employ them to dig ditches for foundations. They would agree to remove asbestos from around heating ducts and to scrape lead-based paint from walls. They would pour hot tar for roofs, handle beakers in methamphetamine labs, mow lawns, deliver circulars, clean sewers—anything at all.

The van came, and the Oaxacans climbed into it. They'd have to ride around in it until it was filled to capacity—about seventeen passengers—and then they would be processed at Brown Field Station. They could be detained for a maximum of seventy-two hours, although it was probable that they would be gone before morning. For a while after arresting them, Nunez had no luck. He spotted only "onesies" and "twosies," and because they were far away he didn't bother to go after them. He did chase four men down a hill, but they "bushed up" on him, vanishing into the mesquite scrub. Then he spent fifteen minutes tailing a suspicious car and keeping in contact with a fellow-agent, who finally stopped the driver and reported that he was "a Japanese gentleman with a valid passport."

And then Nunez was distracted. Somebody was walking toward him at a brisk clip, reversing the usual order of things. The man approached the Blazer, took off his knit cap, and grinned broadly, as if he'd bumped into an old pal. When Nunez asked for his documents, he fumbled in a pocket, then struck himself in the forehead with the palm of a hand—*ay, caramba!*—and said that he had left them at his uncle's house in San Ysidro. The story delighted him out of all proportion to its merits. It was clear that he'd been drinking. Drunks were always wandering across the mesa, often just because another drunk in a *pulque* shop had dared them to, and they wasted everyone's time. The man tried a few more excuses, but he could not invent one that please Nunez, and at last he collapsed into a rueful posture of acceptance and sat down to wait for a van.

The night dragged on. There were more arrests, but they were ordinary. Then, at about eleven o'clock, Nunez received a call on his radio informing him that a big bunch of Salvadorans, as many as twenty of them, were being rounded up. This made him sigh. Central Americans required a lot of paperwork, and he'd have to put in about forty-five minutes with each of them. His shift would stretch into the wee hours. The Salvadorans would all ask for political asylum, whether or not they were genuine refugees, and by the time a court date was set they would be working somewhere—and if they weren't working they wouldn't show up in court. Such job-related frustrations subject agents to constant stress and cause some of them to burn out. Some have marital problems, some have problems with booze, and some, who lack Nunez' equanimity, get headaches from patrolling the mesa in the dark and realizing that they often have no idea where Mexico ends and California begins.

In the last ten years, more and more Oaxacans have crossed into San Diego County, leaving behind one of the poorest and most fractious states in Mexico. There are five hundred and seventy villages in Oaxaca, all of which date from the pre-Conquest period, and all of which have remained fiercely independent. The villages have their own rules and laws, which take precedence over the country's civil codes. And sometimes an extended family within a village will have its own subset of rules and laws, which contradict all the other rules and laws. Disputes are part of everyday life in Oaxaca. Some of them have been raging since the time of Cortés. They center on communal land rights, and lead to altercations, fistfights, and small-scale battles. Tradition matters deeply to Mixtecs and Zapotecs, and, in the face of grinding poverty, it is becoming traditional for the men of both tribes to look for work on American farms where their friends and relatives have worked in the past.

The farms around San Diego are disappearing rapidly, though, and the men often arrive at their destination and find condominiums where the beans and tomatoes used to be. Yet some farms with a history of hiring Oaxacans are still around, such as the one in Carlsbad, where some Mixtecs work. It is a big spread, surrounded by suburban developments, and it has a hundred acres planted with strawberries. The Mixtecs earn three dollars and sixty-five cents an hour to hoe the fields and to harvest the fruit, but there isn't always something for them to do, and they may have a week or two of inactivity. They aren't as disconcerted by this as Americans might be, since they're accustomed to hardship and know how to make it through a slack period. They behave as they might in their home village, staying close to camp and using their free time to relax, playing cards for pennies and nickels or conversing in the sunshine.

The Mixtecs live on camps out of economic necessity, fear, and ignorance, and also for the comfort of being near their own people. The apartment rents in Carlsbad are way beyond their reach, and, besides, the Mixtecs are saving money to take back to Oaxaca. If they have any English at all, it will be limited to "yes" and "no" and "O.K.," and when they go out in the streets they frequently get confused and are afraid to—or don't know how to—ask questions. Many of them have documents, but they are still uneasy, and believe that they might be deported at any moment. They never bank any of the cash they make, storing it instead in their underwear or in their bedrolls or in the baseball caps they love to wear. Thieves descend on them sometimes, including youth-gang members looking for a score. The growers in the county use private security forces to patrol their farms and keep out trespassers, and the guards are responsible for protecting the workers, too, whether or not the workers have asked for protection.

The Mixtec camp in Carlsbad is home to about sixty men. It is built in a dry creekbed below the fenced strawberry fields, in a grove of oaks, bay laurels, and pungent eucalyptus trees. The men live in shacks made of scavenged lumber and cardboard. Some of the shacks have been around for a decade. The Mixtecs are short, but they can seldom enter the doorway of one of their shacks without bending over. If a man in camp has a mattress, he is doing well. A man with a mattress, a chair, some bedding, and a framed religious picture might be considered rich. There are no toilets available, and no electricity or running water, so trash and excrement lie about, despite the Mixtecs' attempts to be tidy. They buy most of their groceries from a quilt truck they call a *fayuca*, or a "roach wagon," paying too much for canned goods and worrying that they'll get sick because they're not eating fresh vegetables. For sundries, they go to a woman, Doña Elvira, who keeps a shop in a tract house up the road. She lets Mixtecs use her telephone in an emergency. At night, they sit outdoors on her patio and watch programs on a black-and-white TV.

For most of the year, the Mixtecs don't mind the camp, but when winter comes they suffer mightily. They have kerosene lanterns and candles to light their shacks, but are constantly knocking them over and starting fires. Sometimes they try to heat a shack with charcoal briquettes, or with kindling. They stuff magazines and newspapers into the walls for insulation, much as people do at La Libertad, holding the material in place with thumbtacks or chicken wire. On the day I visited the camp, I saw a United States government publication for immigrants that was jammed between some plastic and some cardboard, with the pages turned to a paragraph that began, "The United States has fifty states. Rhode Island is the smallest state." A Mixtec was standing nearby, and when I asked him, in English, about Rhode Island, he nodded, smiled, and said, "Yes, O.K."

My guide at the camp was Roberto Martinez, the regional director of the American Friends Service Committee, whose offices are located in San Diego's Logan Heights barrio, around the corner from some safe houses. For the last few years, Martinez has involved himself in the lives of migrants, both legal and illegal, and has been keeping a record of various abuses committed against them by the Border Patrol, the San Diego police, and vigilantes. There are dozens of migrant camps in the county, and Martinez knows them all and drops by them on a regular basis to hand out donated blankets, sweaters, and food. He likes this aspect of his job, because it gets him out into the fresh air. In his opinion, the Mixtecs' camp isn't a particularly bad one. At other camps, men live in "spider holes," digging a pit and then covering the top with leaves and branches. The Border Patrol rarely raids any camps, and neither do any of the county agencies that might be expected to care about them. Martinez isn't sure why this is so.

The Mixtecs were taking it easy the morning I was there. They'd just finished planting some strawberries and now had to wait for the weeds to grow. They were doing their laundry in buckets of water carried down from Doña Elvira's, and hanging the wash on tree limbs to dry. They had a rusty basketball hoop nailed to a tree, but they couldn't play, because their ball was punctured and flat. The Mixtecs ranged in age from about sixteen to about sixty, and they had inky hair and were dressed in very clean clothes, given the circumstances of their lives. They seemed to have only two emotions—extreme pleasure or extreme misery. They smiled in such an open, unaffected, and generous way that they appeared to be in on all the cosmic secrets, but, I gathered, they're also capable of falling into a vicious funk and committing acts of mayhem, especially if they've been drinking. There was no alcohol in the camp. There were no women, either, but prostitutes have been known to pay calls. All the men wore cheap digital watches, and nine out of ten wore baseball caps that said, across the crown, such things as "SWAT" and "OLD FART" and "CALIFORNIA HIGHWAY PATROL."

Martinez asked the men if they were all from the same Oaxacan village, and they nodded and said, "*Sí, mismo pueblo.*" Then he asked if they had papers. The nodded again, but not with as much enthusiasm, and a couple of them remembered chores they had to do, and vanished into shacks.

It was Martinez' guess that about three-quarters of the men were in the country legally. Since Congress passed the Immigration Reform and Control Act (IRCA), in 1986, there have been more documented workers in the States than ever before, and at least seventy-five per cent of the workers at any farm will be legal—although at harvesttime everyone works, papers or no papers. (In businesses other than agriculture, the rate of compliance is much lower.) IRCA hasn't been an unqualified success, however. Some employers use it as a tool for discriminating against aliens: they refuse to hire Hispanic applicants by claiming that their documents look fake. Or an employer may hire somebody whose papers are clearly forged, let him work for two weeks, and call in the Border Patrol on the fourteenth of the month, the day before payday. And there are many crooked lawyers who bilk migrants, charging them five hundred dollars to fill out forms that require only a birth date, a signature, and the remittance of a ten-dollar bill.

In many respects, the most ticklish consequence of IRCA is that it has made a previously invisible phenomenon visible. There have always been plenty of migrant workers in San Diego County, but they have tended to be undocumented and to stay in hiding. A man with papers feels free to roam about, so you now see a lot more migrants on the streets. Even the Mixtecs venture into Carlsbad if they run low on money. They walk a few miles to a 7-11 and stand in front of it, waving at motorists, in the hope that someone will offer them a day job raking leaves or painting a house. If nothing happens by noon or so, they lose their ambition and may lounge around for the rest of the afternoon, as if they were in the *zócalo* in Oaxaca. They sit on curbs or lean against cars and tease each other, and when a pretty woman goes by they lift their eyes and comment appreciatively. If they get sleepy, they take a nap. If they have to urinate, they step behind a bush. It doesn't occur to most of them that they might be causing offense, or that their very presence might be frightening shoppers away from stores.

These groups of documented migrants can be found in any city in Southern California. A few illegal aliens will be mixed in with them, but only a few, and they aren't identifiable at a glance. The men often segregate themselves by nationality—the Guatemalans on one side of a block and Nicaraguans on the other. Mexicans draw very fine distinctions—Jaliscans, say, here and Zacatecans there. The groups can be big—up to three hundred—and also rambunctious, and as their size increases so does the volume of the protests against them. In bedroom communities, irate residents phone the Border Patrol and insist that the foreigners be removed. That puts the Border Patrol in a sort of double bind, which the agents recognize but, as public servants, are compelled not to mention; that is, the migrants wouldn't be standing on corners if some people in Vista and Oceanside and Carlsbad and Encinitas weren't hiring them and paying them—in cash, off the books and way below union scale, and without deducting any taxes for Uncle Sam. So the agents explain to callers that the men, though demonstrably foreign, are only exercising their right to assemble.

In the old days, the Border Patrol ran sweeps to deal with such complaints. Agents came by in a van, grabbed all the Hispanics in sight, and sifted through them later at the station, extending apologies to the few legally documented aliens who happened to crop up among the illegals. They can't do that anymore. An apology is no longer acceptable, and a wrongful arrest brings charges of harassment and may result in a civil-rights suit. Agents in a suburb like El Cajon, northeast of San Diego, must be very cautious about whom they arrest, and how the arrest is conducted, even though they're under pressure from citizens to be more forceful. Throughout the county, there has been a subtle change in the way Mexicans and Central Americans are perceived. Formerly, when an agent was observed hauling in a migrant he might be met with disapproving glances, as if he were bullying a poor person just trying to survive. Now an apprehension outside a convenience store or a pizza parlor is likely to be greeted by applause.

At the El Cajon Station, agents are concerned about a rise in acts of discrimination, and even violence, against migrant workers. They believe that a backlash has set in. This backlash takes many forms, some open and some covert. It can have an absurdist streak, as it does at Fairbanks Ranch, a wealthy subdivision, where D. Wayne Lukas, the horse trainer, stables some thoroughbreds, and where you can buy a midsized mansion on Alydar Court for a million five. Workers loiter by the ranch gates, looking to trim hedges or shovel manure, and periodically some neighborhood matrons give them litter bags of their own, so they won't throw their trash on the grass. Or it can be mean-spirited and life-threatening, as it was at the Carlsbad Country Store, where, two years ago, a butcher and a baker kidnapped a loitering Mexican, bound him with tape, put a paper bag over his head, and left him in the field. The kidnappers' claim that they were making a citizen's arrest for trespassing did not hold up in court.

For people who know San Diego County, the backlash doesn't

come as a surprise. The county is conservative, affluent, and Republican, and the city of San Diego, in particular, has always had a reputation for being tough on Hispanics, even those who were born in the United States. Hispanics constitute nearly twenty per cent of the city's population, but they have never had an elected representative on the City Council, because of the way the districts are gerrymandered. San Diego still depends on the military to bolster its economy, and it is still full of men in G.I. crewcuts who can scan the bay with binocs and tell the CG-47 Aegis guided-missile cruiser from the DD-965 guided-missile destroyer. In San Diego, the nineteen-fifties—an era of golf, highballs, and global dominance—remains a cultural beacon.

Organizations have been formed in San Diego to address the problems at the border. They go by such names as Alliance for Border Enforcement and Stamp Out Crime Council, and they contend that the United States is not enforcing the immigration laws on its books. They have statistics to show that illegal aliens are a drain on the county's resources. Its hospitals, its schools, its jails, and its welfare programs must all accommodate migrants, whether or not they are documented, and the expense, these organizations maintain, is debilitating. They resent the drug smuggling and the associated crime, and they're obsessed by the idea—for which there is no evidence—that terrorists are entering the country. The most militant individuals want to put troops on the border, or to build a wall or an electrified fence from San Ysidro to Otay Mesa. In an attempt to dramatize the need for greater vigilance, members of some of the organizations often drive in a caravan to San Ysidro, park on Dairy Mart Road, and aim their headlights at the Tijuana River levee, "lighting up" the border and exposing the aliens about to cross.

In the suburb of Del Mar, in San Diego County, there is a Oaxacan camp right off a two-lane road, across from Evergreen Nursery, where most of the men work. The men here are Mixtecs—about twenty-five of them in all—but their shacks are cruder than the ones in Carlsbad, more battered and wind-pierced, filthier. The Mixtecs live on brushy land without any shade trees, and the camp smells of decaying garbage, not eucalyptus or bay laurel. In the brush you find crushed beer cans and empty wine bottles. The shacks are thick with dust, because bulldozers are levelling the earth nearby, preparing it for a new housing tract. That means that the Mixtecs will soon have to move, although no one knows where.

It is strange to stand in the camp and look over your shoulder at the bulldozers and, beyond them, the orderly lines of pink and rose-colored condominiums stretching toward the ocean. In fact, if you're tired or a little disoriented—if you've been crossing the border yourself—you can forget exactly which country you are in. At quitting time, when the Mixtecs return from work, one of them begins strumming a guitar, while a woman—the only one around—goes from shack to shack borrowing ingredients to make a *caldo de res* for her lover. Her feet are bare, and she has on a new cotton dress that clings tightly to her body. The man with the guitar sighs and wishes aloud that he had a chicken to eat, or at least some tequila to drink.

Samuel Solano shares a shack at the camp with three others from his home village, sleeping on a cheap sleeping bag that pours out cotton stuffing. He has shoulder-length hair and a full beard, and if you tell him, as a joke, that he looks like a hippie he enjoys it very much. He works only three days a week at the nursery, because he doesn't yet have documents. He has applied for them, though, and carries around a creased and dirty envelope that contains photocopies of some formal letters pertaining to his request. His wife, also a Mixtec, is across the border in Ensenada, less than a hundred miles away, with their four children, and, in season, she picks tomatoes. Samuel wants to visit his family, but he doesn't dare cross over, because he isn't sure he could get back in. The risk is too big, he says, scratching at his beard, so he plans to wait for his documents to arrive. That might happen in the new year, he thinks. Then he will go south for a while, until it's time to leave his wife and head north once again.

BORDERLINE CASES

Border rats, my mother used to call us. She meant it as a joke, but there was some truth in what she said, for my family has lived along the Mexican border, in Arizona and Texas, since the 1940s. I am the only one who went away. And that was a long time ago.

Article by Earl Shorris, free-lance writer, from *Harper's* 281:68–75+ Ag '90. Copyright © 1990 by *Harper's*. Reprinted with permission.

Lately, there has been news from the border. The politics of Central America play out in the papers, repercussions are said to be felt along the Rio Grande, but I do not know what the reporters mean; there is no dust in the teeth of the stories. I decided to go back, to find out what had happened to home.

Returning, traveling 2,000 miles west from the East Texas Gulf Coast—along the Rio Grande and then through the desert to the Pacific—I expected the remembered place, where the rich country and the poor met in an ironic embrace of hope and commerce. Instead, I came across the dark side of home: a long line of violence and needless cruelty, beginning in a cluster of concentration camps and ending at Tijuana in an open sewer.

The border had never been a gentle place. But the nature of its rages has changed. In the past, violence had the good manners to stay off Main Street. Now I saw signs of it everywhere. It is the view from the living room of my sister's house. Between her windows and the nearby canyons of the Sierra Madre a chain-link fence topped with barbed wire has been erected, for when the sun goes down, crowds of desperate people come across the river and through the canyons to rob the houses and steal the cars of the rich.

The war between the U.S. Immigration and Naturalization Service [INS] and the tens of thousands of people without papers who come across the border every day is a brutal business done to no one's credit. The INS's Border Patrol is a failed police agency, a mismanaged collection of 3,800 sour agents who have no effect on the international drug trade and whose presence barely slows the rate of illegal crossings into the United States. (According to INS publicists, the agents capture at least one third of all people who enter the country illegally; if so, the border must be a busy place, for there may be as many as 10 million undocumented people in the United States.)

When I was a young man living along the border, murder was a modest business done between rivals and lovers behind closed doors. Now hundreds of bodies are found along the line every year. The deaths take place in public, as if murder had lost its shame. Most of those who die have no documents. Local police and Border Patrol agents kill some of them. Others die trying to cross the freeways under the protection of night. So many have been run down in and around San Diego that California now posts signs advertising drivers to watch out for people crossing.

Bandits and *cholos* (young hoodlums) do most of the killing.

That's the rumor, and in this case I think rumor is a good detective. A highschool kid in Chula Vista, California, told me that whenever the *cholos* from his school need money, they look for undocumented people, because they are so easy to rob. And sometimes, he said, the *cholos* hunt immigrants, especially the Indians who live in burrows out in the hills east of Oceanside, just for fun.

No one knows for certain how many are killed; the unknown dead lie somewhere in the desert. No one counts the useless cruelties, the physical and psychological beatings of the border. I have no numbers to offer. My own history puts me in danger of overstating the case. The best I can do is give you a few samples of what one border rat saw when he went home.

Brownsville, the Texas Key shelter. I first saw the Nicaraguan woman coming across the lawn from the south security post. She walked quickly, at a shopkeeper's purposeful pace. Her skirt, which was still wet at the hem from crossing the river, was too long, and her low-heeled pumps were stretched out of shape by the journey, gapped at the instep. She was as round as a barrel and as proper as geometry. Her glasses were rimless, fixed to her nose by wire and will. Her hair was light brown and blond and gray, pulled back tightly, gathered at the neck, trailing halfway down her back.

Without stopping to ask directions, she headed straight for the "intake desk." The young man on duty welcomed her and began filling out the usual documents.

She gave her name and date of birth: January 5, 1933. Although she was no more than four and a half feet tall, she seemed bigger, for she stood very straight, still a member of the great company of sergeants, the Latin American bourgeoisie.

"*Su destino?*" he asked.

Miami. My son is in Miami.

We'll help you to telephone him. Do you know his number?

"*Me robaron en el camino,*" she said. The Spanish consonants squeezed her face into an infant's grimace. Tears came. The bandits had taken everything, she said. Even the paper that had her son's number.

Beatriz, the shift supervisor, came out of an inner office. She was a foot taller than the Nicaraguan lady, and heavy. With one great arm Beatriz hugged the little woman. She held her close and stroked her arm; she cradled her. Then she led her down the corridor to the nurse's aide on duty. In the security of white uniforms and the smell of antiseptics, the little lady told of her experience on the other side of the border, of the men who had violated her, of how she had wept and bled and wandered for a month, alone at first, then working here and there while the physical wounds healed and the shame receded and she made herself ready to try again to cross the river.

After the woman left the examining room, the nurse's aide, whose heart knows no limits but who is as crude as a used truck, made jokes about rape. Then, for no apparent reason, her eyes narrowed and her face turned cold. She said that there are places in Mexico on the way to the border where every woman who passes through is raped. She shook her head. There is no way to know how many refugee women had been raped. Half of them? Three fourths? The Nicaraguan woman was a city dweller, she could talk about her experience. Modesty makes such frankness impossible in an Indian.

Bayview, Texas, the Immigration and Naturalization Service Processing Center. The camp lies well to the north of the Rio Grande, covering 317 acres in the flatlands beside the Gulf of Mexico. At the end of a long skein of narrow unmarked roads it appears abruptly, as if the horizon had parted to reveal the widely separated buildings, partially obliterated by the glare of the sun. Only a small sign identifies the place known as El Corralón, the big corral, the great animal pen, the concentration camp.

Two chain-link fences, topped with barbed wire and separated by a corridor of sand and brown grass, surround the camp. Television cameras watch the corridor and the corners, look into the barracks and the exercise yards; the entire camp is under constant electronic surveillance.

Bright orange jumpsuits identify the prisoners, all the prisoners alike: men and women, Guatemalans, Hondurans, Salvadorans, Nicaraguans (Contras, Sandinistas, Somocistas), young, old, criminals, schoolteachers, drug dealers, union organizers, shopkeepers, peasants. The first rule of El Corralón is the rule of we and they—the aliens wear orange. Since they all look alike, they appear to be nobody; yet they glow like traffic signs or like ripe fruit among green leaves, so they have no privacy. They are observed but unknown. Aliens.

They come by the busload. And wait. In the bus and then in long lines. Each person's name becomes a shout, an electronic rumbling on the public-address system, a handle, no longer a name, a thing by which the handler takes hold. They come wearing tennis shoes, T-shirts, blouses still redolent of cooking fires,

blue jeans, embroideries. The camp commander says he can tell a
person's country of origin by his clothing. The guards take the
clothing away first. Public showers and examinations follow. Each
person submits his body for inspection, feels a stranger push and
part his hair in search of lice.

Then nothing. The days are given to waiting. Some prisoners
clean the barracks, some do the laundry; they work to get
through the days. But the days go on too long. It is a prison
without sentences; one can post a bond of $1,500 to $3,000 and
be discharged in two or three days. But people without money
can remain for months and months while the courts consider
their appeals for political asylum.

Outside their barracks, two women in orange jumpsuits lay in
the dust and dead grass, resting their heads on a concrete walk-
way. They had been in El Corralón for a long time. One spoke
lazily to the camp commander as he walked by, asking about her
case. He had no news. He smiled politely. His gleaming boots, the
knife-crease of his trousers passed within inches of her head.

Trouble comes, the camp commander said, when anxiety
takes over. After a hearing before a panel of INS agents, trou-
blemakers are put into isolation cells. They have no right to counsel, there is no due process.

Human rights groups scrutinize El Corralón, but always from
outside, basing their work on love and hearsay. They have sued in
the federal courts and won relief for Salvadoran refugees in *Or-
antes* v. *Thornburgh,* but the papers on which he rights of prisoners
are printed cannot compensate for the capriciousness of the
federal immigration judges. These men, the lowest order of
federal judges, hear the pleas of prisoners who seek asylum. In
the little courtrooms of the camp there are no juries and often no
lawyers, just the prisoner, an interpreter, a tape recorder, and a
bored judge.

One afternoon I watched a Honduran refugee plead before a
thin, balding judge. The Honduran said he had been involved in
organizing labor in his country when three men approached him
on the street one day and whispered to him to stay out of the
labor movement.

The interpreter translated.

What were their names? the judge wanted to know.

The interpreter translated.

The Honduran said he didn't know. It was dark, the men had
stood behind him.

You don't even know their names, the immigration judge

asked, and yet you left your country because they talked to you on the street? He punished the pleading man with sarcasm.

The Honduran tried to explain that such men do not give their names.

The judged rolled his eyes and groaned.

It seemed the Honduran would be deported, but no one could be certain: The judges administer policy, not law, and U.S. immigration policy changes frequently and without warning. Generally, those fleeing countries in which the government is supported by the United States—El Salvador, Honduras, Guatemala—find it difficult to gain asylum. On the other hand, many Nicaraguans who claim to have fled from the Sandinistas complain that the U.S. government has treated them unfairly by refusing to grant asylum, even though one quarter of all Nicaraguans seeking asylum last year were granted entry, a high percentage when compared with other Central American countries. When the number of refugees increases, the percentage of those granted asylum seems to decrease. How the defeat of the Sandinistas will affect the Nicaraguans is not known. Caprice rules, not law. Trouble comes, the camp commander said, when anxiety takes over.

For a few months at the end of 1989 it was INS policy to move people quickly out of El Corralón, releasing them on bond or their own recognizance. The policy changed in the spring when the number of refugees increased. To protect the borders of the United States, the INS said, it would follow a new policy. Releases would stop. Hearings would be speeded up. Big tents, like those used for revival meetings, would be set up on the grounds. The population of El Corralón, which was designed to hold 1,200 adult males and females, would be expanded. The new limit would be 10,000.

Crowding, Primo Levi wrote, was one of the useless cruelties of the camps he knew.

San Benito, the Texas Key shelter for refugee families. Hundreds of men, women, and their children live together in one great room. No walls, no partitions, not more than a few feet of space separates the families. Each family is a clump on the open floor, and every clump represents an attempt to make a room of cardboard boxes, footlockers, and opaque object. All fail; there is no place where a baby can sleep unmolested in the afternoon, nor is there any structure to contain whispers, dreams, or an act of love.

The human and electronic voices of San Benito rise to the

rafters of the barnlike building and roll around there, gaining power; the naked, white wooden walls give back nothing but noise. A public-address system squawks above the din. It is the sound of the camps. After a while the noise and the anonymity of incessantly public life cracks the constructs of reason. As the months go by, some people lose the ability to sleep, others complain of bad dreams. Uncontrollable anxiety possesses one member of the family and infects all the rest.

The Martínez family—six tiny people from Guatemala, looking like darkly Oriental dolls, the mother with a touch of rouge on her cocoa-colored cheeks—live in a huddle of boxes on the floor of the shelter. They have no relatives in the United States and no money. The $1,500 to $3,000 bond is an insurmountable barrier for them; they will have to wait in San Benito until the INS judges their request for political asylum.

On the way to the border they were robbed twice. After the first robbery they got more money from home, but with only a tiny stake they could not afford a "coyote," someone to guide them through the bandits along the Rio Grande and into the United States. They were surrounded by men on horseback armed with machetes. One of them grabbed the youngest Martínez child and raised his machete over his head. He demanded everything—money, rings, earrings, belts, shoes—in exchange for the girl's life. *Hasta sus zapatos,* they say about the bandits who work the border: They take everything from the innocents, right down to their shoes.

So Señor Martínez unbuttoned his trousers and reached inside his underwear to the secret pocket his wife had sewn for him there and gave the bandits everything. He saved only the paper the guerrillas had delivered to him in his village, demanding that he join them, for he knew that the paper—which contained a threat from the communists—was his hope for political asylum, his evidence.

He showed me the paper, he read from it, but he could not concentrate on politics; the robbery occupied his mind, the men on horseback, the machetes. The bandits had made them all lie face down on the ground. Martínez remembers the machetes, his child. "I would die for my children," he said again and again, as if this willingness to die had become his reason for existence.

Along the Rio Grande near Brownsville. Sergio Ramírez, a man who sits like a hunting animal, looked through the window, searching for footprints, discarded clothing, the plastic bags in which emigrants carry dry clothing while crossing the river. As the van moved along the levee beneath the bridge to Matamoros, Ramírez saw two men half hidden in the brush beneath steel supports. Frank López, his partner, drove the van a few yards downriver. Ramírez climbed the steep side of the bank, loosening his .357 magnum in its holster. He approached the men, put them up against the side of the embankment, patted them down, found nothing.

"Glue sniffers," he told his partner. "It was all over their face. If I'd of known, I would have told you to come with me."

"Those bastards are superhuman," López said to me. "I've seen three, four men beat the shit out of one of them, still couldn't subdue him."

They were sure the glue sniffers had hidden weapons somewhere in the grasses under the bridge; they knew that before the night was over someone crossing the river would be caught and driven up into the shadows where the bandits do their work. But they could not wait.

Farther down the river, where many people pay fifty cents to a man who brings them across in a rubber raft, we passed a place where the rocks were still stained with the blood of an emigrant who had resisted the bandits. López himself worries about the bandits, especially after dark, when the roaring, rattling Border Patrol van makes a good target. Sometimes the bandits stand on the opposite bank of the river, he said, showing their weapons to *La Migra* and laughing.

"*La Migra,*" he said, "*la pinche Migra.*" He paused, as if to turn the insult over in his mind, to examine all the aspects of it, to taste the venom: "*Pinche Migra.*" Fucking Immigration.

Back in the city, López and Ramírez drove through the downtown streets near the river. The fixtureless storefronts selling secondhand clothing by the pound and the cheap jewelry and appliance stores had closed. In the dark, the streets belonged to the Mexican transvestites, men who cross the river carrying their costumes and makeup in waterproof bags, then dress and go to work in the streets. Ramírez called out the window to them, "*Oye, chula,* how can someone so ugly do any business?

"*Orale,* guy, let's go."

The transvestites have no papers, but no one arrests them, no one touches them: "They're unpredictable," Ramírez said. "They scratch and bite, and they might have AIDS."

The shift was quiet, slow for a weekend night, until someone crossed the river and set off one of the many seismic sensors. The dispatcher gave the sector number over the radio. López drove to a building near the highway and parked the van behind it. Ramírez climbed out and walked to the edge of the building, moving carefully, staying in the shadows. He stuck his head out quickly to look around the side. Nothing. He knew someone was coming: a trembling refugee? a group of drug runners carrying automatic weapons? The sensor gave no indication. It registers a football. Something heavier than a dog. No more information than that. He waited, looked, and looked again.

Then: *"Arriba las manos!* Up against the wall. Shut up! Shut up!"

Ramírez screamed at the shapes, kept on screaming, shining his flashlight, pushing them, pushing, screaming. There were three of them, and they were just boys. Ramírez shone his light on the seat of their pants. It showed the outline of their underwear, which was still wet from crossing the river. López drove up in the van and they put the boys inside. There was no conversation. López drove down to the river. At the bridge back to Mexico, Ramírez let them out. He spent a moment with them in front of the truck, making empty threats, then herded them across.

Ramírez says that when he picks up people he calls "wets," they often appeal to him, one Latino to another, to let them go. He never does. They are not Americans, he says; he has no feeling for them, no connection to them; he particularly despises the refugees from El Salvador who refuse to fight for their country. In considering this it is useful to know that Sergio Ramírez was born in Baja California, the son of a man who entered the United States illegally.

Pharr, Texas, Colonia Las Milpas. As many as 100,000 people live in unincorporated communities called "colonias" along the border. Most of the colonias have no sewerage or running water. Perhaps the most eminent of the people who live in the colonias, surely the most dramatic, is a seventy-year-old woman who was a schoolteacher in Mexico some generations ago, Carmen Anaya. She is an accomplished orator, a woman whose voice modulates from a whisper to a rage of indignation in the space of a sentence:

"There was a heavy rain. Because we have no drainage and no sewers, there was no place for the water to go. It came up to the houses, which were level to the street. The *casitas* [outhouses] were flooded. The worms and the black water came out. The worms crawled up the walls of the houses to the windows.

"The children walked and played in the black water. The filth caused them to get sick, rashes broke out on their skin. When I saw this, I went to town and told the people who are responsible for sewers and drains to come and see what had happened.

"When they arrived, I said to them, 'Get into it. Get out of your cars and put yourselves in it.'

"One showed me his boots, his fine new boots. He said that he did not want to walk in the filth with his fine new boots. He cared more for his boots than the children."

El Paso, along the river. In the vans used by the Border Patrol at El Paso, the backseats have been removed. Undocumented people sit or crouch on the floor, sometimes for hours, while the agents do their work, racing through the streets and out along the rough, rutted roads near the river, chasing more Mexicans.

For many years, teams of Border Patrol agents and local police burst into cantinas frequented by Latinos in South El Paso, near the border, lined up the patrons, and demanded to see proof of citizenship. Native-born Americans of Mexican descent were often arrested, piled into Border Patrol vans, and held in prison cells until they could prove their citizenship. The practice slowed after civil rights lawyers won an injunction in a U.S. District Court.

According to the Binational Center for Human Rights, the Mexican consul in El Paso claimed there were 2,000 abuses of human rights in the state of Texas in 1988 alone. All the victims were Mexicans or Mexican-Americans. The majority of abuses took place along the border.

Border Patrol agents say that the treatment of undocumented people along the Texas border is more humane than the California. "Why do people criticize us?" one of them asked me. "We're just doing our job. We don't bring all these people here. It's a political problem."

Vista, California, the canyons southeast of town. When we broke out of the wooded area and began climbing, there was suddenly the blue-white light of the undiminished moon. We could see everything—the hills, the tomato field ahead and above, and more woods. Sergio Mendez led the way, climbing quickly to the level of the tomato field. We crossed over the low plastic fence that bordered the field and walked across the rows. After the field, which was on one of the few flat places, we came to a steep drop. At first we tried to climb down, but we quickly realized that it was impassable, a tiny canyon. Mendez turned west, looking for a place to cross or descend. In his fleece-lined denim jacket and workman's pants, he was a cube of a man, thick and strong, an *indígeno*, he

called himself, of the Mixtecs—the Cloud People, whose civilization flourished in Oaxaca a thousand years ago. His fingers were
short, but his hand was so wide and thick that I could not grasp it
properly when we helped each other down the side of the hill.

He moved quickly, he knew the way, although there was now
no trail or other marking that I could see in the moonlight. At
another place, deeper in the trees, he saw a passable place and we
climbed down. Mendez went first, finding the hand and
footholds. I came after, trying to pick the same places. There was
a little jump at the end into the soft dirt of the woods.

Then we moved through a deeply wooded area, following a
clearly defined path. I heard voices and smelled a cooking fire
somewhere down the hill. Mendez moved faster, certain of his
bearings. It was dark among the trees where the moonlight did
not penetrate. The dogs rushed out at us there, snarling and
barking. There were three, possibly four dogs. They surrounded
Mendez, who hissed at them and called ahead in a soft voice to
people he thought might know him.

A man came out of the darkness to silence the dogs. Mendez
and I followed him down the hill to the lean-to where the smell of
the cooking fires originated. Five men sat inside the lean-to,
which was warmed by two fires inside metal drums. There was no
light but a candle flame and the little glow of the fires in the
drums. The men did not sleep in the lean-to. It was a place for
cooking and talking. They slept farther out on the hill, in places
they had dug into the ground; not in caves but in burrows, holes
dug at the base of a tree.

There were two older men and three young ones. The young
ones did not have papers, which made them nervous at first. They
stayed back, at the edge of the candlelight. Mendez spoke of
his business, of laws and rights, of the need to preserve the Mixtec
culture; then the men and I talked.

Tens of thousands of Mixtec Indians have come from the
villages of Oaxaca to work and live in Baja California and in the
towns across the border. Mendez said they are despised in Mexico
and in the United States because they are small and very dark-
skinned. In Mexico they have become the labor force of the Valle
de San Quintín, the gigantic complex of Japanese-owned truck
farms, where people live inside barbed-wire enclosed com-
pounds, eighteen to a room, existing in something he described as
slavery or what others have told him is a concentration camp. On
the U.S. side, the Mixtecs live in constant fear of attack from *cholos*
or white racists. Not far from where we were sitting, a Mixtec had

been found with his throat cut. Down on the main road, in back of a grocery store, two Mixtecs had been grabbed from behind, blindfolded, robbed, and beaten.

Between July 31 and August 14 of 1989, seven murders, shootings, and stabbings of migrant workers were reported to police in the little cluster of farm towns in San Diego County. It is the way of life here, the risk men run to earn enough money to send home to their families in Oaxaca or Baja California. Generally, they suffer in secret, silent except among themselves. If they are sick, the hospitals turn them away; if they are robbed or beaten or shot, the police turn them over to the Border Patrol. None of these men speaks English, many are more comfortable in Mixteco than Spanish.

The men inside the lean-to said that when they go out to work during the day, they sometimes come back to find that the *cholos* have been there, and everything of value is gone. Even so, they are glad to be alive and whole. They make the only possible adjustment: If they cannot defend their personal belongings, they will have none. They live for winter, when they can go home.

I asked them why they did not bring their families across the border. One man answered by describing his village in Oaxaca. Another man said he did not want his children to live in the United States because there was nothing here for them but drugs, violence, and rock and roll.

San Ysidro, the U.S. side of the border. A twenty-three-year-old Mexican man was shot by a Border Patrol agent, who said the man had thrown a rock at him. In his defense the man said that he had picked up the rock and threatened the agent after the agent grabbed his pregnant wife by the hair, pulled her down to the ground, and stepped on her belly. A jury in a U.S. District Court found the wounded man not guilty of throwing a rock.

Fifteen years ago the Border Patrol began hiring Mexican-Americans. Instead of changing the agency's racist attitudes, it added the more brutal racism of the dark-skinned overseer, the one who proves to his white masters that he is loyal and who separates himself from his own people by brutalizing them. Everywhere along the California border the response to violence has been to create more violence. The Border Crime Prevention Unit formed jointly by the San Diego Police and the Border Patrol shot twenty-six people, all Mexican citizens, in its first five years. Nineteen of them died. The level of violence connected with the unit is astonishing; in less than six years of operation the entire unit has been suspended twice, both times after a rash of killings.

The battle has gone on so long the roles of the police and the bandits have blurred. Here, at the edges of the countries, the social order no longer holds.

Tijuana, Baja California, Cañón Zapata. A long, deeply rutted road leads down into the canyon. It is strewn with garbage, made almost impassable by stones and by sudden breaks in the steep slope. On the left, the houses of the old colonia have been constructed in a style peculiar to Tijuana: The backs rest against the slope of the hill and the fronts are held level by foundations made of discarded automobile tires.

On the right, as the road falls sharply down through the rounded hills, the shell of an automobile, covered with rust from the roof to the base of the fenders, sits starkly against the north sky, orange and monumental.

No line, no fence, no river marks the boundary between the United States and Mexico here—only a row of small stones halfway down the side of one of the hills. By late afternoon, seventy-five or a hundred people had gathered. More filtered down through the hills and between the houses as the daylight weakened. Tables and cooking fires had been set up in the flat places on the hill. Women dressed against the cold in layers of clothing cooked fried chicken, beans, hot coffee. A peddler wandered among the waiting people selling blankets, scarves, beans, and small bottles of tequila.

The only customers were the people without papers; they are everybody's customers, everybody's prey; they belong to the coyotes—who guide them to the other side of the river for $100 or all the way to Los Angeles for $350—and to the glove sellers and tequila peddlers and coffee and chicken sellers, even to the waifs who walk the hills selling Chiclets. If the emigrants try to cross without a coyote and they have bad luck, they will become customers of the *cholos*, who will leave them picked clean, barefoot, beaten, and raped, able only to crawl back into Mexico.

As the sun went down behind the hills, leaving parts of the canyon in sudden shadow, people began looking over at the long ridge to the north, to the place called the soccer field, where Border Patrol agents waited in a pale green van and a four-wheel-drive truck, watching, waiting for the first of the emigrants to file down the path between the hills into the deep shadows of the floor of the canyon from which they would make their run.

The emigrants stood or sat in small groups, waiting until it was time to go. Although the number of people on the hills increased rapidly with the coming of the dark, there was very little noise. Only those who were not going across spoke; all the rest were quiet, waiting.

The coyotes appeared then, counting their chickens. Somewhere down in the darkness the *cholos* waited. The emigrants knew this was the existential place, without law or family, outside the rules of order, beyond prediction. A young woman made jokes, insouciant in the dangerous moment. She had put on makeup and had her hair done before crossing the line; she wore white tennis shoes. Beside her, three more women huddled inside their blankets. One was terrified. She said she knew no one on the other side, she had no job, no place to go. I wrote out the name of a sanctuary in Los Angeles. "If you get that far," I said, "you can rest there for a few days and get something to eat. This is my name. The priest is my friend." She took the paper and folded it and reached inside her blanket to hide it in her blouse. She cried a little over the paper. Then she drew the blanket tightly around herself, as if it could shield her from what was to come.

The danger is real. By the time they get across the border into the United States, most of the emigrants will have been robbed, beaten, extorted, or raped by bandits or Mexican police. The Binational Center for Human Rights in Tijuana puts the percentage of such victims at sixty-five.

At dark a man in a shiny warm-up jacket, his wife, and three children started down the narrow path into the deepest part of the canyon. The woman carried a baby slung across her back in a rebozo. All the others carried plastic grocery bags. Up on the hill the coyotes nodded to their customers to get ready. Near the stones that mark the boundary, the woman who knew no one on the other side folded up her blanket and prepared to go. The emigrants bent quietly, moving like animals through the night, atavistic shapes, bent low to the ground, neolithic runners in postmodern shoes.

Tijuana, Baja California, Salón del Pueblo. The ugliest town had put on a gaudy dress. Neon and mirrors decorate the downtown streets; the richest citizens attend shopping malls filled with chain stores from across the border; a cultural center, like the one in Ciudad Juárez, with shops and theaters, ingests tourists; the rich, newly arrived from Mexico City, live in high-rise apartments and hilltop houses in parts of the city known as the elegant zones. The street vendors, Indian women from Oaxaca, have been removed from the areas the tourists frequent—they are too Mexican, the merchants say, too poor, too short, too dark.

Tijuana is a boomtown, the boosters claim, selling 1 percent unemployment, a million and a half inhabitants, and a glorious future. The annual meeting of the Border Commission on Human Rights held last March revealed a different picture. It began with reports by the delegates, all of them from human rights organizations working along the border. Roberto Martínez, of the American Friends Service Committee Border Program in San Diego, and Victor Clark Alfaro, of the Binational Center for Human Rights in Tijuana, chaired the meeting. The delegates spoke, rolling out their litanies of people detained, arrested, tortured, killed. Could the figures be true? One hundred and nine documented cases of the torture of children by Mexican police in Tijuana. Eight hundred and twenty-six "disappeared" people in Mexico. Fifteen hundred dead along the California border between 1984 and 1989.

It was mostly understatement, they said; the statistics are no good. Undocumented people in the United States do not go to the police to make complaints; they are afraid of being deported. Central American refugees in Mexico cannot wait for six or ten months until a bandit or rapist comes to trial; they are going north.

The next day the revelations and accusations made at the meeting were front-page news in Mexico, where the government is said to control the media. Not one word about the commission appeared in a leading paper in the United States. The border remains unconsidered. There is still no policy which would permit an orderly entry and exit for those who come to work or shop but not to immigrate. Nor is there any way for people to seek temporary asylum here; to live and work without fear until conditions at home improve. To distinguish between sojourners and immigrants would be a step in the direction of a truly civil society on the U.S. side of the border. In Mexico, the innocent poor will have to defend themselves.

FROM YUKON TO YUCATÁN

To hear George Bush tell it, a free-trade pact between the U.S. and Mexico would be the next best thing to a free lunch.

Article by S. C. Gwynne, staff writer, from *Time* 137:20–1+ Je 3 '91. Copyright © 1991 by the Time Inc. Magazine Company. Reprinted with permission.

Abolishing trade barriers between the two nations would unleash a flood of new investment that would create hundreds of thousands of jobs on both sides of the border and help stanch the tidal wave of illegal immigration from Mexico into the Southwestern states. The only downside would be temporary "dislocations" in a few American industries until they can adjust to new economic realities.

But to the President's equally passionate adversaries, the proposed North American free-trade agreement would be a disaster. It would cause devastating job losses and a further decline for struggling U.S. manufacturing industries. It would raise the specter of an environmental catastrophe equivalent to a 2,000-mile Love Canal along the U.S.-Mexico border. And it would increase America's vulnerability to Asian competition by allowing the Japanese to take advantage of Mexico's cheap labor and use that country as a staging area for a new surge of exports to the U.S.

The enormous gulf between these competing visions of the future has produced one of the hottest legislative battles of the year—and the most feverish trade debate in memory. It pits a muscular coalition of protectionist Democrats, Big Labor and environmental groups against free-market Republicans, much of corporate America, and a high-profile Mexican government team backed by squadrons of big-time lobbyists and public relations firms.

The issue came to a head last week when both houses of Congress, after heated arguments, passed resolutions extending the so-called fast-track authority that U.S. Administrations have long used to negotiate international trade agreements. Translated from Washington-speak, fast track would authorize the President and his Trade Representative, Carla Hills, to cut a deal with Mexico without congressional meddling. The lawmakers would have the power to vote down a treaty once it is reached, but not to alter it.

At stake in this showdown is Bush's vision of a North American free-trade zone stretching from the Yukon to the Yucatán. If he is able to add a Mexican pact to the free-trade agreement concluded with Canada in 1988, the effect would be to consolidate 360 million consumers into a $6 trillion market, 32% larger than the European Community. The question being posed by skeptics is whether the pact will provide the benefits Bush predicts, or instead increase America's already dire trade deficit, which is expected to reach $75 billion this year. Both economic theory and historic fact support Bush. The Soviet Union's imploding economy is a good example of what happens when a country closes its doors to trade through tariffs, import quotas and other constraints. Mexico, in contrast, offers perhaps the best current example of the benefits that can occur when a country lowers trade barriers. Since the mid-1980s, Mexico has taken a number of daring, unilateral steps to shed the shackles of protectionism. It has slashed its maximum tariff rates from 100% to 20%, and its average tariff from 25% to 10%, while scrapping other nontariff barriers to imports. Seeking a larger role for free enterprise, the country has put many of its 1,155 inefficient state-owned companies up for sale to private interests.

Result: after years of negative growth, Mexico's economy is expanding at a brisk 4% annual rate. Inflation has plummeted from 160% in 1987 to about 25%. The boom has created new markets for U.S. exports, which have more than doubled, from $12.4 billion in 1986 to $28.4 billion last year, creating an estimated $264,000 new jobs in the U.S. in machinery, equipment and agricultural sectors. Mexico is America's third largest trading partner (after Canada and Japan), importing $295 per capita from the U.S., vs. $266 for the European Community.

According to separate studies by the University of Maryland, the accounting firm Peat Marwick and the International Trade Commission, a free-trade agreement would accelerate these welcome trends. The University of Maryland study, for example, predicts that the U.S. economy would gain 44,500 jobs in the first five years of a free-trade pact. The big winners would include producers of machinery and metals, chemicals, plastics and rubber. The losers: clothing, construction, parts of the fruit and vegetable business, furniture, leather and glass.

Mexican industries, notably capital goods like machine tools, would suffer considerably from U.S. competition at first. But those losses would be more than balanced by a flood of new investment from the U.S., Japan and other nations. That influx could help offset Mexico's burdensome $97 billion debt, for which there are few prospects of forgiveness.

The pact's opponents look at the evidence and reach opposite conclusions. They fear that Mexico's low wages (averaging $2.32 an hour, vs. $14.31 for American workers) will tempt U.S. companies to move vast numbers of unskilled and semiskilled manufacturing jobs south of the border. A recent study by the General Accounting Office, for example, found that employment in the

U.S. furniture industry dropped 10% in the past year. All those jobs were lost when 28 wood-furniture makers moved to Mexico in search of cheaper labor and less restrictive environmental rules. Florida's fruit and vegetable growers claim the plan would "annihilate" 8,700 agricultural jobs and billions of the state's farming revenue. According to the United Automobile Workers, 75,000 jobs have already been lost to Mexico.

Those who would try to protect low-skilled jobs have good reason to fear the agreement. Even though Mexicans are far less productive than their American counterparts, there is no arguing with the competitive advantages of cheap wages. Just how American workers would be affected by more open borders can be measured by what has happened to the 2,000 plants along the U.S.-Mexico line that enjoy barrier-free trade. Nine out of 10 of those plants—known as *maquiladoras*—are owned by U.S. companies; they employ 465,000 Mexican workers, who are mainly engaged in assembly of electronic, automotive and textile products for export to the U.S. Those are, in fact, jobs that have gone south. And while American manufacturers argue that this kept jobs from moving to Asia, that is small comfort to displaced, unskilled American workers.

Democratic Senator Bob Kerrey of Nebraska, who supports free trade, says the only solution is for the U.S. to come to grips with the deteriorating competitiveness of its work force. "There's a much larger issue here," says Kerrey. "If all I do is focus on low-skilled jobs lost in textiles or small-scale manufacturing, I'd be missing the point, saying, well, I'm just going to protect those jobs. I believe free trade is good for us in the long run, but I also believe that we have to address the issue of worker education and training and readjustment."

Another fear expressed by critics is that a free-trade agreement, which will have the effect of locking in all of Mexico's liberalizations, will end up simply providing the Japanese with opportunities to invest in plants that will export to the U.S. That would squarely contradict one of the Bush Administration's primary aims: to create a trading bloc in the western hemisphere to compete with the formidable bloc being created by Japan in Asia.

"[Mexican President] Carlos Salinas de Gortari has said Mexico wants Asian investment," says Clyde Prestowitz, president of the Economic Strategy Institute, a Washington think tank. "He wants it in high-value-added, high-technology industries [that will] be exporting to the U.S. What we emphatically don't want to do is to make Mexico safe for Japanese investment." Prestowitz' solution is for the U.S. to induce foreign investors to export certain percentages of what they make in Mexico to third countries.

Whatever else it does, a Mexican free-trade agreement seems likely to accelerate the decline in the number of American manufacturing jobs, which provided 35% of U.S. employment in 1948 but now account for only 17%. In time, say economists, both technological advances in the U.S. and competitive pressures from low-wage countries will mean the loss of most of America's unskilled or semiskilled manufacturing jobs.

One of the major arguments against the proposed pact is not economic but ecological: the *maquiladoras* have an unenviable track record of pollution, which is affecting the health of Americans across the border. Says Stewart Hudson of the National Wildlife Federation: "The *maquiladora* program is a case study of the kinds of environmental catastrophes that can happen where trade and investment rule." The biggest fear of environmental groups, which include Environmental Action, Greenpeace and Friends of the Earth, is that the leaks and spills and pollution of border rivers such as the New River and the Nogales Wash will turn the border into a cesspool, and that Mexico will end up exporting to the U.S. both its pollution and products made in environmentally friendly ways.

Bush's victory on Capitol Hill last week was the result of some uncharacteristically deft political maneuvering on the domestic front. He has succeeded in splintering both textile and environmental lobbies, while mollifying fence-sitting Democrats such as Richard Gephardt by assuring them that the issues of environment, rules of origin covering foreign investors in Mexico, and adjustment programs for displaced workers will be addressed before any agreement is signed. Bush also cornered the Democrats into choosing between two important constituencies, labor and Hispanics. Just as Bush hoped, the Democratic National Committee recently denounced fast-track authorization, which put them on the side of the shrinking constituency, against the growing one. "The party is not looking at the numbers," said a Democratic Congressman who supported fast track. "They're choosing the protectionist label over a community that will be the largest ethnic minority in 10 years."

Although last week's vote cleared away the biggest obstacle to negotiating a trade agreement with Mexico, it will be some time before Congress gets to vote on an actual agreement. When it is completed, it is likely to be so loaded with adjustments for threatened industries that very little pain will be felt in this country for a long time. And the benefits, according to most economists, will be felt most keenly by the next generation.

III. MIGRATION FROM SOUTHEAST ASIA

EDITOR'S INTRODUCTION

The articles in this section consider the immigrant group of Southeast Asians, who have become an increasing presence in America in the last two decades. This group includes mainland Chinese, Hong Kong Chinese, Vietnamese, Laotians, Cambodians, Koreans, Filipinos, and Japanese. On the whole, Southeast Asians have assimilated well into American life, though among some Americans there is resentment toward Japan as an economic superpower perceived to be a threat to our position in trade, manufacturing, and technology. To some degree, this prejudicial attitude toward Japan carries over in attitudes toward the other Asian groups. Either latent or overt racism affected American views of Asian immigrants in the nineteenth and in much of the twentieth centuries, when they were admitted in conspicuously smaller numbers than were Europeans.

The opening article in this section, by Robert L. Funster writing in the *State Department Bulletin*, consists of the text of two addresses he gave before the Families of Vietnamese Political Prisoners Association and the UN High Commissioner for Refugees Orderly Departure Program. In these talks, Funster, a State Department official, speaks of the negotiations pursued by the U.S. State Department with representatives of the Vietnamese government for the release of former officials of South Vietnam held in reeducation camps. As a result of the talks, Vietnam made a commitment to permit 6,000 people to depart legally each month, with the U.S. accepting half of this number initially. In a following article in *America*, Bartholomew Lahiff argues that the U.S. should make every effort to receive refugees presently lodged in camps in Southeast Asia. The Chinese, he points out, have one of the lowest crime rates of any ethnic group, and are among the highest achievers in American schools and universities.

In the third article, Kenneth Labich in *Fortune* indicates that since the Vietnam War ended in 1975, the U.S. has taken in nearly a million Southeast Asian refugees, more than 500,000 of whom were Vietnamese. More recently, however, quotas for

Southeast Asian refugees have fallen sharply, to no more than 50,000 in 1989. Labich believes that the number should be increased, especially in view of the many uprooted Chinese refugees seeking asylum in the West. In the past the Chinese have assimilated well into American life—entering the labor force quickly, doing well in school, working hard, and moving upward in society. Labich also states that U.S. immigration officials' approval or rejection of the applications of those in Asian refugee camps follows no real logic. On the one hand, a strong feeling exists that immigrants with relatives in the U.S. should be favored; but on the other hand many believe that those with especially desirable skills should be given priority.

The next article in this section, by John Schwartz in *Time*, discusses the transformation of Los Angeles as the "Eastern Capital" of Asia. Although Hispanics make up Los Angeles's largest and fastest growing minority group, the city is also the home of considerable numbers of Filipinos, Vietnamese, Koreans, and other Asians. A 70-square block section called Koreatown forms a special ethnic enclave within the city; and Monterey Park, a well-to-do suburb, has a population that is 50 percent Asian. Moreover, Los Angeles is a center of trade with Asia; three-quarters of the downtown office space is foreign-owned or -controlled, nearly a third of it by the Japanese. Yet striking as the Asian presence in L.A. is today, it will be stronger still in the future. By the year 2000 it is estimated that Asian immigrants in the U.S. will number 12 million. The final article, an excerpt from *Civil Rights Issues Facing Asian Americans in the 1990s*, deals with the bigotry and violence experienced by Asian Americans.

ASPECTS OF U.S. RESETTLEMENT PROGRAMS FOR VIETNAMESE REFUGEES

Address, November 14, 1987

I am deeply honored by your invitation to share this evening with you in support of the Vietnamese political prisoners and to

Two addresses by Robert Funseth, U.S. Senior Deputy Assistant Secretary for Refugee Programs, given respectively to the Families of Vietnamese Political Prisoners Association and to the UN High Commissioner for Refugees Orderly Departure Program. From *Department of State Bulletin* 88:58–60 My '88. Copyright © 1988 by *Department of State Bulletin*. Reprinted with permission.

be asked to address you. I have the greatest respect for your noble cause and the greatest admiration for your personal courage in sustaining your heartfelt efforts and in maintaining your hope in the face of tremendous emotional hardship and torment.

Sitting together to share a meal is one of the most venerated of traditions in the history of the human family. It is, therefore, right and proper that we should experience together this profoundly symbolic act as we commemorate and rededicate ourselves to the freedom of your husbands, your fathers, your brothers, and your relatives and our Vietnamese colleagues and our friends.

You will all remember that in September 1984, Secretary Shultz made the historic announcement of President Reagan's great humanitarian initiative aimed at bringing all of the "reeducation" camp prisoners and their qualifying family members to the United States. You will also recall that, sadly, the Vietnamese authorities backed away from their initial willingness to negotiate with us to implement the President's program. We profoundly regret that change. We sincerely hope it will change.

When it was my privilege to speak briefly at your solemn commemoration in April at the U.S. Capitol—which marked the 12th anniversary of the imprisonment of your loved ones—I reaffirmed our readiness to resume bilateral discussions with Hanoi at any time. Six weeks ago, in his testimony before the Congress of the United States, Secretary of State Shultz again reiterated this pledge on behalf of the government.

And this evening I stand before you to reaffirm with the strongest possible words and feelings our firm commitment to continue our steadfast efforts to bring about the release and resettlement in the United States of all the former and current "reeducation" camp prisoners and their accompanying family members who wish to be resettled in America.

Proposals To Hasten Resettlement and Reunification

I believe you all know that we have urged the Vietnamese Government to allow all the prisoners who have been released from their "reeducation" camp prisons to apply to leave Vietnam through the Orderly Departure Program (ODP) and to approve their applications for exit permits. Since our formal presentation of the President's initiative to the representatives of the Vietnamese Government in Geneva in 1984, 270 former prisoners and over 1,000 of their accompanying family members—for a total of nearly 1,300 persons—have been allowed to come to the United States. Perhaps some of you are here this evening.

However pleased we are that these 1,300 persons have been permitted to leave, we remain greatly disappointed that there are 11,000 other Vietnamese—including 2,280 former prisoners—whose names we have sent to the Vietnamese, who have not been given permission to leave, as well as many, many others who still have not come to our attention.

In your association's letter to me, you noted the September announcement in Hanoi of the release of 480 political prisoners and asked that we consider five specific proposals that might hasten their resettlement and reunification with relatives in the United States. Please allow me now to respond directly to each of your proposals.

First, you asked that we: "continue to press Vietnam to release the prisoners for resettlement in the United States."

We have done so. We are doing so. We will do so. Our policy is clear; our objective is clear. We have declared, again and again, our readiness to negotiate the release of all political prisoners, and we intend to keep trying. I will once more be leading the U.S. delegation to the annual meetings with the Vietnamese in Geneva 3 weeks from now, and I pledge that we will again use these bilateral meetings to reaffirm strongly President Reagan's humanitarian initiative for the release of the "reeducation" camp prisoners and for their resettlement in the United States.

Second, you asked that we: "assure that, if these political prisoners are allowed to emigrate, adequate budget and resettlement numbers are available to take care of this increased requirement."

You always have our assurance to do this. We stand prepared to take all necessary steps, in consultation with the Congress, to ensure that we have the necessary money and refugee admission numbers to resettle any and all of these prisoners the Vietnamese authorities allow to emigrate and who wish to be resettled in the United States.

Third, you asked that we: "assure that letters of introduction (LOIs) are issued to any of the recently released political prisoners who do not have such a letter as soon as the names of these political prisoners can be identified."

Again, you have our assurance. When we are informed of the identity of recently released prisoners, the American Embassy in Bangkok is instructed immediately to review the files and issue LOIs wherever needed.

Fourth, you asked that we: "be prepared to establish a bilateral program with Vietnam to process the political prisoners if necessary and required by the Vietnamese."

You ask that we be prepared to establish a bilateral program. We have already had direct bilateral meetings with the Vietnamese in 1984, 1985, and 1986. I can assure you that we are fully prepared to establish such a bilateral program if this is necessary. It may not be necessary. Our current Orderly Departure Program mechanism and the initiative we have put to the Vietnamese representatives for these prisoners would be perfectly sufficient without the establishment of a separate program. Through it, we have resettled 1,300 former prisoners and their families. However, if the Vietnamese authorities indicate that they would prefer to establish such a bilateral program with us for these prisoners, we are ready to discuss the modalities of such a program without further delay.

Finally, fifth, you asked that we: "provide to the Vietnamese community, in writing, clear guidelines on what family members can accompany."

We appreciate that clear guidelines on accompanying family members are of great importance to all of you. Our office has already provided your president with a written explanation of the current guidelines. If additional information or clarification is required, we will be more than happy to provide that as well, and we are always available to answer any of your questions.

Resumption of the Orderly Departure Program

I am pleased to be able this evening to give you some good news about the Orderly Departure Program itself. It is working again, and we are encouraged by the way things seem to be going. After 18 months of persistent U.S. diplomatic activity, we succeeded in July in reaching an agreement with the Vietnamese Government for the resumption of interviews for the ODP. In September, a parallel agreement was reached on a bilateral program with the Vietnamese Government for the Amerasian children. Two interview trips to Vietnam by teams of U.S. consular and INS [Immigration and Naturalization Service] officers from the American Embassy in Bangkok have now been successfully completed. Each resulted in the interview and approval of over 1,000 persons. We now expect to be making further interview trips on a reasonably regular basis, and we hope for similarly positive results.

I am sure that all of you are aware that at the beginning of 1986, the ODP suffered a severe setback. At that time, the Vietnamese authorities unilaterally suspended the interviewing of new ODP applicants for the United States and sharply cut back the ODP program for all other participating countries. We conducted a series of meetings with Vietnamese officials over the next 18 months, during which we urged that interviewing be allowed to resume and during which we made proposals on how the interviewing process could be improved and accelerated once it was resumed.

In July of this year in Hanoi, the Vietnamese Government accepted our proposals and agreed to a resumption of interviewing in Ho Chi Minh City. Since then, we have twice sent interview teams to Ho Chi Minh City. I am very pleased to be able to report to you this evening that these trips have been, in our view, successful, and we are encouraged by the way they have gone and, indeed, by the very good cooperation which the Vietnamese officials in Ho Chi Minh City have extended to the U.S. officials.

Let me explain briefly how the interview process has changed and why we believe it could result in faster departures from Vietnam for those we are able to interview and approve. Before the end of 1985, the interviewing was done for us by UNHCR [UN High Commissioner for Refugees] personnel. The results of the interviews were then taken back to the American Embassy in Bangkok, where they had to be reviewed by U.S. consular and immigration officers. Under the new U.S.-proposed procedures, U.S. consular and immigration officers are going directly to Ho Chi Minh City to conduct the interviews in person. This means that, hopefully, most cases can be adjudicated on the spot, subject to satisfactory medical examination results, with final approval normally occurring within only a few weeks after the interviews take place. Since there is no longer a long backlog of people waiting for flights, we hope that the first of those approved in September will be able to join their relatives in the United States before the end of the year.

There still remain some unresolved processing problems. As you know, the ODP office at the embassy in Bangkok issues letters of introduction on behalf of applicants whose files are sufficiently complete and who have either an approved Form I-130 petition which is "current," or nearly so, or who have been tentatively approved for travel. The United States has provided to the Vietnamese authorities the names of everyone to whom we have issued an LOI. In August of this year, after the Vietnamese Government agreed to the resumption of interviewing, the American Embassy sent them a new consolidated list of everyone to whom an LOI had been issued who was still in Vietnam. That list contained about 95,000 names. We hope that the Vietnamese authorities will increasingly draw from these U.S. lists of persons who have already been issued LOIs.

For most of the time that interviewing was suspended, the Vietnamese Government did not issue any exit permits—or issued only a very few. The good news is that they have, in recent months, resumed issuing some exit permits again. So we will make this one suggestion for something you can do: if your relatives in Vietnam have LOIs but do not have exit permits, we would suggest that you urge them to reapply now, either for an exit permit or for an appointment for an interview. The chances for favorable action on a request may be better than they have been for some time. Urge your family members in Vietnam to take a copy of their LOI to the appropriate authorities and try again now. They may not be successful, but they may be.

U.S. Commitment to Refugee Resettlement

Our mission is not to posture. Our mission is to bring about the freedom of your relatives and to obtain Vietnamese agreement for their resettlement in the United States. Therefore, we must be discreet and careful in what we say in public. We leave the polemics to others. When we meet with the Vietnamese authorities on this unresolved humanitarian issue we must be sober, sincere, and serious—and we are.

There is, we believe—based on the recent positive developments concerning the Orderly Departure Program—some reason to be hopeful that there may be better news ahead about the "reeducation" camp prisoners and their prospects for being allowed to leave Vietnam for resettlement here.

In June, in an address to the foreign ministers of the Southeast Asian countries meeting in Singapore, Secretary of State George Shultz declared that the United States would support the countries of first asylum for the long haul, including the continuation of a substantial American refugee resettlement program. In September, this pledge was made concrete in President

Reagan's formal proposal to the Congress and subsequent determination to set the first-asylum admissions ceiling for FY [fiscal year] 1988 at 29,500 and the ODP ceiling at 8,500, for a total of 38,000 persons.

Commitment is, indeed, the watchword of U.S. refugee policies and programs. We are committed to humanitarian ideals as a nation. We are committed to helping refugees who are the victims of oppression in this world. We are committed to generous refugee admissions programs in order to offer hope and new lives to the thousands and thousands who have lost their homes. And we are committed to fighting for the freedom to emigrate of those still imprisoned for their beliefs. Your loved ones are uppermost in our thoughts and actions, and we commit ourselves—and re-dedicate ourselves again this evening—to unceasing efforts to obtain their freedom.

Address, December 3, 1988

Mr. High Commissioner [Jean Pierre Hocke], we would like first to express appreciation to you and those of your organization for your efforts and interest on behalf of the UNHCR's Orderly Departure Program. The sponsorship by UNHCR of this very important annual consultation and your personal participation again this year as chairman is a significant manifestation of the commitment of UNHCR to do everything possible to ensure that this program becomes truly a viable, safe, and orderly alternative to clandestine, dangerous departures from Vietnam as envisaged in the 1979 memorandum of understanding between the Socialist Republic of Vietnam and the UNHCR. We believe that your recent visit to Hanoi contributed in an important and helpful manner to the renewal of this vital program.

The United States is greatly encouraged by the resumption of processing of applicants for resettlement in our country which has occurred in the past months and by the recent increase in approval for other countries. We are here to build on that progress. We salute the good will and cooperation demonstrated by the Government of the Socialist Republic of Vietnam and its representatives, the UNHCR, the ICM [Intergovernmental Committee for Migration], and all other parties involved. Together, we now have the opportunity and the challenge for a new beginning—to restore departures to the levels achieved in 1984 and 1985, when, for the first time, more Vietnamese left via the ODP than risked clandestine, dangerous departures. But our goal must be to go beyond those levels. We, therefore, welcome the Minister's [Vietnamese Vice Minister for Foreign Affairs Tran Quang Co] clear statement that his country does not wish its citizens to become "boat" people.

It is useful to recall on this occasion that the memorandum of understanding recognizes both "family reunion and other humanitarian cases." It provides that selection of those persons authorized to leave Vietnam is to be made on the basis of lists of persons submitted by the Vietnamese Government and lists of persons submitted by the receiving countries. The 1979 memorandum also affirms the central role of the UNHCR.

U.S. Commitment to the ODP

On behalf of my government, I reaffirm the steadfast commitment of the United States to the UNHCR Orderly Departure Program within the terms of the 1979 understanding. This American commitment was further strengthened by all of the Members of the U.S. Congress in a 1987 resolution unanimously endorsing the program's provision for departures from Vietnam for both family reunification and for humanitarian reasons.

Vietnam's Southeast Asian neighbors also recognize the central humanitarian role of the Orderly Departure Program. At their June meeting in Singapore, the Foreign Ministers of the Association of South East Asian Nations strongly urged the Government of the Socialist Republic of Vietnam to take measures to remove the causes of clandestine departures from Vietnam and to cooperate earnestly with the UNHCR and the resettlement countries to ensure the success of the Orderly Departure Program.

Alternative to the Perils of Clandestine Flight

Since 1980, the Orderly Departure Program has enabled more than 130,000 persons to depart Vietnam safely and in an orderly way to build new lives in new homelands, with over 60,000 coming to my country. In 1984, more than 28,000 persons departed Vietnam under this program, and in 1985, more than 26,000. In those years, the Orderly Departure Program truly was becoming an alternative to the perils of clandestine departure. Sadly, this is not now the case, with clandestine departures now exceeding departures under the Orderly Departure Program. However, with the recent renewal of the program, we are hopeful that it will once again become the principal means for persons to depart Vietnam.

Amerasians and Prisoners

At our consultations in 1984, I had the honor to announce on behalf of my government two special humanitarian initiatives of the President of the United States. One called for the admission to the United States of all Amerasian children, their mothers, and close family members from Vietnam who wished to be resettled in the United States. The second called for the resettlement of all the so-called reeducation camp inmates and their qualifying family members who also wished to be resettled in the United States.

We are very pleased that recent steps have been taken to fulfill the intent of the initiative on behalf of Amerasians. We remain, however, profoundly disappointed that the Vietnamese authorities have not as yet responded positively to our initiative on behalf of the reeducation camp prisoners—a population of compelling concern to the international community.

This afternoon—as was done at this consultation last year—I once again reaffirm that we are ready to resume discussions with the Government of the Socialist Republic of Vietnam on this important issue. Our humanitarian goal must be to develop ways to receive these prisoners or former prisoners and their immediate families who wish to be resettled in the United States. We are hopeful that the cooperative spirit reflected in the recent resumption of the Orderly Departure Program and Amerasian Program will now manifest itself in addressing this profound, unresolved humanitarian issue.

In a special act of amnesty, the Vietnamese authorities recently announced the release of 480 persons from "reeducation" camps—persons who had been incarcerated since 1975 and who held positions under the former government. We appreciate, applaud, and welcome this humane gesture of amnesty by Vietnam. We invite the Vietnamese authorities to allow any of this group who wish to be resettled in the United States or in any other country to be accorded priority in the ODP on special humanitarian grounds. We also reaffirm our request that all former "reeducation camp" prisoners be allowed unhindered access to the Orderly Departure Program.

Conclusion

This year's international meeting is a significant consultation. My delegation is looking forward very much to continuing consideration of this very important humanitarian undertaking in meetings tomorrow with the Vietnamese delegation led by Vice Minister Co.

A PLEA FOR SELFISHNESS

Last year, I conducted a seminar in American History at the Ateneo de Zamboanga, a Jesuit institution of higher education in the southwestern tip of the Philippines. One of my teaching tools was "Dreams of Distant Shores," a superb videotape provided by the U.S. Information Service. This film, narrated by the actor James Whitmore, tells the story of European immigration to the United States, from 1890–1915. During those years, 16 million people poured through Ellis Island in the New York harbor.

The video had a strong attraction for me. As a boy growing up in Jersey City I could see the Statue of Liberty from our kitchen window, and I often swam in the narrow band of water that separates Ellis Island from Jersey City. But the tape's interest was based on more than familiar scenes. My mother and father and several of my uncles were among those 16 million newcomers whose descendants comprise almost 50 percent of all Americans.

Most of those immigrants brought with them nothing more than the clothes on their backs and one or two pathetic bundles of baggage. They met with a welcome less than warm. Immigration officials were usually brusque, and the new arrivals were herded like cattle from station to station. Perhaps there was no other way to do it.

The coldness followed them from Ellis Island. Micks, Wops, Polacks, Bohunks and Kikes encountered hostility not only from the masses of men-in-the-street, but also from politicians, jour-

Article by Bartholomew Lahiff, S.J., teacher of history at the Ateneo de Manila University in the Philippines, from *America* 163:40–1 Jl 14–21 '90. Copyright © 1990 by *America*. Reprinted with permission.

nalists and pseudo-scientists like Madison Grant, author of a widely circulated attack called *The Passing of the Great Race*. More than one voice shouted: "We are being swamped. These foreigners will take our country away from us!"

It could be pointed out that these foreigners became in fact the parents of future national leaders—justices of the Supreme Court, governors of states, educators, scientists and influential church people. But that might obscure rather than make a more important point. Civilizations are kept going, not by the actions of a few great persons, but by the routine efforts of millions of ordinary people doing ordinary things like earning a living, raising a family, paying taxes, obeying the law and supporting schools, hospitals and churches. Almost all those who landed at Ellis Island did just these ordinary things and did them extremely well. The decision to admit those immigrants was one of the wisest the United States ever made. Thank in no small part to those newcomers, the United States came through the ordeal of two world wars and is today the richest and most powerful country in the world.

At the end of the 20th century, however, neither the United States nor the world are much like what they were in 1900. Immigrants no longer see the Statue of Liberty; it is too far from the airports. Ellis Island is now a museum. But immigrants still come, although not in their former numbers nor mainly from the European countries that were sending them a century ago. Now they come from Latin America and, since the United States is part of the Pacific Basin, they also come from the Far East.

The United States has been particularly fortunate in its Asian immigrants. Like the Japanese before them, the Koreans, Chinese and Filipinos who have arrived more recently have one of the lowest crime rates of any ethnic group. They will certainly make a contribution to U.S. society out of all proportion to their numbers. The Chinese are among the highest achievers in our universities. If there is a lazy Korean in the United States, he or she belongs on the list of endangered species. And what large U.S. hospital could function without its contingent of Filipino doctors, nurses and medical technicians?

In the light of this beneficial experience, the United States should be recruiting more immigrants from Asia, and there is one group it should especially welcome. This is the group made up of refugees now lodged in camps around Southeast Asia. These people had the courage and the faith to risk everything in the sort of perilous ocean voyages that have claimed the lives of unknown thousands. In the Philippines I have met some of them who are awaiting their fate in a camp in Bataan, near the old World War II battlefield.

What kind of people are they? They are like Lien, a woman who cooked for three priests working with the refugees and managed to convert the most ordinary collection of rice, fish and vegetables into a variety of delicious meals. She had spent four days at sea in an open boat before reaching Thailand, where she stayed in a camp for several months. Eventually she arrived in Bataan, where I said good-bye to her on the day she left for California. Lien adamantly rejected all suggestions that in the United States she concentrate on getting an education. She was determined, instead, to find a job, save her money and bring her parents to join her.

Or again, there are refugees like the teen-age girl whose story had the violent drama of a Hieronymus Bosch painting. When her boat was seized by Thai pirates, the men aboard were killed and the women repeatedly raped. After several days, these women were slashed and dumped overboard. With the aid of an upturned bucket, the girl floated for she knows not how long. She was picked up at last by some Thai fishermen and brought to a refugee camp. She told her story in a calm, dignified manner, without rancor or bitterness. She is looking forward to starting a new life in whatever country will be fortunate enough to receive her.

There are also refugees like the quiet-spoken young man who taught himself navigation by studying books. With a few dozen men, women and children as brave or as foolhardy as himself, he then set out in a cockleshell boat and reached safety. Depending upon one's point of view, he was either the beneficiary of a miracle or a fugitive from the law of averages.

Finally, there are refugees like the children I joined around their camp bonfire one night. Without costumes, props or stage, they put on skits that had their audience convulsed with laughter. A nine-year-old girl, playing to perfection an imperious lady-of-the-house, was hoodwinked by her oh-so-stupid servant. A seven-year-old boy dared to challenge the huge wrestler who had just posted a string of four victories. With one hand behind his back, the champion disdainfully took on his undersized opponent. When the challenger "threw" him and the champion was carried off "unconscious," the kids howled for several minutes.

Their bittersweet past has shown that these people are brave, resourceful and determined to be free. Crowded into the camps, they may look no more like the stuff from which nations are made than did those poorly clothed hordes that swarmed into Ellis Island 80 or more years ago. But it is as certain as such things can be, that the children of these East Asians, or their grandchildren if it should take that long, will greatly enrich the United States.

They look longingly across the Pacific to the country of the Golden Gate. Life has not done them any favors, so they expect none. All they want is a place where they can work, bring up their families and live out their lives in peace. In short, they want a chance to be numbered among those millions who keep civilization from sinking into chaos.

It could be argued that Americans should accept these refugees out of loyalty to their own U.S. tradition, or out of the compassion that is part of their post-Christian ethos, or out of the debt they owe the East Asian people who trusted them.

Such pleas would make eminent sense. But the plea here is to out-and-out selfishness. The United States should open its doors to these prospective immigrants before nations like Canada, France, Australia and Norway seize the chance. It should welcome these East Asians precisely because of the contribution they can make to American life during the rest of this century and into the next. Like their fathers, grandfathers and great-grandfathers, the descendants of the Ellis Islanders should recognize a good thing when they see it. If they let this opportunity slip away, they and their children will be the losers.

LET'S LET ASIANS IN

A consensus is building in America that it's time to accommodate many more Asian refugees yearning to be free of repressive political systems and economic hardship. As Chinese flee gunshot brutality, Vietnamese escape oppression, and Hong Kong's citizens press to leave before China takes over their colony in 1997,

Article by Kenneth Labich, staff writer, from *Fortune* 120:89–90 Jl 17 '89. Copyright © 1989 by *Fortune*. Reprinted with permission.

the U.S. faces an uncommon opportunity to enrich its melting pot with new thousands of energetic, potentially productive citizens.

America's recent record on accepting Asian immigrants, especially Vietnamese, has been commendable. The U.S. has taken in nearly a million Southeast Asian refugees since the war ended in 1975. More than 500,000 were Vietnamese, with most of the rest from Laos and Cambodia. Mainland Chinese have lately emigrated to the U.S. at the rate of about 25,000 annually. Canada, Australia, and France have absorbed many Southeast Asians as well.

Britain is another story. Foreign secretary Sir Geoffrey Howe recently demanded that the thousands of Vietnamese flocking to Hong Kong be forcibly sent home. He argues that Hong Kong is already overwhelmed with refugees. British officials have also said that even longtime residents of the crown colony would not be welcomed into the U.K. after 1997. If that decision stands, fumed the *Spectator,* the influential and generally pro-Thatcher British journal, the Prime Minister "will have presided over the most discreditable British policy of the 20th century."

Not just discreditable, but plain dumb. U.S. hospitality to Asians over the years has been amply rewarded. Beyond the famous immigrants who have soared to prominence—computer tycoon An Wang, superconductivity genius Ching-Wu Chu, architect I. M. Pei, among many others—the anonymous masses by and large have integrated well into U.S. society. They have demonstrated the classic attributes of the upwardly mobile: hard work, perseverance, respect for education. Southeast Asians who arrived between 1975 and 1979 were paying well over $170 million in federal income taxes annually by 1986. Says Robert Bach, a sociologist who has worked extensively with Southeast Asian refugees: "These are people who enter the labor market quickly. The young people, on average, are doing well in school. There is no reason to believe this population will become part of the underclass."

The Asians' firm grasp of the capitalist system makes clear the absurdity of the notion that letting in ambitious immigrants somehow costs Americans jobs. "Immigrants create more jobs than they take away," says Demetrios Papademetriou, the U.S. Labor Department's director of immigration policy and research. "They invite more investment, create their own businesses, and act as consumers. They make a contribution in every little niche."

But U.S. immigration policy toward Asians needs fine-tuning.

The most obvious problem: Quotas for Southeast Asian refugees have fallen sharply. The U.S., which admitted almost 170,000 Southeast Asians as refugees in 1980, plans to let in about 50,000 of them this year [1989]. The policy change reflects America's waning feeling of obligation toward Southeast Asian refugees as the Vietnam war recedes into the past. The press of people hoping to leave the region remains far greater than the quota.

Equally problematic is the creaky bureaucratic machinery of immigration. Only close family members of U.S. citizens are exempt from country-by-country quotas. The rest receive priority ratings according to their relationship with relatives already in the country, their professions, or their work skills. Once rated, they must wait their turn until their number comes up—and that can take years. For example, the spouse of a resident alien from the Philippines can expect to wait seven years before being admitted to the U.S. Would-be immigrants with no relatives in the U.S. and no scarce professional skills can still qualify by proving that they fled their home countries because of political persecution. This provides no openings for the many Hong Kong residents who fear persecution in the future. And people suspected of simply hoping to improve their economic lot are out of luck.

The trouble is that an immigrant's real motives are often all but unfathomable, so officials' decisions under current rules are often arbitrary. For many of the 170,000 or so Southeast Asians crammed into inhospitable refugee camps throughout the region, the process of trying to insinuate themselves onto some official's approved list can resemble a Kafkaesque nightmare. Father Henry Beninati, an American Maryknoll missionary who serves as chaplain at a Vietnamese refugee camp in Pusan, South Korea, describes the frustrations of his flock as "simply horrible, sometimes overpowering." A U.S. immigration official visits Father Beninati's camp every six months or so, conducts a few quick interviews, then approves some applications and rejects others according to no obvious logic. The randomness of it all is especially dispiriting. "Increasingly these are people without hope," says Father Beninati. "They feel they are expendable."

The U.S. Congress and various immigration experts have been locked in a spirited debate over how to evaluate potential immigrants (FORTUNE, May 9, 1988). The argument is basically between those who want to continue favoring immigrants with relatives in the U.S. and others, citing national interest, who contend that the U.S. should copy Canada and other countries by pushing to the head of the line would-be immigrants with desirable skills. Senators Edward Kennedy (D-Massachusetts) and Alan Simpson (R-Wyoming) recently drafted compromise legislation that would retain most family preferences while increasing the numbers that could be admitted as "independent immigrants" with needed skills.

These reforms eventually could allow a few more Vietnamese and other Asians to hurdle the bureaucracy, but without major changes many thousands more still will be blocked. Given the wretched conditions most face in the refugee camps, at least some officials must be tempted to suggest simply loading up the lot and hauling them to U.S. shores. But, say perceptive immigration experts, such a dramatic gesture could produce continuing cycles of human suffering. By emptying the camps, these experts contend, the U.S. would encourage more Asians to leave homelands such as Vietnam, Cambodia, and Laos, from which it is difficult or impossible to emigrate legally, and make extremely perilous journeys to Hong Kong, Thailand, and elsewhere. Among the certain results: more at-sea rapes, robberies, and murders as more hapless refugees fall prey to roving pirate bands.

The answer instead, some U.S. immigration experts argue persuasively, is bigger quotas and faster growth of so-called orderly departure programs, in which U.S. officials travel directly to home countries—not refugee camps—for interviews with potential immigrants. Overlooked amid the brouhaha over Britain's intransigence on refugees was Vietnam's commitment to permit 6,000 people to depart legally each month. The U.S. will initially take in about half of those, perhaps boosting its share to three quarters before long.

Americans wishing to help Asian refugees who have been approved by the Immigration and Naturalization Service can sponsor them through various relief agencies, such as the U.S. Catholic Conference. Americans unmoved by the refugees' thirst for liberty might consider pragmatic reasons for at least allowing more of them in on their own. According to the U.S. Bureau of Labor Statistics, the number of jobs in the U.S. will increase 19.2% by the end of the century, while the labor force will increase only 17.8%. The bureau suggests that labor shortages will be especially severe in such sectors as health care, retailing, and business-support services. Asians have proved their worth as employees and citizens and would help fill the gap. They are obviously needed. Happily, more Americans have come to realize that they should also be wanted.

THE 'EASTERN CAPITAL' OF ASIA

In Los Angeles you can drive across the Pacific without getting your tires wet. Just fold the top down and cruise down Olympic Boulevard into Koreatown. The neighborhood looks like L.A. but reads like Seoul, with precious few signs in English. The tantalizing aroma of smoking meat wafts out of a Korean barbecue restaurant—one of nearly 100 eateries in the 70-square-block area. Driving past Buddhist temples and bustling mini-malls, you swing over to the San Bernardino Freeway and head east to Monterey Park, a well-to-do suburb where half the population is Asian. Before running out of gas you could visit Japan, Vietnam, Thailand and the Philippines. Now peer through the smog at the skyline. According to the Los Angeles Times, three-quarters of downtown L.A. office space is foreign owned or controlled, nearly a third of it by Japanese. Says Jack Lewis, associate professor of international business at the University of Southern California, "Los Angeles is the eastern capital of the Pacific Rim."

L.A. is once again giving us a glimpse into our future: in the decades to come, virtually all Americans will feel the dual impact of Asian immigration and investment. Japan Inc. continues to reshape our cities, buying up billions of dollars' worth of buildings and businesses. It is remaking our workplace, employing more than 250,000 Americans to produce everything from Nissan cars in Smyrna, Tenn., to chocolate biscuits in York, Pa. Other deep-pocketed Pacific Rim nations will surely follow. Asian immigrants—who will number as many as 12 million by the year 2000—could affect America more profoundly than any group since the first boat people crossed over on the Mayflower. Americans not directly touched by these trends will feel them indirectly. Lester Thurow, dean of the Alfred P. Sloan School of Management at the Massachusetts Institute of Technology, says the

Article by John Schwartz, staff writer, from *Newsweek* 111:56–8 F 22 '88. Copyright © 1988 by Newsweek, Inc. Reprinted with permission.

United States may be in for humbling lessons our neighbors have already learned: "If you were raised in Canada, you know that what those crazy Americans do has more impact on your economy than your economy in Ottawa does." Our huge national indebtedness, Thurow warns, could leave the nation even more vulnerable: the "danger is that we'll be treated like Mexico and we'll be told how to run our own country."

For Americans who can capitalize on ties between East and West, the Pacific boom will carry growing opportunity. Asia hands who have studied the region, know its key players and understand its cultures will become increasingly influential in everything from business and politics to law, academia and the arts. Alice Young, an American-born child of Chinese diplomat parents, recalls that when she took Japanese in college, people thought her eccentric—as if "one was studying Mahayana Buddhism from the sixth and seventh century. Interesting, but quite useless." Today, at 37, Young is a partner in the prestigious law firm of Milbank, Tweed, Hadley & McCloy in New York City, with an office that commands a stunning view of New York Harbor and the Statue of Liberty. Young heads her firm's Japan Corporate Group, conducting business for the Asia-conscious firm throughout the Pacific Rim.

As the Pacific Century comes to be, the economic forces shifting the world's geopolitical balance will be played out from coast to coast. The western tier of the United States is fast eclipsing the East, a trend recently noted by journals such as The Atlantic Monthly. The ports of Long Beach and Los Angeles handled 58.6 million tons of cargo in 1986, surpassing the 21 million that moved through the Port of New York and New Jersey. Fifteen years ago bank deposits in cities like Chicago and San Francisco dwarfed L.A.'s; today only New York exceeds it if savings and loan deposits are added in. New York's days of banking supremacy may also be numbered: while the Big Apple's deposits rose less than 7 percent between 1980 and 1986 (to $192 million), deposits in the City of the Angels leaped 65 percent to $145 million, according to Jack Kyser, chief economist for the Los Angeles Area Chamber of Commerce.

Tatami mats: Asia accounts for much of the wealth tilting westward. According to a report by the University of California at San Diego's new Graduate School of International Relations and Pacific Studies, a stunning 82 percent of California's $80 billion in annual trade is with Pacific Rim countries. California already has absorbed more than 40 percent of the total Japanese investment in the United States and boasts more than 750 subsidiaries of Japanese firms. The state has nine Japanese-affiliated banks with more than $10 billion in assets. Eight of Japan's biggest car companies and South Korea's Hyundai set up their headquarters around Los Angeles.

Asian money is fast transforming many other parts of the country beyond L.A. In all, the Japanese will gobble up some $10 billion worth of U.S. real estate this year, according to Grubb & Ellis Brokerage Services. They are best known for high-profile, high-dollar ventures like Chicago's $76 million Hotel Nikko, a luxury hostelry that features special $750-per-night Japanese suites complete with tatami mats. Japanese investors have also quietly made inroads into almost every sector of the U.S. economy—even agriculture. Last October a Japanese Coca-Cola bottling company plunked down $1.2 million for a 214-acre almond orchard. The Japanese will buy $100 million worth of California almonds this year for snacks such as slivered almonds with dried sardines.

Businesses are priming themselves to go after a piece of the Pacific action. Insurance giant John Hancock is investing in an Indonesian insurance company, while ETL Testing Laboratories, founded by Thomas Edison, puts products through rigorous Japanese safety tests to speed them through Japanese customs. Nineteen Wall Street investment-banking firms have Tokyo branches. Merrill Lynch also has offices in Hong Kong, South Korea and Singapore, with a Taiwan branch in the works.

Despite Washington's penchant for Japan-bashing, state and local governments are also scrambling for Asian cash. Announcing a new study, Duome & Associates, Ltd., says states are vying for Japanese investors at "an almost frenetic pace," sending trade delegations and politicians on courting missions. Today at least 35 states have liaison offices in Tokyo and Osaka. States have gone incentive-mad; Illinois offered automaker Mitsubishi $88.2 million to attract Diamond-Star Motors, a joint venture with Chrysler. Some of the money will fund a weekend Japanese school and the extensive testing Mitsubishi requires of job seekers. With 15-hour direct flights to Tokyo, Atlanta has become something of a hub for Japanese investment, having attracted 168 companies—a $650 million investment. "Never mind geography," said an Atlanta Constitution editorial. "Georgia can become a Pacific power."

Will to succeed: Students, too, are gearing up to meet the Asian challenge. Although the figure of 23,000 students taking Japanese in American colleges still pales in comparison with the 275,000 taking French, that represents a 45 percent jump from 1983. The interest goes beyond language: the Japanese Business Society, a course at the University of California, Santa Barbara, has never been more popular, reports Frank Gibney Sr., a UCSB adjunct professor and president of the Santa-Barbara-based Pacific Basin Institute. "The kids are fighting to get in."

Many Americans don't have to go to school to learn about Asians; they have only to look around their hometowns. While Hispanics make up Los Angeles's largest and fastest-growing immigrant group, the city is also believed to be home to the largest communities of Filipinos, Vietnamese and Koreans outside of their respective nations of origin. Vast ethnic and financial differences separate the Japanese and Korean groups from the poorer Vietnamese and Filipinos, but almost all the immigrants show an awesome will to succeed. Four years ago Korean Sam Lee heard there was opportunity in El Paso, so he bought a map, loaded a van with goods and left L.A. for Texas. Now Lee's Discount Store is one of nearly 50 Korean-owned shops, many with Spanish names like Casa Toro and Casa de Dama, which cluster near the bridge to Juarez and sell everything from underwear and Walkmans to ginseng.

Bumper stickers: As their numbers increase, Asian-Americans are sure to overcome cultural differences and become a more cohesive political force. The moving and shaking has already begun in Los Angeles: after failing to get a newly drawn council district to encompass all of Koreatown in 1986, local Korean activists backed Chinese candidate Arthur Song against black incumbent Nate Holden. Song lost, but Holden mended fences by appointing a Korean aide, former Song aide Charles Kim. Two other council members also appointed Korean aides. Diplomacy was in scarcer supply in Monterey Park, where a rancorous dispute that ostensibly concerned development revealed a racist taint: some local cars now sport bumper stickers showing an Asian caricature stamped with a circle-slash symbol.

Bigotry might diminish over time as successive generations of Asian-Americans become more assimilated, moving out of concentrated neighborhoods. "It's less easy to stereotype someone you know personally than someone halfway around the world," says Robert Oxnam, president of The Asia Society in New York.

The generations that lived through three wars in the Pacific are giving way to one that associates Asia with Sony Walkmans and Honda Accords. Gibney says his students have "almost total receptivity" toward working for Asian companies someday. "The Pearl Harbor syndrome just doesn't seem to be there."

Asia's mounting influence over America won't always be greeted so cheerfully. Many Asian-Americans complain that prejudice still holds them back. Despite considerable academic achievement, Asian-Americans "have not been as successful in the marketplace as professionals," according to Oxnam. According to figures collected by the Equal Employment Opportunity Commission, in 1985 Asian-Americans accounted for 4.3 percent of professionals and technicians but just 1.4 percent of officials and managers. Asian-Americans could even become victims of their own success in higher education, as schools debate whether the "overrepresented" Asian students should be subject to quotas in order to keep other minorities and even whites from being squeezed out of colleges. At UCLA, where Asians make up upwards of 18 percent of the student body, Anglo students joke that the school's initials really stand for "United Caucasians Lost Among Asians."

Other Americans focus their anger on a dangerous import: Asian gangs from Hong Kong, Vietnam and other Asian nations. Run like businesses, with tens of thousands of members, syndicates with names like 14K and Bamboo Union are following the lead of legitimate businesses by going multinational. Notorious tongs, U.S.-based Chinese groups, control gangs such as New York's Ghost Shadows and Flying Dragons. "Business" ranges from heroin importation and gambling to extortion rackets in Brooklyn and prostitution rings in California. Their numbers are building as 1997—when Hong Kong changes hands —nears.

No matter what the salubrious effects of Asian money flowing into the United States, the specter of foreign ownership and competition continues to give many Americans chills. Citing the "curious combination of awe, dread and admiration" that dominates discussion of Japan's competitiveness, Richard Samuels, director of MIT's Japan Science and Technology Program, warns that manufacturers outside the United States could have a "predatory effect." However, Samuels says, "name calling, baiting and making excuses are not going to fix the problem." Wariness may be appropriate, nonetheless. As the price of investment, the Japanese tend to demand training for their employees—effectively buying U.S. know-how for a fistful of rapidly depreciating dollars.

'Delightful partners': For some American businessmen, however, familiarity breeds respect. New York builder John Tishman has entered several partnerships with the Aoki Corp., a construction-and-development firm that owns luxury hotels like New York's famed Algonquin. "They have been delightful partners," Tishman says. He and Aoki president Hiroyoshi Aoki have become personal friends, and Tishman says, "I'd rather have Mr. Aoki's word than a 100-page document written by our own attorneys." He says jokingly, "Maybe they'll take us over in the year 2050—but what do I care?"

Many other Americans will join Tishman in making the best of the Pacific Century, if only because they will have little other choice. If xenophobia drives Pacific business away, the money will just flow elsewhere: a great deal of Japanese manufacturing is already going to less expensive nations like Mexico and South Korea. American consumers aren't about to stop wanting the best goods at the lowest costs. And U.S. companies will need to keep studying the successes of their Asian counterparts if they are to stay competitive. For Americans, pursuing fruitful partnership while protecting U.S. interests will be *the* balancing act of the Pacific Century.

BIGOTRY AND VIOLENCE AGAINST ASIAN AMERICANS

Many Asian Americans are forced to endure anti-Asian bigotry, ranging from ignorant and insensitive remarks, to stereotypical portrayals of Asians in the media, to name-calling, on a regular basis. Asian Americans are also the frequent victims of hate crimes, including vandalism, assault, and sometimes even murder. Although incidents of bigotry and violence against Asian

An excerpt from Chapter 2 of *Civil Rights Issues Facing Asian Americans in the 1990s*, A Report of the United States Commission on Civil Rights, February 1992, pp. 22–45.

Americans are reflections of a broader national climate of ethnic, racial, and religious intolerance, they are also reprehensible outgrowths of ingrained anti-Asian feelings that reside to a greater or lesser extent among many members of American society.

In 1986 the U.S. Commission on Civil Rights published a report on acts of bigotry and violence against Asian Americans. The Commission report documented many examples of bias-related incidents against Asian Americans and noted some of the factors contributing to anti-Asian activities. That report concluded:

[A]nti-Asian activity in the form of violence, vandalism, harassment, and intimidation continues to occur across the Nation. Incidents were reported in every jurisdiction visited by Commission staff and in other parts of the country as well. . . . The United States is a multiracial, pluralistic society built on the principles of freedom, justice, and opportunity for all. We cannot allow these principles to be violated in the case of Asian Americans by anyone. Rather, we must ensure that persons of Asian descent are guaranteed the rights promised to residents and citizens of this Nation.

More recently, the Civil Rights Commission issued a general statement on intimidation and violence in America. The Commission statement identified several factors that contribute to racial intimidation and violence, including:

1) racial integration of neighborhoods leading to "move-in violence";

2) deep-seated racial hatred played upon by organized hate groups;

3) economic competition among racial and ethnic groups;

4) insensitive media coverage of minority groups; and

5) poor police response to hate crimes.

All of these ingredients play a role in anti-Asian bigotry and violence. For instance, economic competition among racial and ethnic groups is undoubtedly one of the underlying causes of the tensions between Asian American businessmen and many of their customers across the country. Unbalanced media coverage, such as coverage that fosters the model minority stereotype, has also contributed to anti-Asian sentiments. Asian Americans, like other minorities, are increasingly becoming the targets of organized hate groups, as evidenced by the activities of anti-Indian Dotbusters in New Jersey and the recent killing by skinhead associates of a Vietnamese youth in Houston.

Anti-Asian bigotry and violence also has its own unique causes and manifestations, however. . . . [T]he United States has a long history of prejudice and discrimination against Asians. In recent years, underlying anti-Asian sentiments have been aggravated by the increased visibility of Asian Americans due to a large influx of immigrants and refugees from Asia. The Asian population grew from 1.5 percent to 2.9 percent of the United States population just in the decade between 1980 and 1990. Since Asian Americans are heavily concentrated geographically, the increase in the Asian population in some communities has been much more dramatic. For example, in Lowell, Massachusetts, the Cambodian population increased from a negligible percentage to roughly 25 percent of the population after 1980. Many California communities have been similarly affected by Asian immigration.

High rates of immigration have also magnified the linguistic, cultural, and religious differences between Asian Americans and others residing in their communities. As more and more new immigrants have arrived from Asia, the percentage of the Asian American population that is native born with native-born parents—who consequently are native speakers of English and are more easily assimilated into the broader American culture—has declined. Not only do most new immigrants have limited English proficiency, reducing the potential for communication between them and their non-Asian counterparts, but they bring with them cultures and religions that are unfamiliar to the American public. These differences often generate misunderstandings that contribute to anti-Asian sentiments.

Because of their limited English proficiency and/or because of difficulties in acquiring the credentials required to pursue their chosen professions in the United States, many Asian immigrants are unable to find jobs in the professions for which they were trained in their countries of origin and turn instead to self-employment as a means of earning a living. For instance, 17 percent of foreign-born Korean men working in the United States in 1980 were self-employed. Many Asian immigrants operate small retail stores or restaurants in economically depressed, predominantly minority neighborhoods. The entry of small businesses owned by Asian Americans into these neighborhoods and their apparent financial success often provokes resentment on the part of neighborhood residents, who wonder why the business does not hire locally and often suspect that the Asian businesses are receiving special government subsidies. Contrary to these misperceptions, however, most small Asian businesses are family-owned and operated and cannot afford to hire nonfamily members: all the workers are family members, who work long hours for low pay. Furthermore, beyond short-term welfare and training programs offered only to those who are refugees, Asian immigrants are given very little government aid that is not generally available to all Americans, and, with limited exceptions, the government does not give Asian immigrants or refugees special help in opening their businesses. Furthermore, they do not typically receive much bank financing: they usually raise the capital for their businesses by pooling the resources of family and friends. Aggravating the resentment of Asian business owners are cultural and linguistic differences between immigrant business owners and residents of the neighborhoods they serve that lead the residents to perceive Asian Americans as rude and unfriendly. The boycott of several Korean businesses in New York City discussed below as well as a recent boycott in Los Angeles are examples of how racial tensions surrounding immigrant businesses can affect entire communities.

The general tendency to view all Asians as alike and the stereotype of Asians as foreigners make Asian Americans particularly vulnerable to the vicissitudes of the United States relations with Asian countries. Over the past half-century, the United States has frequently been at war with Asian countries (e.g., Japan, North Korea, Vietnam, and the Cold War with China), fostering in many Americans resentment and hatred of Asian nationals that, for some, carried over to their attitudes towards Asian Americans. In recent years the public's resentment of Japan's economic success, seemingly at the expense of our own, has added to historic anti-Asian sentiments. Many in the American public associate all Asians, regardless of their national origin, residence, or citizenship, with Japan's economic success and resent them accordingly. The killing of Vincent Chin, discussed below, is an example of how this resentment can erupt into violence.

Finally, the common stereotype of Asian Americans as a "model minority" also leads to increased racial tensions. Although most Americans are familiar with the widely discussed academic and economic success of some Asian Americans, they are largely unaware of the social problems, poverty, and high school dropout rates affecting many other Asian Americans. As in the case of Asian-owned businesses, apparent success, whether real or illusory, leads to resentment and aggravates any previously existing anti-Asian sentiments.

Thus, to a large extent, existing anti-Asian sentiments in this country have been compounded by a lack of knowledge about Asian Americans on the part of the general public. The inaccurate "model minority" and "foreigner" stereotypes, the misperception that Asian immigrants receive unfair subsidies from the government, and the public's unfamiliarity with the diverse histories, cultures, and socioeconomic circumstances of Asian Americans all contribute to anti-Asian feelings.

This [excerpt] updates the 1986 Commission report by providing recent examples of anti-Asian incidents, including violent incidents against individuals, housing-related incidents, incidents targeted at places of worship, incidents targeted at Asian-owned businesses, racial harassment on college campuses, and anti-Asian slurs made by public figures. . . .

Recent Incidents of Bigotry and Violence Against Asian Americans

This section documents recent cases in which anti-Asian bigotry led to violence, harassment, vandalism, intimidation, and racial slurs.

Violent Incidents

Two racially motivated murders of Asian Americans in the 1980s have been etched into the national consciousness as examples of racism against Asian Americans: the murder of Vincent Chin in 1982 and the murder of Jim (Ming Hai) Loo in 1989. These killings are prominent examples of racially motivated violence against Asian Americans, but they are not isolated incidents. Racially motivated violence leading to injury and sometimes to death occurs with disturbing frequency across the country and affects many different Asian groups. This section discusses five examples of anti-Asian violence: the murders of Vincent Chin, Jim Loo, Navroze Mody, and Hung Truong, and the mass killing of Indochinese school children in Stockton, California.

Vincent Chin—The racially motivated murder of Vincent Chin and the inability of the American judicial system to bring his murderers to justice became a vivid symbol and source of outrage during the mid-1980s. The facts of the case are as follows.

On the evening of June 19, 1982, Vincent Chin, a 27-year-old Chinese American, met with some friends in a Detroit bar to celebrate his upcoming wedding. He was accosted by Ronald Ebens and Michael Nitz, two white automobile factory workers, who reportedly called him a "Jap" and blamed him for the loss of jobs in the automobile industry. Ebens and Nitz chased Chin out of the bar, and, when they caught up with him, Nitz held Chin while Ebens beat him "numerous times in the knee, the chest, and the head" with a baseball bat. Chin died of his injuries 4 days later.

Ebens and Nitz were initially charged with second-degree murder but subsequently allowed to plead guilty to manslaughter. In March 1983 the defendants were each sentenced to 3 years' probation and fined $3,780 by Wayne Circuit County Judge Charles Kaufman, who reasoned that the defendants had no previous history of violence and were unlikely to violate probation.

The U.S. Department of Justice brought Federal civil rights charges against Ebens and Nitz to a Federal grand jury, which indicted them on November 2, 1982. On June 18, 1984, Ebens was found guilty of interfering with Chin's civil rights, and on September 18, 1984, he was sentenced to 25 years in prison. However, Nitz was acquitted of the Federal civil rights charges.

Ebens' conviction was overturned by the Sixth Circuit Court of Appeals in September 1986 for technical reasons, including issues pertaining to the admissibility of audio tapes and prosecutorial misconduct (overzealousness) in preparing witnesses. When Ebens came up for retrial in the Eastern District of Michigan, the defense moved for a change of venue on the grounds that Ebens could not get a fair trial in Detroit. The defense motion was granted, and the trial was moved to Cincinnati. The case was retried during the month of April 1987, and this time Ebens was acquitted.

The acquittal of Ebens in the second Federal trial means that neither Ebens nor Nitz ever went to prison for Vincent Chin's killing. Some have speculated that the main reason that the Cincinnati jury acquitted Ebens is that the jury could not comprehend the reality of anti-Asian bias as it existed in Detroit in the early 1980s. Whereas Detroit in the early 1980s was the scene of a massive media campaign against foreign imports, especially those from Japan, a campaign that inflamed anti-Asian sentiments in that city, there had not been the same type of campaign in Cincinnati. Also, there were very few Asians in Cincinnati, and anti-Asian sentiments were not widespread.

Others contend that the Cincinnati jury's acquittal of Ebens reflects a fundamental problem with current Federal civil rights laws. Ebens was charged under Federal criminal civil rights law section 245(b), which prohibits (among other things) the racially motivated interference by force or threat of force with a person's use of public facilities, such as restaurants and bars. Some experts argue that the jury may have been confused about what had to be shown for there to be a civil rights violation under section 245(b): even though the jury may have felt that the attack was indeed racially motivated, it might not have thought that Evens specifically intended to interfere with Chin's use of a public facility (the bar).

Jim (Ming Hai) Loo—Seven years after Vincent Chin's killing, another Chinese American was killed in Raleigh, North Carolina under similar circumstances.

Jim (Ming Hai) Loo, 24, had immigrated to the United States from China 13 years before, was working in a Chinese restaurant, and was saving money so that he could attend college. On the evening of Saturday, July 29, 1989, during an altercation that began in a nearby pool hall, Loo was hit on the back of the head by a handgun held by Robert Piche. He fell onto a broken beer bottle, which pierced his eye and caused a bone fragment to enter his brain, resulting in his death on July 31.

Loo and several Vietnamese friends had been playing pool in the pool hall, when Robert Piche, 35, and his brother, Lloyd Piche, 29, began calling them "gooks" and "chinks" and blaming them for American deaths in Vietnam. Lloyd Piche said, "I don't like you because you're Vietnamese. Our brothers went over to Vietnam, and they never came back," and "I'm gonna finish you tonight." Although the manager forced the Piche brothers to leave the pool hall, they waited outside for Loo and his friends, and attacked them as they left the pool hall. Robert Piche and his brother first attacked one of Loo's friends, Lahn Tang, with a shotgun, but when Tang escaped, Robert swung a pistol at another of Loo's friends, Jim Ta. He missed his intended victim and hit Loo on the head instead.

Although Lloyd Piche made most of the racial remarks, he did not strike the fatal blow. He was sentenced to 6 months in prison for disorderly conduct and simple assault (on Tang), both of which are misdemeanors. In March 1990, Robert Piche was found guilty of second-degree murder and assault with a deadly weapon and sentenced to a total of 37 years in prison. He will be eligible for parole after serving 4½ years. Although Judge Howard E. Manning Jr. gave Piche a stiff lecture, the sentence was less than he could have meted out: under North Carolina law, Piche could have been given life in prison.

Many Asian American community leaders, struck by the similarities between Loo's murder and Chin's, pressed the U.S. Department of Justice to bring Federal civil rights charges against Robert and Lloyd Piche. They were particularly anxious to see a prosecution of Lloyd Piche, who received a minimal sentence despite being the chief instigator of the incident. After a lengthy investigation, the Justice Department announced on March 29, 1991, that it had indicted Lloyd Piche on Federal civil rights charges, but it did not indict Robert Piche. In making the announcement, Attorney General Thornburgh said:

This is a heinous crime committed against innocent patrons of a public facility. Such egregious behavior, especially with death resulting, cannot go unpunished.

This country was built on the freedom to enjoy life, liberty and the pursuit of happiness. When innocent patrons of a public facility are harassed and ultimately killed simply because of their race, religion or national origin, the government has a moral and legal obligation to step in and prosecute.

Lloyd Piche was indicted on eight counts of violating Federal civil rights laws. On July 15, 1991, in a Federal district court in Wilmington, North Carolina, Lloyd Piche was found guilty on all eight counts. On October 15, 1991, Lloyd Piche was sentenced to 4 years in prison and ordered to pay over $28,000 in restitution to the Loo family. Although the Justice Department had sought the maximum sentence under Federal sentencing guidelines, Piche's sentence was less than the minimum sentence (6 to 7½ years) under the Federal guidelines.

There are many similarities between the Loo and the Chin murders. In each case, the victim was a young man spending an evening relaxing with friends in a public facility (a bar in Chin's case, a pool hall in Loo's). In each case, an altercation began inside the public facility, and violence leading to murder erupted outside of the facility. In each case, the victim was killed after being mistaken for or associated with Asians of other nationalities. In Chin's case, his killers were venting hostility against foreign Japanese, and in Loo's case, his murderers apparently mistook him for a Vietnamese. Thus, both Chin and Loo became victims simply because they were of Asian descent.

Together, the Chin and Loo murders underscore the harsh reality of racially motivated violence against Asians. They also signal in differing ways the general public's lack of awareness of and to some extent indifference towards anti-Asian discrimination. The 3-year probation and almost nominal fines imposed by Judge Kaufman on Chin's murderers are suggestive of very little value being placed on an Asian American life. The ultimate failure of the American justice system to convict Ebens of civil rights charges, perhaps partly because of the Cincinnati jury's difficulty in believing in the existence of anti-Asian hatred, also implies that many Americans view racial hatred purely as a black-white problem and are unaware that Asian Americans are also frequently targets of hate crimes. Finally, neither murder was given much national prominence. Chin's killing did receive some national attention, but Loo's killing (in stark contrast to the murder of a young black man in Bensonhurst that occurred at roughly the same time) was hardly covered by the national media and raised no national sense of outrage.

Unlike the Vincent Chin case, Loo's murder resulted in a successful Federal prosecution—the first ever successful Federal civil rights prosecution where the victim was Asian American. If given sufficient attention, the Federal civil rights trial of Lloyd Piche could do much to highlight the racial aspect of Loo's killing and will send a message that anti-Asian racism will not be tolerated by the United States Government.

Navroze Mody—The 1987 killing of Navroze Mody shows that Asians, like other minorities, are potential targets of organized hate campaigns and that anti-Asian violence can be the outcome of such campaigns.

In early September 1987 the *Jersey Journal* published a letter from a group, called the Dotbusters, whose avowed purpose was to rid Jersey City of Asian Indians. There followed numerous racial incidents against Asian Indians ranging from vandalism to assault. On September 27, 1987, Navroze Mody, an Indian, was "bludgeoned with bricks, punched, and kicked into a coma" by a gang of 11 youths, while his white friend remained unharmed. In April 1989 three of his assailants were convicted of assault, and one was convicted of aggravated assault. Murder charges were not brought against any of the assailants.

Although many in the New Jersey Indian community felt that the crime was racially motivated, no bias charges were brought, and prosecutors denied that Mody's killers were Dotbusters. There were reports, however, that two of the youths involved in the Mody killing had attacked some Indian students at Stevens

Institute of Technology 2 weeks previously, but that the police had not filed a report in that incident. Whether or not Mody's killing was racially motivated, coming as it did in the wake of an organized outbreak of bigotry and violence against Asian Indians in Jersey City, it added significantly to the fears of Asian Indians throughout the country. Anti-Indian incidents continued to occur frequently in the Jersey City area for at least a year after Mody's killing.

Hung Truong—A more recent killing of a 15-year-old Vietnamese boy in Houston, Texas, illustrates the threat posed to Asian Americans along with other minorities by skinheads.

Hung Truong moved to the Houston area from Vietnam with his father in 1980. His mother and three brothers remained in Vietnam. On August 9, 1990 at 2 a.m., Truong was walking down the street with three friends, when they were accosted by persons in two cars that stopped alongside them. Several minutes later, one of the cars followed them, stopped, and two 18-year-old men, Derek Hilla and Kevin Michael Allison, came out of the car, one of them carrying a club. One of Truong's friends later testified that the two men had shouted "White Power." They chased Truong, who became separated from his friends, and kicked and beat him with their feet and hands. Allison later testified that Truong had begged them to stop, saying, "God forgive me for coming to this country. I'm so sorry." After Hilla and Allison had left the scene, Truong's friends caught up with Truong, finding him lying on the ground bleeding. Truong's friends went for help, but when the paramedics arrived, Truong seemed okay, and they let him go home with a friend. The following morning at 7:15 a.m. paramedics were called to Truong's friend's apartment. Truong died shortly after arrival at the hospital. Hilla and Allison were arrested and charged with Truong's murder the following day.

Hilla was well known to have racist views and to have skinhead ties. During the January 1991 trial, witnesses described him as a violent man. Although denying that he was a racist, Allison admitted during the trial that he had participated in a couple of fights with skinhead friends and that his parents had kicked him out of the house when they discovered a swastika in his room. He also admitted that the only reason he and Hilla had attacked Truong was because he was Vietnamese.

On January 23, 1991, a Houston jury convicted Hilla of murder and Allison of involuntary manslaughter in Truong's killing. The jury sentenced Hilla to 45 years in prison and gave him a $10,000 fine. The jury also found that Hilla had used his feet as a deadly weapon, which means that he will be required to serve at least one-fourth of his sentence before becoming eligible for parole. Allison was sentenced to 10 years in prison (the maximum allowable prison sentence for involuntary manslaughter) and also was assessed a $10,000 fine.

Although the prosecutor presented the case as a racial killing, neither Hilla nor Allison was tried on a civil rights charge, because Texas law does not provide for additional penalties for racially motivated crimes against persons. Truong's killing has added momentum to a movement to pass legislation that would provide stronger sentencing provisions for hate crimes.

Stockton Schoolyard Massacre—A chilling massacre of school children in Stockton, California, illustrates the tragic consequences of racial hatred.

On January 17, 1989, a gunman dressed in military garb entered the schoolyard at Cleveland Elementary School in Stockton and repeatedly fired an AK47 assault rifle, killing five Indochinese children and wounding 30 others. The gunman, Patrick Edward Purdy, then turned the rifle on himself. The children who died were identified as Raphanar Or, 9; Ram Chun, 8; Thuy Tran, 6; Sokhim An, 6; and Ocun Lim, 8. Four of the dead children were Cambodian, and one was Vietnamese. Almost 60 percent of the pupils at Cleveland Elementary were from Southeast Asian families.

In the days following the massacre, news coverage focused in large part on the rifle used by Purdy, and the incident was a powerful force behind gun control initiatives across the country. Purdy was described as a "deranged young man . . . who nursed an obsession with guns and the military." The possibility that the killings were racially motivated was hardly addressed in the national press. Almost 10 months later, however, California Attorney General John Van de Kamp issued a report on the incident concluding that the killings were driven by a hatred of racial and ethnic minorities. The report observed, "Purdy was filled with hate and anger toward many groups of people, including virtually all identifiable ethnic minorities." It then concluded:

It appears highly probable that Purdy deliberately chose Cleveland Elementary School as the location for his murderous assault in substantial part because it was heavily populated by Southeast Asian children. His frequent resentful comments about Southeast Asians indicate a particular animosity against them.

Housing-Related Incidents

It is not only in public places, such as bars, pool halls, and city streets, that Asian Americans encounter acts of bigotry and violence. They often face harassment and vandalism in their own homes and also experience other forms of intimidation aimed at keeping them from living or working in a neighborhood.

There have been numerous incidents of racist flyers being distributed in neighborhoods where Asian Americans live or work, calling for Asians to go home or be expelled. As an example, anti-Asian flyers were distributed to mailboxes in the Bensonhurst and Gravesend neighbors of Brooklyn during the fall of 1987. The flyers urged boycotting Korean and Chinese businesses and real estate agents involved in selling property to Asians. Both the New York City Commission on Human Rights and the police department's antibias unit investigated the incidents. A survey by the New York City Commission on Human Rights found that 90 percent of Asian-owned stores in the neighborhood experienced serious losses in business after the flyers were distributed, and two Bensonhurst real estate offices mentioned in the flyers were subsequently vandalized. The person or persons responsible for the flyers were never found. In a more recent incident, anti-Asian flyers were distributed this year in Castro Valley/Hayward, California, by members of the White Aryan Resistance.

As many Cambodian refugees moved into New England in the early 1980s, housing-related incidents against them multiplied. In 1981, shortly after he had moved into his new house in Portland, Maine, a Cambodian man was hit on the head by a rock hidden in a snowball thrown by neighbors as he was playing in the snow with his children. When he approached his neighbors, one of them said, "Go back where you came from, gook." Between 1983 and 1987 there were recurrent incidents of violence against Cambodians living in Revere, Massachusetts, and vandalism against their homes, including rocks thrown at windows and several fires that destroyed entire buildings. Similar incidents occurred elsewhere in Massachusetts, such as a fire set by arsonists which left 31 Cambodians homeless in Lynn, Massachusetts, in December 1988.

Such incidents are not unique to New England. In Richmond, California, for instance, following numerous incidents of egg throwing and BB gun shots, eight cars parked outside an apartment complex where several Laotian refugees lived were badly damaged in September of 1990. Nor do they only affect Southeast Asians. In 1987, in Queens, New York, a Chinese family was the repeated target of a group of young people who threw eggs, drove a car into their front gate, and said things like "Why don't you move away?"

Incidents Targeted at Places of Worship

Hate activities have also been directed against Asian Americans' places of worship. One participant in the Roundtable Conferences reported that out of 60 Hindu temples he had surveyed, 55 had experienced some form of harassment or vandalism in the previous 6 months. In a recent example, vandals spray painted hateful messages, including "No Chinks, Go Home to China," on a Chinese American church in Chandler, Arizona, and fired five rounds of ammunition through the church's doors. The incident, which occurred on September 11, 1990, was the second time the church had been attacked within 2 months. The first attack, which also involved spray-painted hate messages and shots, had occurred on August 7. The incident was very upsetting to the Phoenix's Asian American community, which has grown in recent years, and now is 3 to 4 percent of the Phoenix area.

Incidents Targeted at Asian-Owned Businesses

As was documented in the 1986 Commission report on racially motivated violence against Asians, anti-Asian activities are often targeted at Asian-owned businesses. Many Asian Americans, especially Koreans, own and operate small retail businesses, such as grocery stores, laundries, and restaurants, often in inner-city neighborhoods. The apparent success of these businesses occasionally provokes resentment among persons residing in the neighborhood, and resentment leads to harassment, vandalism, and sometimes violence. Two recent examples, one in California and the other in New York, reflect continuing anti-Asian activities directed against businesses owned by Asian Americans.

Castro Valley, California—On November 25, 1989, at about 10:30 p.m., a group of white teenagers both physically and verbally assaulted Asian American employees and an Asian American store owner at a shopping center in Castro Valley, California. In the midst of the scuffle, gun shots were fired, and one of the attackers was hit in the leg. According to sheriff's investigators, the incident was racially motivated and the youths had assaulted the workers "because they did not like Asians." The details of the incident as obtained from newspaper accounts and staff interviews with the victims are as follows.

A Korean American employee at the Laurel Liquors store had gone into an outdoor garbage disposal area to deposit garbage when several youths slammed the disposal site's door shut and locked it. They taunted him, using ethnic slurs, and then let him out and beat him before he ran back to the liquor store.

During this commotion, a Chinese American man, a U.S.-born college graduate, who was helping clean up the Choice Meat and Deli store owned by his father two doors down from the liquor store, came out to see what the problem was. He was attacked by the youths, who knocked him down and kicked him repeatedly. His father, Frank Toy, came out of the meat store carrying a broom handle and tried to help his son. The assailants wrested the broom handle from Mr. Toy, who then went back inside his store and returned with a rifle. Mr. Toy fired two warning shots in the hope that the assailants would disperse. Someone grabbed Mr. Toy and the rifle, knocking him down. The rifle went off a couple of times, and a bullet hit one of the youths in the leg. Mr. Toy managed to drag his son into the meat store and lock the doors, but the assailants kicked the doors in and beat both men severely while hurling racial insults and slurs and claiming that Mr. Toy had shot their friend. The attackers fled moments later when the sirens of approaching sheriff's cars were heard.

The attackers had inflicted enough physical harm to both Mr. Toy and his son to require prolonged medical treatment. The district attorney's office decided not to press charges against Mr. Toy on the grounds that the elder Toy had acted in self-defense. One attacker was arrested and placed on probation by a juvenile court referee. In March 1991 the assailant was taken off probation.

When the local newspaper reported that a lawsuit had been filed against the attackers in March 1990, the Toy family received a telephone death threat, and for several nights the son was followed home by a pickup truck. As a result of the suit and mounting community interest in the case, considerable publicity was generated in the local news media during early summer. In August 1990, some 9 months after the incident, another attacker was arrested. However, charges against this second attacker were later dismissed for insufficient evidence.

The Toys continued to be harassed after the incident. Soon after the November incident, a white man came into the store asking for change. When he was told that there was not enough change, the man went to the Safeway grocery store next door, then came back to Mr. Toy's store shouting, "See this change? We Americans help each other!" On more than several occasions, ice cream and soda were thrown against the store windows during the night.

Mr. Toy also recalls that during the first 4 years of his 10-year ownership of the store, he had to endure a long series of harassing acts by county inspectors, which persisted until he hired an attorney and threatened to sue. The harassment included: 1) not allowing Mr. Toy to put up a neon sign similar to the one on the store next door, 2) telling Mr. Toy that promotional advertisements displayed inside the store were too big and had to be reduced, and 3) asking Mr. Toy to change the color of fluorescent lamps inside the meat compartment, when other stores were allowed to use the same ones as his.

Concerned about the continuing undercurrent of anti-Asian prejudice in the area, declining sales, and most important, his wife's apprehension for the family's safety, Mr. Toy closed his store on June 29, 1990, incurring over a $100,000 loss, and found a part-time job at another grocery store in the same city.

Boycott of Korean Grocers in Flatbush, Brooklyn, N.Y.—On January 18, 1990, a seemingly minor incident occurred at the Family Red Apple Market grocery store (hereafter the Red Apple grocery store) in the Flatbush section of Brooklyn. It quickly led to a year-long boycott by black residents of two Korean American-owned groceries. This boycott forced the owners to the brink of bankruptcy, brought about one of the largest mass rallies of Asian Americans in the history of New York City, and resulted in a flurry of accusations between the offices of the district attorney and the mayor. The handling of the boycott led many Korean Americans to become disillusioned with the political process. The nature of the boycott remains controversial: a committee set up by Mayor Dinkins to investigate the incident (hereafter, Mayor's Committee) concluded it was "incident-based," although the city council's committee on general welfare flatly rejected this characterization and viewed it as racially motivated. The city council committee also questioned the neutrality and credibility of the Mayor's Committee. The incident is a significant one because it illustrates a widespread pattern of racial tensions between immigrant small retail store owners and their minority clients.

The incident that led to the boycott occurred on January 18, 1990. At about 6:00 p.m., Ghislaine Felissaint, a Haitian American resident of Flatbush, was shopping for a few produce items at the Red Apple store. As she was leaving the store to go across the street to another store which seemed to have a shorter line, she was asked to open her bag, and she refused. An altercation erupted between Ms. Felissaint and store employees, the police were called, and she was taken to a nearby hospital emergency room where "she was treated for superficial injuries and released several hours later."

What took place during the altercation is not totally clear, for the two sides have given conflicting versions. According to Ms. Felissaint, the store employee grabbed her by the neck and slapped her. She fell to the floor, and another employee kicked her on her left side and under her stomach. Since the assault, she has had "frequent headaches, and has developed serious gynecological problems. She has not been able to work for five months." At a January 26 meeting held at the police station, the attorney for Ms. Felissaint brought forth further allegations that "the female Oriental [cashier] was heard to say 'I'm tired of the f_____ing black people.'" The police officer who interviewed Ms. Felissaint at the hospital stated that she did not "mention ethnic remarks . . . and the female cashier spoke little or no English."

The store employee's version is somewhat different. According to them, when Ms. Felissaint arrived at the cash register, she had $3 worth of food, but presented only $2 to the cashier. While she looked in her bag for more money, the cashier began to wait on another customer because the line of customers was very long. She became angry, began yelling racial slurs, and then threw a hot pepper at the cashier. The cashier responded by throwing a pepper back at her. This squabble grew, with Ms. Felissaint knocking down boxes of hot pepper, and spitting in the cashier's face. The store manager intervened, appealing to her to calm down and asking her to forget about the $1. When he requested, with his "hands on her shoulders," that she leave the store, she "laid herself down on the floor." Customers began to take sides, some telling her that she should sue, and others advising her to get up and leave.

When the police arrived, they called an ambulance for Ms. Felissaint and, at the insistence of the crowd, arrested Bong Jae Jang, who identified himself as the owner of the store, for committing a third-degree assault. At this point the crowd was becoming "somewhat violent, throwing rocks and bottles at the Koreans. The personnel quickly closed the store."

A boycott of the store began shortly after the incident. According to the police record, at about 7:00 p.m. approximately 40 persons assembled in front of the store:

to protest the assault upon the Haitian woman by the Korean merchants, demanding that the store close permanently. Unidentified spokespersons voiced their opposition to the Korean-American treatment of customers in general, indicating that there have been a number of incidents in which customers have been manhandled and there is a lack of respect to all black customers. When [the store] closed at about 2000 hours the demonstrators moved across the street to 1826 Church Ave, another Korean-owned fruit and vegetable market [Church Fruits and Vegetables].

After closing the Red Apple store, an employee "ran across the street to take refuge from the angry crowd" gathered outside the store. While crossing the street to the Church Fruits and Vegetables store, "he was hit by bottles, rocks and fruits." It is because this employee took refuge in the Church Fruits and Vegetables store that the demonstrators followed him across the street. Although the two stores have been competitors and are in no way connected to each other, a connection was established in the minds of the demonstrators, and Church Fruits and Vegetables also became a target of boycott.

On the following day, there was a demonstration of about 25 persons in front of the Red Apple and the Church Fruits and Vegetables stores. The demonstrators "demanded that the store be closed permanently, claiming that a woman was beaten therein and is now in a coma." The next day, approximately 150 protesters began demonstrating in front of the store, and the crowd grew to about 400 persons by the late afternoon. One demonstrator was arrested for disorderly conduct after knocking over fruit stands and pushing bystanders.

In this manner, the boycott grew in size and gathered momentum. In the months that followed:

The boycott often became volatile and racially charged in tone, resulting in several instances of violence, as the demonstrators, using bull horns and positioning themselves in close proximity to the store entrances, exhorted, and, in certain instances, verbally abused shoppers in order to dissuade them from patronizing the boycotted stores.

Racist leaflets were distributed, and an act of violence by a demonstrator resulted in the wife of one of the store owners undergoing a medical abortion, leading one reporter to name the boycott the "'ugliest crack' in the gorgeous mosaic of racial harmony in the city." The boycott was still continuing at least a year later. In early 1991 demonstrators appeared only on evenings and weekends, but they still were driving away some shoppers.

Several specific developments that occurred subsequent to the January 18, 1990, incident are worthy of special mention:

1) On April 21, 1990, Mayor David N. Dinkins, who was elected on his campaign promise of racial harmony and assumed office 17 days before the start of the boycott, appointed a committee to investigate the circumstances of and climate surrounding the January 18th incident and to make recommendations on resolving the protest and boycott.

2) Because of the continuing protest and its devastating effects on business, the store owners applied for and, on May 10, 1990, were granted injunctive relief by the Kings County Supreme Court. Balancing the protesters' rights to congregate and express their position and the store owners' rights to engage in commerce, the court issued an order that the demonstrators could continue their protest from a distance of not less than 50 feet from the store entrances and directed the New York City Police Department to enforce its provisions. The policy department failed to enforce the May 10 order, however. Because of this failure and the continuing boycott's adverse commercial impact, on June 4, 1990, the store owners initiated a mandamus proceeding to compel the police department to enforce the court order. On June 26, 1990, the court directed the police department to implement its May 10 order. The police department, however, arguing that law enforcement is a matter exclusively committed to the discretion of the police department and that public safety and community relations concerns strongly militated against enforcing the May 10 order, appealed the June 26 decision on several grounds.

3) On September 17, 1990, the State appellate court unanimously concluded that the police department must enforce the lawful order of the court. Specifically, the court noted that the police assertion that to enforce the May 10 order would engender community resentment towards the police or exacerbate the intensity of the protest was unpersuasive. This assertion, the court reasoned, failed to recognize that the court prescribed the mea-

sures as reasonable and necessary after examining the relevant circumstances. Furthermore, the police are not "entitled to unilaterally conclude otherwise by, in essence, abrogating to themselves the ultimate authority to weigh the petitioners' entitlement to effective enforcement of the court's order . . . and state officials are not entitled to rely on community hostility as an excuse not to protect . . . the exercise of fundamental rights."

4) On August 30, 1990, the Mayor's Committee issued its report (hereafter the Mayor's Committee Report). The report concluded that:

a) The boycott was "incident-based," not racially motivated.

b) Although the New York City Police Department did a commendable job of keeping peace in the neighborhood, the police failed to inform the Bias Investigation Unit of the department, even though both sides claimed that racial insults were used, and the police treated the incident "in a light and superficial manner." None of the police officers spoke Korean, French, or Creole, and the police lost "crucial witnesses" because they were more intent on clearing the store than determining what had happened.

c) The mainstream media coverage of the situation was "inflammatory and polarizing," "overly simplistic and in some cases blatantly racist," and did not assist the resolution process.

d) The district attorney's office did not move the resulting court cases as expeditiously as it could have, thereby contributing to the erosion of public trust in the criminal justice system.

5) On the same day that the Mayor's Committee Report was released, August 30, 1990, the District Attorney of Kings County issued a 14-page statement responding to the report, characterizing it as "flawed because of inaccuracy and an incomplete review of facts and circumstances."

6) The New York City Council's Committee on General Welfare (Council Committee) held a public hearing on the report on September 12, 1990, and issued its findings and conclusions in December 1990. The Council Committee observed that the Mayor's Committee Report was "a disappointment to all participants in the situation and to the public who was hoping for a courageous moral stand from its leadership." Specific conclusions were as follows:

a) "From the outset, the Mayor's Committee was apparently unwilling to evaluate critically the facts of the January 18 incident . . . and [its] failure to investigate the protest meaningfully appears to be purposeful." As evidence for this statement, the Council Committee cited the basic fact that the Mayor's Committee failed to interview the protestors themselves regrading their causes for the boycott.

b) The Mayor's Committee failed to attribute racist behavior to the particular groups responsible for the distribution of racist literature. The Council Committee called this failure "baffling," since some of the racist literature was clearly identified with particular groups.

c) "While the goal of resolving the boycott is laudable, it cannot be done at the expense of the constitutional rights of one of the parties, nor the abrogation of the function of the police [as law enforcement agents]."

d) "The City's refusal to enforce the fifty-foot order [for demonstrators not to congregate within 50 feet from the stores] absent the specific direction of two courts is without defense.... The Mayor's failure to direct the police to enforce [the court order] raises questions about his willingness to exercise his authority. The failure of the Committee to criticize this [aspect] is profoundly disturbing."

e) The conclusion that "the protest is incident-based and not primarily racist is contradicted by the facts. This erroneous conclusion adversely affects the rationale behind the Committee's recommendations regarding resolution of the protest."

7) The Mayor's Committee Report was also criticized by the media. For example, a *New York Times* editorial noted, "Cynics suggested the [appointment of the committee] was merely a device to diffuse responsibility for an intolerable display of racism. The report makes even the cynics look starry-eyed.... The Flatbush boycott [is] racist.... The report leaves Mayor Dinkins still seeming to excuse racial picketing. By doing so, he encourages the spread of this pernicious tactic."

8) On September 18, 1990, Asian Americans (primarily, but not exclusively, Korean Americans) held a civil rights rally in front of the city hall. This peaceful rally, officially named by the organizers as "Peace Rally For Racial Harmony," drew a record crowd of near 10,000 persons, the largest rally of its kind in the city. It promoted themes of racial harmony, racial justice, and cultural pluralism. At this rally Mayor Dinkins announced that the city would enforce the court order barring demonstrators within 50 feet from the stores.

9) After the appeals court decision, the police department started enforcing the 50-foot court order, arresting 13 persons for disorderly conduct. On September 21, 1990, Mayor Dinkins visited the two boycotted stores and shopped. His visit was characterized as "directly contradict[ing] his previous position on how to handle the protest ... and adopted instead exactly the tactic that an array of other politicians and opinion-makers had urged on him for months." After the mayor's visit, business at the two boycotted stores took a sharp upswing. Over the following weekend, however, 19 gasoline bombs were discovered on the roof of the

Red Apple store by police officers who were conducting a routine sweep of the building. The police noted, "We don't know who did this or for what purpose, [but] because of the close proximity to the Korean grocery stores, there's a possibility it's connected." Although there were no major boycott-related violence or incidents since the mayor's visit, demonstrators were still appearing on evenings and weekends, driving away some customers, even after one year.

The year-long boycott exacerbated race relations in the Flatbush area and may have led to a violent attack on three Vietnamese American men by a large group of black youths who mistook them for Koreans. In that incident, which took place early in the morning of Sunday, May 13, 1990, as many as 15 youths were gathered outside an apartment building in which the Vietnamese men lived. One of them threw a beer bottle, shattering a plate-glass window in the Vietnamese men's apartment. When the Vietnamese men came out to see what was going on, the youths attacked them with a baseball bat, knives, and bottles, shouting, "Koreans, what are you doing here?" and other racial slurs. One of the Vietnamese men, Tuan Ana Cao, suffered a fractured skull and other severe injuries in that attack. Despite the proximity of the attack to the location of the boycott and the anti-Korean remarks made by the attackers, the police commissioner maintained that the incident was not related to the grocery store boycott.

The Flatbush incident illustrates what can happen when racial tensions are unchecked and racial incidents mishandled by local governments. An incident that might have been managed in such a way as to improve racial relations in New York City instead ended up worsening racial relations and disillusioning many Korean Americans about the American political process.

Harassment of Vietnamese Fishermen

The 1986 Commission report noted a general pattern of friction between Vietnamese fishermen and native fishermen in Florida, Texas, and California. The friction was caused by difficulties in communication, the Vietnamese fishermen's lack of awareness of local fishing regulations, and economic competition between established native fishermen and the Vietnamese newcomers. The report documented many incidents of vandalism and violence arising out of this friction, including Ku Klux Klan activity against Vietnamese fishermen in Texas. The report also pointed to a pattern of using State government action, such as restrictive laws and regulations, against Vietnamese fishermen.

A more recent incident demonstrates that such acts of harassment were not an isolated episode. In 1989 Vietnamese fishermen charged that the U.S. Coast Guard's selective enforcement of a 200-year-old law was being used to harass them and drive them out of the fishing business in California. The Jones Act, enacted in the late 1700s, effectively prohibits noncitizens from owning or operating large boats (heavier than 5 net tons) in U.S. waters. The original objective of the act was to ensure that such boats would be operated by persons predisposed to defend the United States in the event of war. The U.S. Coast Guard apparently began enforcing the Jones Act against Vietnamese fishermen in northern California waters in November of 1987. Most of the Vietnamese fishermen in northern California are permanent residents who have not yet met the waiting period for becoming citizens, and thus could not operate their fishing boats in certain waters under the law. Fines of $500 were levied against fishermen found violating the law, and the Coast Guard threatened to seize boats that were operated illegally. Several fishermen gave up fishing after that, while others continued.

According to the Vietnamese fishermen, the law had not been enforced by the U.S. Coast Guard in recent years, and they believe it was being selectively enforced against Vietnamese fishermen. The U.S. Coast Guard, however, contends that "[h]ere in the San Francisco Bay Area, it has been enforced at the same level as far back as anybody can remember." The Vietnamese fishermen contend further that the Jones Act is unconstitutional, because there is no longer any overriding military need for the law, and its enforcement deprives the fishermen of their ability to earn a living.

On September 27, 1989, the Vietnamese Fishermen Association of America and six individual fishermen brought a suit seeking an injunction to stop the Coast Guard from enforcing the law on the grounds that it is unconstitutional. The next day Judge Orrick of the United States District Court for the Northern District of California issued a temporary restraining order stopping the Coast Guard from enforcing the law while the issue was being litigated. On October 16, Judge Schwarzer, of the same court, denied application for a preliminary injunction on the grounds that the fishermen were unlikely to win their suit on the merits.

The fishermen appealed the denial of a preliminary injunction and at the same time filed an emergency motion for injunctive relief, which was granted on November 15, 1989. At that point in time, it was agreed by the parties that the October 16 decision denying a preliminary injunction would be treated as a decision in favor of the Coast Guard, and on January 24, 1990, the fishermen appealed this decision. Arguments were heard on July 20, 1990.

Before a decision was rendered, however, Congress passed and President Bush signed legislation sponsored by Representative Norman Mineta (D-CA) that would allow permanent resident aliens to operate fishing boats in excess of 5 tons in California coastal waters.

Racial Harassment on College Campuses

Bigotry and violence against Asian Americans extends to college campuses, where the way the incidents are handled reveals much about the underlying climate of the institution. An incident that took place at the University of Connecticut (UConn) at Storrs in December 1987 is illustrative:

On the evening of December 3, 1987, at about 9:30, Marta Ho, Feona Lee, and six other students of Asian descent boarded a bus that was to take them to a semiformal Christmas dance sponsored by two University dorms at the Italian-American Club in the nearby town of Tolland. . . . Marta in a black-and-white, knee-length gown made of silk, which she had borrowed from her sister, and Feona in a full-length, blue silk gown that she had brought from her native Hong Kong. . . . The crowded bus held between 50 and 60 people—some of them drinking and yelling profanities. The group of eight Asian American students found seats scattered toward the rear of the bus. . . . While waiting on the bus parked in front of a dormitory, Feona felt something land in her hair. "At first I thought it was just water dripping from the bus. . . . Then I felt something warm and slimy hit me in the face." She realized it was spit. As she stood up and turned to face her attackers, she was hit again, this time in the eye. "Who did that?" she screamed, "Stop!" . . . When Daniel Shan, one of the eight [Asian American] students, rushed over to see what was wrong, Feona was facing a group of half-dozen young men sitting in the back seats—drinking beer, some of them chewing tobacco—two of whom Shan recognized as football players. When Feona sat down, these two men spat on her, hitting [Shan] as well, and yelling slurs such as "Chinks!" "Gooks," and "Oriental faggots!" Shan and another man in the group, Ron Cheung, approached the two men, demanding they apologize. The two harassers invited them to fight, while one of the two threw a punch at Cheung and missed. Someone separated them, and the bus driver yelled at everyone to "Sit down and shut up!" No effort was made to put the spitters off the bus . . . By the time the bus pulled up to the Club, the harassment had lasted nearly 45 minutes.

The Asian American students tried to salvage the evening by dancing and staying on the opposite side of the room from their antagonists. But one of the two harassers followed them repeatedly elbowing Marta's dance partner, making "animal sounds" and screaming insults. According to one witness, this harasser dropped his sweatpants, mooning her and her partner, and then danced with his penis exposed. Later he urinated on a window and confronted Danny Shan in a stairway, apparently trying to get him to fight. . . . The victims complained to three Resident Assistants [RAs], upperclass students hired by the university as nominal authorities in the dormitories. But they were told "not to spoil a good time," otherwise they "would be written up." When they asked permission to leave the dance, they were told the could not because the RAs were responsible for the victims' safety. . . . Marta and Feona called the Vernon police by mistake instead of the Tolland police. . . . A little before midnight, a squad car drove up. Although the victims thought it was in response to their call, the squad car was responding to another call stemming from an unrelated fight. By this time the dance was coming to an end, and the first bus had arrived to take people home; without making a complaint to the trooper, the group got on the bus and rode back to the UConn campus. . . . A group photograph taken afterward at the dormitory shows the brown tobacco stains on Feona's blue gown and on her wrist.

At the insistence of Marta's sister, Maria Ho, the victims went to the campus police on Dec. 4, 1987 to report the incident. After listening to their story, the officer on duty conferred with his supervisor and told them there was nothing he could do because the incident had taken place in Tolland, outside UConn's jurisdiction, suggesting they take their complaint to state police and the campus affirmative action office, Only after he was confronted with the question, "Aren't you at least going to take a report?" he agreed to take a "miscellaneous" report for future reference.

It was nearly 10:00 p.m. that evening that the victims finally were able to talk to a state trooper in Tolland. The officer advised the victims to go back to campus police because the incident had begun on UConn property. According to the victims, the trooper's response upon being told of the incident was "to laugh." He also said something like, "Boy, this guy must have been drunk out of his mind." Furthermore, Feona recalls, "He asked me, did I see [the man] pull his pants down, and did I see his penis? I said I did, and he asked me, do I really know what a penis looks like?" . . . It was 11:00 p.m. when the victims finally went home after being shunted back and forth all day.

The following Monday, December 7, Maria called the university's Office of Affirmative Action Programs and made an afternoon appointment. When the victims showed up, they were told the case lay outside the office's jurisdiction and referred to the Dean of Students. . . . When Maria called the Dean's office Tuesday, she learned the dean was out and his assistant offered to schedule them for later in the week. Maria then replied that if they did not receive prompt attention, they would tell their story to the newspapers. At that point the assistant invited the students to come to the office to give oral testimony. . . .

After Maria Ho's threat to bring the incident to the press, the pace of the university's response picked up. On Thursday, December 10, the two perpetrators were charged with violating the Student Conduct Code and a hearing was scheduled for the accused. In the meantime, the university's director of public safety determined that the actions that occurred while the bus was parked on UConn property were within his jurisdiction. The victims were summoned back to give sworn affidavits, and warrants were obtained for the arrest of the two accused students for disorderly conduct. Eventually, one of the two accused was expelled from school for 1 year and the other, a star football player, was prohibited from living in the student dormitories but allowed to continue to play for the UConn football team.

To the Asian American community and students, the "administration's treatment of them was as bad as the original incident. Perhaps worse." The frustration at the university's handling led to a protest fast of 8 days by an Asian American faculty member on the campus in the summer of 1988 and to the university senate's passage in September 1988 of a resolution mandating an investigation into the December 3, 1987, incident and the university's response. The university senate's subcommittee on discriminatory harassment, in its report released in early April 1989, noted that the dean of students may have mishandled the disciplinary hearings on the December 1987 incident by violating procedural rules and possibly coercing the victims. Based on this report, the college of liberal arts and sciences faculty passed a resolution requesting that "UConn President John Casteen investigate the allegations and if substantiated, the Dean and his assistant be suspended from participation in any hearing affecting College of Liberal Arts and Sciences students." The subcommittee report also noted serious causes for concern at the Storrs campus: "deep-seated intolerance, a perceived absence of leadership at the top, an atmosphere 'altogether too permissive of harassing behavior,' and lack of trust in the administration." The report found that "deep-seated prejudice at UConn has bred a climate in which harassment based on race, sex, ethnic background and sexual preference is tolerated by administrators, students, faculty and staff members." Commenting on the report, one newspaper editorial noted that "without question, there are harassment problems on the campus. . . . Whether the problem is less or greater at

UConn than at other universities of equal size is not known. What is known is there is a problem of apparent pervasive prejudice and harassment. The cure for the ailment is contained in the report if it is applied to the patient without delay."

By nearly unanimous voice vote, the University of Connecticut's Faculty Senate voted on May 1, 1989, not to suspend the dean of students for his alleged mishandling of the December 3, 1987, incident. Soon after the senate vote, University President Casteen announced that he found no evidence of wrongdoing by the dean of students (who resigned in June 1989 to become vice president of student life at a college in South Carolina). At the same time he instituted two changes in the Student Conduct Code: 1) preventing students found guilty of harassment from playing sports or taking part in other activities for at least one semester, and 2) imposing suspension or expulsion as a possible punishment on every student accused of discriminatory harassment. The president also acknowledged that he should have responded more quickly to the incident: "In hindsight, if I had known more of the incident, I would have or should have acted differently. I would have taken a fairly strong posture."

Racial Slurs Made by Public Figures

When public figures make racial slurs against Asian Americans, they lend an aura of legitimacy to the anti-Asian attitudes held by many in the public and indirectly encourage anti-Asian activities. In a much-publicized incident in 1990, Jimmy Breslin, a prominent columnist for *Newsday*, angered at criticism of one of his columns by a female colleague who is Korean American, publicly referred to her as a "yellow cur" and "slant-eyed." *Newsday* management's apparent reluctance to discipline Breslin after he had made what to some seemed an inadequate apology, provoked accusations that they were operating under a double standard. The situation was further aggravated when Breslin made light of the situation several days later, joking on the air, referring to his nephew's wedding to a Korean woman, "Now does this mean I can't go to the wedding?" The next day, *Newsday* management gave Breslin a 2-week suspension.

Breslin's comment is by no means an isolated incident. In a much less publicized incident, Cliff Kincaid, a Washington, DC, radio personality, referred to CBS television anchor Connie Chung as "Connie Chink." Later, explaining himself, he said, "It's a slang term. It is not a vulgar term," and argued that it was not a term like "honky." Yet, a handbook for journalists, sponsored by the National Conference of Christians and Jews, the Asian American Journalists Association, and the Association of Asian Pacific American Artists, defines the term "chink" as:

racial slur—A derogatory term for Chinese and Chinese Americans that some believe was derived from the Ch'ing Dynasty, which ruled during the period of the first major migration of Chinese immigrants. Avoid except in direct quotes and specific historical references.

Kincaid's ignorance is illustrative of insensitivity in the media to Asian Americans.

Racial remarks made by politicians can be even more damaging, because they suggest that the political process itself is racist. In January 1990, John Silber, candidate for the Democratic nomination for Governor of Massachusetts, called Massachusetts a "welfare magnet" that has "suddenly become popular for people who are accustomed to living in the tropical climate." He was also quoted as saying, "Why should Lowell [Massachusetts] be the Cambodian capital of America? Why should they all be concentrated in one place? This needs to be examined." Cambodian community leaders in Lowell found these remarks demeaning and offensive. They considered Silber's remarks another reflection of the anti-Asian bias that had led to the "English-only" ordinance that had recently been passed by the Lowell City Council. Silber went on to win the Democratic nomination, but in November 1990 he narrowly lost his bid to become Governor of Massachusetts.

IV. THE QUESTION OF IMMIGRATION POLICY

EDITOR'S INTRODUCTION

The last section of this compilation addresses our national immigration policy. Although some may regard the present influx of immigrants with apprehension, fearing that they may take jobs from native workers or overload welfare and social services, most commentators on the subject favor it. The first article of this section, an editorial from *The New Republic*, while acknowledging the scale of current immigration and the problem of providing federal subsidies for refugee settlement in a time of budget constraints, advocates that as in the past the United States open its doors to newcomers.

The second article, from *Commentary* by Ben J. Wattenberg and Karl Zinsmeister, points out that although the new wave of immigrants is large (650,000 legals, illegals, and refugees per year), it is proportionately less than that at the turn of the century: about one-fifth of 1 percent now compared to 1 percent then. The authors also present a number of arguments favoring immigration. Immigrants, first of all, tend to be younger than the general population and thus draw only lightly from Social Security and Medicare programs. They often fill manual jobs for which native workers are in short supply, attract minimum-wage industries, and start new businesses. Furthermore, studies show little evidence that immigrants entering the work force lower the wages of even the most vulnerable native groups, such as low-skill blacks. In addition, the authors call for more individuals to be admitted on the basis of education and occupational skills instead of familial ties in order to take advantage of a talented pool wishing to emigrate to the United States.

Next, Julian L. Simon notes in a related article from *The Public Interest* that arguments against immigration raised by groups such as lobbyists and organized labor are based on misinformation. Simon maintains that in the years ahead, due to a lowered birth rate, the size of the labor pool will lag behind the needs of American business and industry, leaving a gap that a young generation of immigrants can fill to keep America competitive in an international marketplace. Simon claims that legislation passed by congress in 1990, which increases the number admitted from 600,000 to 750,000 per year, does not go far enough. Needed are more skilled immigrants, such as top scientists. Permanent resident visas should also be issued to foreign students, especially those studying science and engineering.

Finally, an article by Peter Skerry, also from *The Public Interest,* takes a less positive view of the new wave of immigration. Conditions today, he reasons, are not the same as they were at the turn of the century, when immigrants were eager to be assimilated as Americans, and institutions were able to inculcate in them a sense of shared national identity. Today immigrants flowing into the country are more apt to define themselves along their ethnic and racial lines, contributing to a more divided American society.

KNOCK KNOCK

"Let my people go." That's what Moses said to Pharaoh. What the United States and its allies have been saying to the contemporary pharaohs is "Let *your* people go." And they have begun to do just that. Suddenly there is a panic throughout the West. How in the world are we going to cope with hundreds of thousands, and soon perhaps millions, of men and women, young and old, who will be free to leave the Communist countries from which hitherto there had been no exit? For 28 years the Berlin Wall has symbolized that cruel policy of sealed borders. We in the West, of course, made the most of it politically, taunting the red regimes for having to keep their subjects from voting with their feet.

But our indignation was safe and easy, since our bluff was not called. In Asia we have let masses of wretched escapees from Marxism-in-power languish in camps, not only homeless but stateless, which (as Hannah Arendt has shown) also means utterly rightless. Most of the Eastern and Central Europeans probably will fare rather better than the Vietnamese and the Cambodians did. They are white, after all. Still, dispossession does not yet

Editorial article, from *The New Republic* 201:7–8 O 2 '89. Copyright © 1989 by *The New Republic.* Reprinted with permission.

evoke much practical sympathy in Europe. Notice how little notice has been taken of the Turks of Bulgaria, who did not leave voluntarily but have been expelled—300,000 of them in recent months—penniless, before our very eyes in these very days into an indifferent world.

This journal has always maintained that America should open its doors ever more widely to those who aspire to be Americans. Perhaps we can no longer have the completely open borders we once had, but at the very least current immigration and refugee ceilings can be doubled and redoubled. We favor a more open door not simply as a way of relieving the distress among other peoples and in other societies. We favor it because we believe that many of the distinguishing strengths of this country derive from its foreign strains, and that new immigrants can contribute to America just as past immigrants have done.

Alas, the drift of public policy is not in that direction. To be sure, the United States has moved decisively in recent decades away from the invidious ethnic and racial preferences that governed early immigration practices. And during the last quarter century we have also been far more responsive to political refugees than other societies. But immigrants are limited to about 600,000 a year, with a complicated point system used for deciding who is most worthy of admission. Refugees—those deemed to be fleeing political oppression, as opposed to merely seeking economic opportunity—are a separate category. Last year [1988] we admitted 76,000 refugees. We have admitted 75,000 already this year [1989]. President Bush proposes increasing that to 125,000 next year, but is requesting enough money for only 84,000.

But the world is awash with refugees—an estimated 14 million of them. Some are victims of unbelievably brutal governments; others are the human refuse of routine economic and even nutritional want. Asking whether their motivation is "economic" or "political" is to make an absurd distinction: impossible as a practical matter, and morally irrelevant in any event. Often the causes of collective and individual misery go together, as in Haiti. Nevertheless, when a Haitian family risks its life to come to America in an old boat and is apprehended on the seas, our laws do not recognize them as refugees.

The category of refugee is narrowly defined. It is also arbitrarily defined. For a while Cubans were axiomatic refugees. Within numerical limits so were Indochinese. Since we don't admit everybody, choices are always made, hard choices. Perhaps necessary choices. The choices are especially difficult this year. There is the budget constraint: refugees receive federal subsidies for resettlement. But the sheer number of refugees is what really overwhelms. The intensified repression in China alone is bound to create a wave of new refugees that will affect the fate of other refugees and would-be refugees. In a world as nasty as ours the status of refugee—the moral claim that attaches to it—is always relative.

While the Bush administration tries to create a fair refugee policy, Congress has passed legislation that would grant Jews and evangelical Christians from the Soviet Union virtually automatic classification as admissible refugees. The State Department estimates that in 1990 at least 100,000 Soviet Jews would apply and qualify. Given the severity of the world refugee situation, this legislation, promoted by Senator Frank Lautenberg of New Jersey and Representative Bruce Morrison of Connecticut, both Democrats, is nothing more than special pleading.

With the dramatic changes taking place under *glasnost* and *perestroika,* there is reason to question whether any residents of the Soviet Union wanting to leave the country should still be considered refugees. Treating them as such may be close to an obsolete concept. (They always can apply as immigrants, going through the arcane and time-consuming procedures just like everyone else.) But in the case of Soviet Jews there is a second consideration. Those who are allowed out are not in the position of having no place to go. Israel was always willing—eager—to take them in. In fact, part of the romance that surrounded Soviet Jewish "refuseniks," those who couldn't get out, was that they wanted to "go home." Even those who settled elsewhere (and 90 percent in recent years have come to America) left the Soviet Union under the legal fiction that they were going to Israel. Any Soviet Jew who can get an exit visa can still go to Israel, a democratic society where he can lead a free, if somewhat exasperating, life. In this sense also no Soviet Jew is properly a refugee. He may prefer the United States, but he is far better off than the hundreds of thousands with no place to go.

There is nothing inherently hypocritical about America's insistence that everyone should have the right to leave his country, just because we cannot (or at least do not) make room for everyone who exercises that right. Nevertheless, more room ought to be made. While most continue to be excluded, however, decency requires reserving precious spaces for those who have no place else to go.

THE CASE FOR MORE IMMIGRATION

For the first time in a quarter-century, and only the fourth in our entire history, Congress is attempting a comprehensive update of our immigration laws. The Senate has already passed a bill and the House of Representatives is now deliberating on a version of its own. If, in concurrence with the President, they produce legislation, it could be the most important action taken by our government in this decade. It would not only change the blend of the American clay, it would significantly influence any number of powerful issues, from competitiveness to national purpose. Immigration policy, in short, critically affects the relative position and prosperity of the United States, both domestically and on the international scene.

I

The first thing to be said about current immigrant flows to this country is that in historical terms they are fairly moderate. While the actual number of foreign citizens now entering the U.S. may seem high—about 650,000 per year, counting legals, illegals, and refugees, and subtracting out-migration—it amounts all in all to an annual increase in the population of only about one-fifth of 1 percent. At the turn of the century, by contrast, when immigration was at its height, it increased the U.S. population by about 1 percent per year. Furthermore, the fraction of our current population that is foreign-born is not only well below earlier U.S. peaks, it is lower than the present levels in several West European nations, and considerably below the proportions in other immigrant nations like Australia and Canada.

Article by Ben J. Wattenberg, senior fellow, and Karl Zinsmeister, adjunct fellow, at the American Enterprise Institute in Washington, D.C., from *Commentary* 89:19–25 Ap '90. Copyright © 1990 by *Commentary*. Reprinted with permission.

The extent of *illegal* immigration to the U.S. seems particularly subject to exaggeration. In early 1986, the U.S. Bureau of the Census, in its first official estimate, concluded that there were about two million undocumented aliens in the country as of 1980, and that approximately another 200,000 had entered each year thereafter. This figure was much lower than the ones trumpeted by many alarmists. (The Census Bureau also concluded during the 1980's that about 160,000 persons, most of them foreign-born, emigrated from the U.S. every year.) And today there appear to be at least somewhat fewer illegals arriving than in the past. Since passage of the Immigration Reform and Control Act of 1986, the Immigration and Naturalization Service has reported a significant reduction in the number of persons caught illegally crossing U.S. borders, with the 1989 figures falling 54 percent below the 1986 totals.

This does not mean that illegal immigration is not a problem, or that strict measures may not need to be implemented to deal with it, ranging from forgery-resistant Social Security cards to more border guards. But the point is that even with illegals taken into account, the numbers of people now entering the country are not distressingly high. In fact, they are lower than what, in our judgment, a wise policy would dictate.

II

Before considering what such a policy might look like, however, we need to attend to the arguments *against* substantial further immigration to this country.

The most widespread such argument is that America already has enough people, or too many people, or will soon have too many people unless the flow of new residents is stopped.

Yet according to medium-variant ("most likely") projections by the Census Bureau, at current levels of birth, mortality, and immigration, the U.S. over the next fifty years will experience relatively slow population growth, then slower growth, then no growth, and then decline. This is due primarily to the fact that, for fifteen years now, fertility rates have been below the replacement level. Even an immigration moderately higher than the current level would still leave us on a slow-growth path toward population stability in the next century.

The future can, of course, change. Suffice it to say that under current conditions there is no long-term population explosion under way in this country. Claims that immigration is going to bring about a standing-room-only America, or anything close to it, are bunk.

Beyond that, the risks and benefits of our current demographic trends are open to debate. Though much attention has been paid to the dangers of overpopulation and overimmigration, little notice has been directed to the dangers of stasis or decline. Over the last two centuries, America's prosperity and growing influence have coincided with the most significant long-term population boom in history. In the century to come the population of the planet as a whole will double; is it wise for America to be a no-growth player in a high-growth world?

A second, related argument against immigration focuses on potential damage to the environment. Former Colorado Governor Richard Lamm put the view clearly:

With current levels of immigration, we will always be forced to use our resources at a faster and faster rate, to try to expand our economy to make room for more and more workers, to try to spread our suburbs, cutting down the forests and clearing out the farms that used to surround our cities.

The biologist Garrett Hardin recently blamed immigration for the fact that "Traffic problems are being replaced by rush-hour gridlock. Safe drinking water is scarcer every year. Forests are being killed by acid rain."

Statements like these are flawed in many respects. To begin with the issue of resource depletion, the truth is that regardless of the level of population, we have always been and will always be "running out" of resources, but we will never hit empty. Under any intelligent market-based system, resource use is not a matter of draining down inherited reserves but a complex process of inherent rationing, constantly evolving new applications, and substitutions based on what makes economic sense plus what is feasible with contemporary technology. Among the once-dwindling resources that are now in "oversupply" are flint for arrowheads, farmland, acetylene for lamps, high-quality vacuum tubes, latex for rubber-making, trees usable for schooner masts, good mules, and copper ore. Moreover, as the economist Julian Simon has noted, the real costs of nearly all natural resources—measured in hours of human labor needed to acquire one unit—have fallen steadily and sharply in recent decades.

Similarly, ecological degradation is caused in large measure by what people do or fail to do, not by how many people there are.

Within the last two decades, since America began spending significant sums on abatement, pollution has declined even as population has gone up. Recent concern about environmental trends like carbon-dioxide build-up and alleged ozone depletion are particularly irrelevant to the immigration question. If, as some worry, an individual person adds to global warming, it does not matter whether that person is in South Korea or New York (unless it is beneficial for Third Worlders to stay poor, thereby using less energy).

As for the perceived crowding that so inflames environmentalists, much of it is an effect not of numbers *per se* but of living in a land of growing affluence. If American suburbs are expanding outward, if national parks are host to more and more visitors, if once-favorite beaches and vacation spots have been "discovered," all that is largely owing not to a surfeit of Americans but to the unprecedented amounts of discretionary earnings at their command. Disposable income per capita, adjusted for inflation, has gone up by about 50 percent in the last twenty years; in the same period, the number of second homes has doubled. We now have about one car per adult. More than twice as many Americans take vacations abroad today as did in 1970.

This can make for crowded airports and difficulty in finding a parking spot. By any decent standard, however, these are good things, a function of greater choice and opportunity for Americans of all classes. They are not a result of letting in too many immigrants.

A third argument in opposition to immigration is that immigrants constitute a big drain on social spending.

A series of recent economic studies challenge this notion. Immigrants tend to be disproportionately young, and as a result they draw very lightly on Social Security and Medicare—by far our largest social programs. Nor do they draw much more than natives on other kinds of welfare spending, like Aid to Families with Dependent Children, food stamps, and unemployment compensation. In all, immigrants actually consume smaller amounts of public funds than do natives for about their first dozen years in the U.S. After that, levels tend to equalize.

What is more, within eleven to sixteen years of coming to America the average immigrant is earning as much as, or more than, the average native-born worker. Immigrant *families*, who typically have more working members, outstrip native families in income in as little as three to five years. In this way, immigrants become above-average tax*payers*. Viewed strictly in terms of fiscal flows and social-welfare budgets, then, immigrants tend to represent a good deal for the nation.

A fourth argument directly contradicts the third: immigrants are such zealous workers that they deprive natives of scarce jobs. Here, too, major studies by the Urban Institute and by the Rand Corporation paint a different picture. Immigration to a given area can be quite compatible with job growth, and even with wage increases. Indeed, one finds little evidence of higher unemployment or of a serious depressive effect on wages even among the most vulnerable native groups—low-skill black workers or American-born Hispanics—when there is a rise in the proportion of immigrants in the local labor market.

Immigrants seem generally to complement rather than compete with native workers. They often fill manual or specialized jobs for which domestic workers are in short supply. They sometimes attract minimum-wage industries which would otherwise have located elsewhere. They stimulate activity in the service economy. They start new businesses. As anyone who has lived in a neighborhood with such businesses can attest, these enterprises are largely original: far from driving someone else from a job, many immigrant entrepreneurs carve a narrow foothold for themselves out of the rubble of empty buildings and unserved needs.

A fifth and final argument against immigration, perhaps the most venerable of all, is cultural: immigration on a large scale will eventually disrupt societal coherence, "swamp" the national culture, and imperil our sense of shared history and unity. Benjamin Franklin was an early articulator of this view; the targets of his ire were Germans, whom he criticized as clannish, ignorant, and intent on maintaining their own language. Since Franklin's time, the targets have varied—Irish, Italians, Jews, Hispanics, and others have each taken their turn—but the charges have remained remarkably consistent.

Yet, Benjamin Franklin and a host of other critics notwithstanding, the integration of immigrants into the national ethos has not proved notably difficult in the past. We did not develop a German-language province, or any other separate enclaves; new arrivals, certainly after a generation or two, have tended to disperse fairly broadly across the land. Immigrants have not succeeded in introducing monarchism into this country, or for that matter Bolshevism (to mention only two once-widespread fears).

Our founding fathers, were they able to pay a visit, would find many of our basic social and political institutions rather familiar. American ethnic history has for the most part followed the wise old dictum, "In all things essential, unity, in other things diversity."

Now, it could be argued that this generally healthy pattern has changed somewhat over the last twenty-five years. American politics has increasingly come to be conducted in terms of what the sociologist Nathan Glazer has called "ethnic populism"—one bloc against another, with the national interest perceived as nothing more than an aggregate of group appeals. This has made many Americans defensive, and probably less charitable toward the idea of large immigrant flows with their implicit threat of Balkanization. Then, too, there is the changing makeup of those immigrant flows themselves. Increasing proportions come from Asia, Latin America, the Muslim world, the Caribbean, and Africa, places where historical, religious, racial, and political traditions are often quite different from those of the majority of Americans.

There is no ignoring the unsettled feeling many people experience upon walking into a New York City subway car or a Los Angeles public school—the feeling of being, as the saying goes, "in a Third World country." Mass public opinion in America has never been pro-immigration, and may be less so today as immigration from European nations has dwindled. That is understandable enough; within a properly tempered political system citizens should not be made to feel like strangers in their own land.

But there are many grounds for reassurance. Data from California, for instance, show that somewhere between a quarter and a third of all Hispanics marry "Anglos"; us-vs.-them politics becomes much harder to sustain when it is difficult to tell the sides apart. Moreover, the powerful forces of Americanization are far from dead. More than 90 percent of U.S.-born Hispanics are now entirely fluent in English, and more than half of that group speaks *only* English. Young Hispanics aged twenty-one to twenty-five who are either native-born or have been in the country for more than ten years have reading scores comparable to the all-U.S. average.

Continued emphasis on English-language proficiency and other essentials of the collective American identity is obviously wholly desirable, not only from the perspective of the larger American interest but from the point of view of immigrants anxious to make progress in society. Militant advocates of linguistic and cultural separatism are, as it happens, out of step with the actual practices of most immigrants. It is in fact newcomers who often have the most powerful interest in the creation of common cultural ground—one reason Spanish is not going to become California's co-official language is that new Californians from Korea, Taiwan, the Philippines, Vietnam, the USSR, India, and Cambodia would not stand for it.

When it comes, finally, to a sense of shared national values, in the United States this has almost never been based on common blood but rather on specific traits and attitudes, both real and idealized. And the simple fact is that those traits and attitudes— self-reliance, a disciplined work ethic, strong family attachments, religiosity, an inclination toward entrepreneurship, a stress on education, independence of mind, an appreciation of individual liberty—are often notably prominent among immigrants to this country. It is no accident: in some large measure, after all, they come to America because they admire what America stands for.

International pollsters tell us that Americans are more patriotic, more willing to fight and die for their nation, and prouder of their heritage than residents of other industrial countries, even the most homogeneous ones. Our common ground derives from the surpassing power of deeply held principle. The democratic and individualistic values associated with that principle have proved and continue to prove assimilable by immigrants.

III

These, then, are some of the reasons why we need not fear additional immigration to the United States. Beyond these, there are other reasons why, especially in the period just ahead, we should positively welcome it.

In a normal labor market new people not only "consume" jobs, they also "create" jobs through their labor and their buying. That is usually justification enough for not being overly concerned about "job-stealing." But the United States is not at present experiencing a normal labor market. The unemployment rate stands not much above 5 percent (which is near "full employment"), and the supply of young workers is shrinking (due to earlier depressed fertility).

Many, though not all, economists believe we may be entering an era of long-term labor deficit. Business cycles may rise and fall, they maintain, but the long-term trend will probably be one of too few qualified workers for the positions available. From mid-1985 to 1990, eleven million new jobs opened up while the total working-age population grew by only five million. If that squeezing trend continues, it will become harder and harder for employers to fill positions.

In some areas, grave labor shortages have already surfaced, and not just at entry levels. As once-young workers get older and low-fertility cohorts become a more significant part of the workforce, recruitment problems are shifting upward in the employment chain. Nationwide surveys find that one of the biggest problems facing American companies today is hiring and retaining employees.

A future of more jobs than workers may sound like a happy circumstance, but it reflects imbalance for which there can also be penalties. One such penalty is deteriorating service, and an increase in underqualified, rude, and weakly committed employees. Another is the cancellation of expansion plans for many businesses. Still another may be the advent of wage inflation, which could damage not only the U.S. but also other nations in both the Western and developing worlds.

Many of these dislocations could be avoided by immigration, a superb smoother of economic and demographic swings. Immigrants flow not to areas of labor surplus but to the regions and the occupations where demand is greatest. In this way they serve as a natural shock absorber in the U.S. labor market.

The most immediate beneficiaries of immigrant enterprise, moreover, are often the very individuals who are assumed to be their competitors—the poor. Ghetto stores are perhaps the clearest example. In vast stretches of low-income inner cities all across America, the most striking fact of life, aside from the staggering crime incidence, is the underprovision of basic services. In Washington, D.C., for instance, in the large poor neighborhood east of the Anacostia River, home to a significant portion of the city's population, there are only a handful of decent sit-down restaurants and grocery stores. Block after block passes unpunctuated by commercial operations. To obtain even the simplest of goods and services often requires a long bus ride.

The absence of provisioners is not conspiratorial, but "rational." With the harassments of crime and the low spending habits of the residents, only long hours of unpleasant work can make inner-city businesses succeed. And in Anacostia, as in many other places, it is largely immigrants who are opening establishments in the commercial desert. It is easy to downplay the significance of their contribution, and their motive is not altruism. But for residents who can buy milk and newspapers and hay-fever pills at 2 A.M. where before there was nothing, they make a significant addition to the quality of life.

Beyond a strong dose of the enterprising spirit, immigrants typically bring something else to the country, and that is their youth. The United States is in the midst of becoming a significantly grayer nation. Census Bureau projections show median age rising from thirty-three to forty-two over the next forty years. Just from 1990 to 2000, the number of young adults aged twenty-five to thirty-four is expected to drop from 44 million to 37 million. The ratio of working-age taxpayers to elderly people will shrink from the 5:1 of today to 2.5:1 in 2030.

The cultural effects of such a demographic shift are uncertain, although anyone who has recently visited Vienna or Stockholm will have noticed the very different quality of a society in which one out of five, one out of four, one out of three citizens is over age sixty-five. Less uncertain are the economic effects. Social Security and Medicare have become the largest single component of the federal budget, and one of the most important elements of U.S. macroeconomic policy generally. Because the generation born roughly since the late 1960's is so thin compared to its predecessor, the Social Security system faces some painful readjustments in coming decades as the baby-boom generation reaches retirement age. And the decline in the ratio of prime-age workers to retirees is being further compounded by spiraling health-care expenses, coupled with the inexorable lengthening of life spans. As a result, we face a future of more taxes, fewer benefits, or both.

Restoring some demographic equilibrium to the system by more nearly balancing the number of workers and retirees would lessen the need for tax increases or benefit reductions for many decades. While new pro-natal tax policies would be very useful, changing native birth rates is difficult, and there is a long lag between the arrival of the extra child and his entry into the productive workforce. Immigration, however, can begin to ameliorate these imbalances fairly quickly. Each payroll-taxpaying immigrant adds thousands of dollars per year to the Social Security trust funds.

Of course, immigrants provide our society and economy with

other, more ineffable, benefits than these. It is often said, for example, that America's future depends on our ability to cultivate strengths and bolster weaknesses in an increasingly competitive global arena. Even though current immigration policies give inadequate consideration to occupational qualifications—a subject to which we will return—the U.S. still gets more than 11,000 engineers, scientists, and computer specialists per year. We also get future practitioners of these professions; of the 40 finalists in the 1988 Westinghouse high-school science competition, 22 were foreign-born or children of foreign-born parents: from Taiwan, China, Korea, India, Guyana, Poland, Trinidad, Canada, Peru, Iran, Vietnam, and Honduras. In Boston, 13 of the 17 public-high-school valedictorians in the class of 1989 were foreign-born. Researchers at San Diego State University report that "immigrants and refugees to the U.S.—whether from Asia, Europe, or Latin America—are systematically outperforming all native-born American students in grade-point averages despite . . . English-language handicaps." Beyond the specific contributions made by such people, we may also consider the salutary shock effect their presence in our schools could have on young native-born Americans.

Immigration, then, can bring us significant numbers of bold creators and skilled workers. It can diminish whatever labor shortages may be coming our way. Immigration can keep America from aging precipitously and fill in the demographic holes that may harm our pension and health-care systems. Immigration can energize whole communities with a new entrepreneurial spirit, keeping us robust and growing as a nation. At a time when the idea of competitiveness has become a national fixation, it can bolster our competitiveness and help us retain our position as the common denominator of the international trade web. And as most Americans continue to believe that we have a mission to foster liberty and the love of liberty throughout the world, immigration can help us fulfill that mission through successful example.

IV

None of this means that Americans lack the right to define the membership of their nation. Of course they do. Nor is every immigrant a bonus, as witness the castoffs from Cuba's jails and asylums, the nearly 10,000 aliens now serving time in federal

prisons, and the 50,000 more who have committed crimes but
have been released or sentenced to probation.

It is clear enough that recent policies have not always produced the optimal immigrant stream. Deportation of undesirable
individuals could be greatly speeded, and careful selection of
future citizens is well within national prerogatives. American immigration, after all, is one of the world's greatest buyer's markets—many fine candidates are lined up for each spot—and we
need only specify more carefully what we are looking for.

Unfortunately, the incentives in current laws not only make
for an inefficient system, but they often cut against our interests.

Since 1965, when the system was overhauled to end forty
years of quotas that were unfair to residents of many countries
outside Western and Northern Europe, our criteria for accepting
immigrants have more and more boiled down to family connections—what has been called the nepotism standard. Nearly 90
percent of all nonrefugee immigrants now come to the U.S. in the
name of "family unification," a category which carries no skills or
educational requirements. That has tended to give a big advantage to residents of a handful of Asian and Latin American countries where extended kinship ties are strong. (Two-thirds of all
immigrants come from the following fifteen countries, and one-
third from the first four alone: Mexico, the Philippines, Haiti,
Korea, China, the Dominican Republic, India, Vietnam, Jamaica,
Cuba, Iran, the United Kingdom, El Salvador, Canada, and
Laos.) The nepotism standard has left little room for immigrants
valued on other grounds. Today, only about 5 percent of immigrant visas go to persons qualifying specifically on occupational
merit.

Yet there is no good reason why our immigration laws should
fail to serve our social and industrial needs. In perhaps overly
romantic homage to our notion of America as an open sanctuary
for the world's huddled masses, we have been strangely reluctant
to design immigration policy in order to maximize the contribution it might make to our economy and society. There is no basis
for such reluctance, especially in light of the fact that over the
years we have consistently taken in more refugees and immigrants than all other nations combined. Without eliminating the
humanitarian thrust of our current policy, without cutting down
(indeed, while probably widening) existing immigrant streams,
we can substantially increase our total acceptance of immigrants

and allot a good portion of the available slots with both eyes squarely on the national interest.

The economist Barry Chiswick has produced a useful plan for the reform of our visa preferences, and the proposals that follow build upon the program he has sketched in *Regulation* magazine.

As under current policy, we propose that refugee visas be allotted independently, and adult citizens of the United States be able to bring in any bona fide spouses, minor children, or parents without limit (but not more distant relatives, who would be judged under meritocratic criteria). These two categories together—refugees and immediate family—would make up a little more than half of the yearly total of immigrants to the United States. All other entrants would be selected through a skill-based system, with points awarded for years of school completed, apprenticeship or vocational training, knowledge of English, high professional status or special educational achievements, and some carefully drawn blueprint of occupational demand in the U.S. Extra points could be given if a spouse also had scoreable skills, and as a continuing partial boost to extended family members, the presence of relatives in the U.S. willing to guarantee financial support could also count in an applicant's favor. Entrepreneurial talents and willingness to invest capital would be recognized, and extra points would be granted to young workers.

At the end of each year's scoring process, the available entrance slots would be filled simply by accepting, in order, the top scorers on the list. This is similar to the way Canada, Australia, and New Zealand already select most of their immigrants, with a great deal of success. It is a fair, rational alternative to the unjust, helter-skelter preferences now in place, and it would open up immigration channels to a much wider range of applicants across a broader spectrum of countries.

Moving to a more merit-based system would quickly increase the average qualifications of new arrivals to the U.S. That in turn would produce favorable ripples throughout our labor force, within our universities and laboratories, and all across American society. One example: the educational profile of current U.S. immigrants is exaggerated at both the top and the bottom—the fraction of recent immigrants who have a college degree is significantly higher than among the U.S. population as a whole, but so is the proportion with grade-school-only educations. A point system would enlarge the number of highly educated immigrants even further, and somewhat reduce the number of lightly educated ones.

This is appropriate. Chiswick points out that recent adult male Mexican immigrants have arrived with an average of 7.5 years of total schooling. Unskilled, weakly educated immigrants may earn much more here than they could in their countries of origin, and so find themselves personally better off, and they also can make valuable economic contributions—from maids, bus-boys, and gardeners, up the occupational ladder as far as aspiration and ability allow. But they do little to improve immediately the overall competence of the American workforce. Under the system proposed here, there would continue to be ample room for such hard-working but undereducated immigrants. It is very unlikely, however, that a seventh-grade education would continue to be an *average* level of achievement.

Another advantage would flow from the fact that most immigrants have already had their educations completed elsewhere. In terms of the costs of schooling alone, even the relatively small number of professional and technical-occupation immigrants we currently accept are worth an estimated several billion dollars annually. Raising the average educational level of future immigrant cohorts would swell this figure dramatically.

Large benefits would also accrue every time we attracted an immigrant with proven financial skills and capital. The payoff is double: we gain the nest egg and, even more important in the long run, the talent. America does not nationalize investments, but investors frequently nationalize themselves (as it were). This tendency might be encouraged. In Canada a program to bring in venture capitalists has been in place for ten years, providing Business Immigrant visas to individuals willing to sink at least the equivalent of about a quarter of a million U.S. dollars in a new enterprise. In 1988, according to Canada's Employment and Immigration Office, 3,258 foreign-born entrepreneurs pumped nearly $2 billion into such new enterprises, creating an estimated 15,000 jobs.

V

It is a sign of progress that Congress has taken at least some short steps in the direction of more meritocratic criteria in the immigration bills now under consideration. In something of a breakthrough, the new Kennedy-Simpson legislation passed by the Senate sets up a scoring system to allot a substantially higher number of visas (to a total of 150,000 per year) to people who possess special skills or hold doctorates. Among other changes, it also earmarks 4,800 visas for people who bring at least $1 million and create ten jobs upon their arrival, and 2,000 slots for immigrants who bring $500,000 and promise to invest in a depressed area.

Yet even while these modest efforts have been mounted, non-merit-tested visas for non-immediate family members continue to be a big part of the system. In particular, an amendment to the Senate legislation sponsored by Senators Hatch and DeConcini guarantees a special quota of 216,000 annual entrance permits, to be distributed outside any point system or merit test to nonimmediate relatives like siblings, nieces, nephews of U.S. citizens as well as to relatives of permanent resident aliens. This very unsound proposal would tend to block further movement toward a more balanced mix of criteria for immigrant selection.

Still, the Senate has established the beginnings of a better system—and somewhat increased the total number of expected immigrants. Equally important, the Congress as a whole has made some small progress toward addressing the problem of European immigration. The 1965 immigration reform had the effect of unfairly curtailing European entrants to 10 percent of the total incoming flow. Yet ours is a heavily European nation, and so long as our immigration policies leave hardly any room for arrivals from the original sources of our culture, those policies will lack broad support.

This is an especially appropriate moment to increase sharply our acceptance of East European and Soviet immigrants. By adding a new program of Liberty Visas we could provide 150,000 legal slots annually to people who for decades have been doubly impeded by Communist governments that would not let them out and now by an America that does not let them in because they have no family connections. But demand also exists in Western Europe, particularly in Great Britain and Ireland but also in Germany, Spain, Greece, and elsewhere. A bias of twenty-five years' standing could be ended by making available a special allotment of 75,000 legal slots annually for immigrants from democratic Europe. Both of these programs would be designed to terminate after ten years. By then, a stream of European entrants (many of them skilled and highly educated) would have been established, representing somewhere around 25 to 35 percent of our new arrivals, a fairer and much more balanced figure than present ratios.

Although wildly varying numbers have been floated, basically what the proposed Senate bill seems to establish is a system which, while moving toward a merit-based selection process, adds only a modest number to the total of new immigrants. The proposal of Congressman Bruce Morrison (D.-Conn.), chairman of the House subcommittee dealing with immigration, adds more, but without an individual-merit point system. The proposal sketched here would yield an overall increase of 250,000—probably somewhat more than Morrison—with a merit system.

VI

We have long since passed the point when we could hope to be a nation in the tribal sense. We are ethnically, religiously, and racially diverse. This does not always make for easy relations, but there is no changing it. Moreover, there are compensations for our diversity in the form of our unmatched dynamism and our capacity for successful synthesis. Adaptability is our strong suit, something we are better at than any other people. This is in some significant measure thanks to our immigrant tradition. Our more recent immigrants have made America the first truly universal nation in history. We now come from everywhere.

Our many generations of working pluralism, derived in such large measure from broad immigration, have demonstrated the effectiveness of free values to peoples from all corners of the globe. That an increasingly integrated world more and more lives by our own code is no accident. To a great extent the shift toward universal liberty has been inspired by hard-earned, sometimes painful, but ultimately triumphant day-to-day American practice.

Americans are properly proud of this historical role, and politicians or political parties that have failed to take it into account have suffered for their lack of understanding. Americans believe they seek not just prosperity for themselves but the fulfillment of a national purpose. Wisely designed immigration policies can help in pursuing that national purpose.

But our immigration policies ought not be conceived as some kind of messianic international public service. From our inclusionism we reap rich fruits, bolstering our numbers, enhancing our competitiveness, increasing our influence. A nation like ours functions best when confident, welcoming progress and growth, and demonstrating a willingness to absorb the lessons of outsiders. It wounds itself when it turns inward—excluding foreigners, protecting its markets, resisting fresh ideas and infusions. We would dilute both our own prosperity and our reason for being were we to fail to extend, and widen, our gangplank to the world.

THE CASE FOR GREATLY INCREASED IMMIGRATION

By increasing somewhat the flow of immigrants—from about 600,000 to about 750,000 admissions per year—the immigration legislation passed by Congress late in 1990 will improve the standard of living of native-born Americans. The bill represents a sea change in public attitude toward immigration; it demonstrates that substantially increasing immigration is politically possible now. That's all good news, and we should celebrate it.

The bad news is that the legislation does not *greatly* increase immigration. The new rate is still quite low by historical standards. A much larger increase in numbers—even to, say, only half the rate relative to population size that the United States accepted around the turn of the century—would surely increase our standard of living even more.

The political problem for advocates of immigration is to avoid the letdown to be expected after the passage of this first major legal-immigration bill in a quarter-century. And since the new law seems to contemplate additional legislation (by providing for a commission to collect information on immigration), it is important to educate the public about how immigration benefits the nation as well as the immigrants.

Increased immigration presents the United States with an opportunity to realize many national goals with a single stroke. It is a safe and sure path—open to no other nation—to achieve all of these benefits: 1) a sharply increased rate of technological ad-

Article by Julian L. Simon, author and teacher of business administration at the University of Maryland, College Park, from *The Public Interest*, No. 102:89–103 Winter '91. Copyright © 1991 by National Affairs, Inc. Reprinted with permission.

vance, spurred by the addition of top scientific talent from all over the world; 2) satisfaction of business's demand for the labor that the baby-bust generation makes scarce; 3) reduction of the burden that retirees impose upon the ever-shrinking cohort of citizens of labor-force age, who must support the Social Security System; 4) rising tax revenues—resulting from the increase in the proportion of workers to retirees—that will provide the only painless way of shrinking and perhaps even eliminating the federal deficit; 5) improvement in our competitive position vis-á-vis Japan, Europe, and the rest of the world; 6) a boost to our image abroad, stemming from immigrants' connections with their relatives back home, and from the remittances that they send back to them; and 7) not least, the opportunity given to additional people to enjoy the blessings of life in the United States.

All the U.S. need do to achieve these benefits is further to relax its barriers against skilled immigrants. Talented and energetic people want to come here. Yet we do not greatly avail ourselves of this golden opportunity, barring the door to many of the most economically productive workers in the world.

If immigration is such an across-the-board winner, why aren't we welcoming skilled and hardworking foreigners with open arms? These are some of the reasons: 1) The public is ignorant of the facts to be presented here; it therefore charges immigrants with increasing unemployment, abusing welfare programs, and lowering the quality of our work force. 2) Various groups fear that immigrants would harm their particular interests; the groups are less concerned with the welfare of the country as a whole. 3) Well-organized lobbies oppose immigration, which receives little organized support. 4) Nativism, which may or may not be the same as racism in any particular case, continues to exert an appeal.

The Dimensions of Present-Day Immigration

The most important issue is the total number of immigrants allowed into the United States. It is important to keep our eyes fixed on this issue, because it tends to get obscured in emotional discussions of the desirability of reuniting families, the plight of refugees, the geographic origin and racial composition of our immigrant population, the needs of particular industries, the illegality of some immigration, and so on.

The Federation for American Immigration Reform (FAIR)—whose rhetoric I shall use as illustration—says that "[i]mmigration to the United States is at record levels." This claim is simply false: Figure I shows the absolute numbers of legal immigrants over the decades. The recent inflow clearly is far below the inflow around the turn of the century—even though it includes the huge number of immigrants who took advantage of the 1986 amnesty; they are classified as having entered in 1989, although most of them actually arrived before 1980. Even the inclusion of illegal immigrants does not alter the fact that there is less immigration now than in the past.

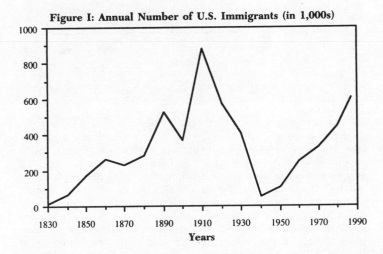

Figure I: Annual Number of U.S. Immigrants (in 1,000s)

Economically speaking, more relevant than these absolute numbers is the volume of immigration as a proportion of the native population, as shown in Figure II. Between 1901 and 1910 immigrants arrived at the yearly rate of 10.4 per thousand U.S. population, whereas between 1981 and 1987 the rate was only 2.5 per thousand of the population. So the recent flow is less than a fourth as heavy as it was in that earlier period. Australia and Canada admit three times that many immigrants as a proportion of their populations.

Figure II: Immigrants to the U.S. per 1,000 Inhabitants

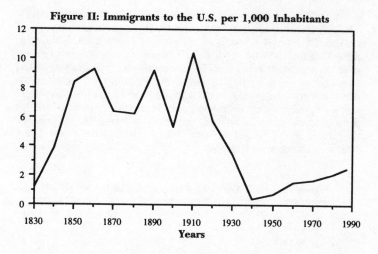

Years

Another way to think about the matter: in 1910, 14.6 percent of the population was born abroad, but in 1980 less than 6 percent of us were. Not only is the present stock of immigrants much smaller proportionally than it was earlier, but it also is a small proportion considered by itself. We tend to think of ourselves as a "nation of immigrants," but less than one out of fifteen people now in the U.S. was born abroad, including those who arrived many years ago. Who would guess that the U.S. has a smaller share of foreign-born residents than many countries that we tend to think have closed homogeneous populations—including Great Britain, Switzerland, France, and Germany? We are a nation not of immigrants, but rather of the descendants of immigrants.

Furthermore, the absorption of immigrants is much easier now than it was in earlier times. One has only to read the history of the Pilgrims in Plymouth Colony to realize the enormity of the immediate burden that each new load of immigrants represented. But it is the essence of an advanced society that it can more easily handle material problems than can technically primitive societies. With every year it becomes easier for us to make the material adjustments that an increase in population requires. That is, immigrant assimilation becomes ever less of an economic problem—

all the more reason that the proportion of immigrants now seems relatively small, compared with what it was in the past.

Unfortunately, despite recent changes favoring skilled immigrants, our present admissions policy remains largely nepotistic. Most visas are granted to foreigners who have family connections here. Even with the 1990 legislation, the U.S. will admit only about 110,000 people—perhaps 20 percent of all immigrants— on the basis of their job skills. Compare our policy with Australia's, which admits almost 50 percent of its immigrants according to "economic" criteria, and only 30 percent as relatives of citizens. Many of those whom we admit via family preferences also are skilled, of course, but it would be beneficial to us as well as fair to deserving foreigners to admit more people on the basis of merit alone. Indeed, George Borjas of the University of California at Santa Barbara has presented evidence that the economic "quality" of immigrants with given levels of education has declined in recent decades—though the magnitude of the decline remains controversial; the likeliest explanation for the decline is an increase in the proportion of immigrants who are admitted as relatives rather than on their merits alone. On the other hand, Harriet Duleep of the U.S. Civil Rights Commission has recently shown that despite the different admissions policies of the U.S. and Canada (which uses a point system), immigration affects the economies of the two countries similarly—probably because families carefully evaluate the economic potential of relatives before deciding to bring them in.

For years, phony inflated estimates of the stocks and flows of illegal immigrants were bandied about by opponents of immigration in order to muddy the waters. Since the 1986 Simpson-Mazzoli law's amnesty we know that the numbers are actually quite modest, much lower than even the "mainstream" estimates cited in the press. So that scare no longer serves as an effective red herring for opponents of immigration.

Malthusian and Other Objections

Now let us consider the costs and benefits of immigration— even though economic issues may not be the real heart of the matter, often serving only as a smoke screen to conceal the true motives for opposition. Only thus can one explain why the benefits of immigration do not produce more open policies. Because opponents of immigration wield economic arguments to justify their positions, however, we must consider their assertions.

Malthusian objectives to immigration begin with "capital dilution." The supposed "law of diminishing returns"—which every economics text explains should not be thought of as a law—causes output per worker to fall. The "law" is so marvelously simple, direct, and commonsensical that it easily seduces thought—especially among academics, for whom such abstractions are bread and butter. Its simplicity also makes the Malthusian notion excellent fare for the family newspaper. In contrast, the arguments that demonstrate the inapplicability of Malthusian capital dilution in the context of immigration are relatively complex and indirect. As a consequence, simple—though incorrect—Malthusianism easily attracts adherents.

Nowadays, however, the most important capital is human capital—education and skills, which people own themselves and carry with them—rather than capitalist-supplied physical capital. The bugaboo of production capital has been laid to rest by the experience of the years since World War II, which taught economists that, aside from the shortest-run considerations, physical capital does not pose a major constraint to economic growth. It is human capital that is far more important in a country's development. And immigrants supply their own human capital.

The main real cost that immigration imposes on natives is the extra capital needed for additional schools and hospitals. But this cost turns out to be small relative to benefits, in considerable part because we finance such construction with bond issues, so that we operate largely on a pay-as-you-go basis. Immigrants therefore pay much of their share.

The supposed cost that most captures the public's imagination, of course, is welfare payments. According to popular belief, no sooner do immigrants arrive than they become public charges, draining welfare money from the American taxpayers, and paying no taxes.

Solid evidence gives the lie to this charge. In an analysis of Census Bureau data I found that, aside from Social Security and Medicare, about as much money is spent on welfare services and schooling for immigrant families as for citizens. When programs for the elderly are included, immigrant families receive far *less* in public services than natives. During the first five years in the U.S., the average immigrant family receives $1,400 in welfare and schooling (in 1975 dollars), compared with the $2,300 received by the average native family. The receipts gradually become equal over several decades. Arthur Akhbari of St. Mary's College in Canada has shown that recent Canadian data produce almost identical results. And Duleep's finding that the economic results of Canadian and U.S. immigration are quite similar, despite the different admissions systems, adds weight to the conclusion that U.S. immigrants pay much more in taxes than they receive in benefits.

Of course there must be some systematic abuses of the welfare system by immigrants. But our legislative system is capable of devising adequate remedies. Even now there are provisions in the Immigration and Naturalization Act that deny visas to aliens who are "likely to become public charges" and provide for the deportation of immigrants who have within five years after entry become public charges "from causes not affirmatively shown to have arisen after entry."

As to illegal immigrants and welfare, FAIR typically says that "[t]axpayers are hurt by having to pay more for social services." Ironically, several surveys—for example, one by Sidney Weintraub and Gilberto Cardenas of the University of Texas— show that illegals are even heavier net contributors to the public coffers than legal immigrants; many illegals are in the U.S. only temporarily and are therefore without families, and they are often afraid to apply for services for fear of being apprehended. Illegals do, however, pay taxes.

Some cities and states with disproportionately high immigration do incur significant costs and complications when immigrants first arrive. They deserve sympathy and perhaps federal assistance, though officials should note that immigrants' federal taxes will later effectively pay for such temporary assistance.

The Non-Threat of Displaced Native Workers

The most dramatic argument against immigration—the bogeyman in the mind of organized labor, which has been its most powerful political opponent since the nineteenth century—has been that foreigners take jobs held by natives and thereby increase native unemployment. The logic is simple: if the number of jobs is fixed, and immigrants occupy some jobs, there must be fewer available jobs for natives.

In the shortest run, the demand for any particular sort of worker is indeed inflexible. Therefore, additional immigrants in a given occupation must to some degree lower wages and/or increase unemployment in that occupation. For example, the large recent influx of foreign physicians increases the competition that U.S. physicians face, lowering their earnings. But because immigrants come with a variety of skills, workers in most occupations feel little impact. And in the longer run, workers in most occupations are not injured at all.

A good-sized body of competent recent research shows that immigration does not exacerbate unemployment, even among directly competing groups; in California, for instance, immigrants have not increased unemployment among blacks and women. And the research, done by several independent scholars from a variety of angles, uses several kinds of data. For example, Stephen Moore and I systematically studied immigration's effects upon overall unemployment, by looking at the changes in unemployment in various U.S. cities that have experienced different levels of unemployment. We found that if there is displacement, it is too little to be observable.

The explanation is that immigrants not only take jobs, but also create them. Their purchases increase the demand for labor, leading to new hires roughly equal in number to the immigrant workers. Immigrants also create jobs directly by opening new businesses. A Canadian government survey of immigrants, which should also describe U.S. experience, found that almost 5 percent—ninety-one of the 1746 males and 291 single females in its panel sample—had started businesses within their first three years in Canada. Not only did they employ themselves, but they also employed others, creating a total of 606 jobs. Thus the total of 2037 immigrants personally created roughly 30 percent as many jobs as they collectively held. Furthermore, these numbers surely rose rapidly after the three-year study period; after one year seventy-one self-employed immigrants had created 264 jobs, compared with the ninety-one immigrant entrepreneurs and 606 jobs observed after three years.

We can interpret this result as follows: even if one native Canadian was pushed out of a preexisting job by every five immigrants—an improbably high number—this effect would be more than made up for by the new jobs, occupied by natives, created by the immigrants' business.

The businesses that immigrants start are at first small, of course. But surprisingly, small businesses are the most important source of new jobs. And immigrant entrepreneurs tend to succeed in a dynamic economy, because they are innovative and mobile.

Furthermore, potential immigrants are well aware of labor-market conditions in the U.S., and they tend not to come if there is little demand for their skills. Natives tend not to be harmed even in the few industries—like the restaurant and hotel businesses—in which immigrants concentrate, because natives do not want jobs in these industries. Evidence for this comes from experiments conducted by the Immigration and Naturalization Service and San Diego County. In one case, 2154 illegal aliens were removed from jobs, but the California State Human Resources Agency had almost no success in filling the jobs with U.S. citizens.

Wages are admittedly pushed downward somewhat in industries and localities in which immigrants are concentrated. Barton Smith and Robert Newman of the University of Houston found that adjusted wages are 8 percent lower in the Texas border cities in which the proportion of Mexicans is relatively high. Much of the apparent difference is accounted for by a lower cost of living in the border cities, however. And because immigrants tend to be heterogeneous in their skills, their presence does not disproportionately affect any particular industry; and of course salaries rise in the occupations that few immigrants enter. (Indeed, if immigrants were spread evenly throughout all occupations, wages would not fall in any occupation.) At the same time, immigrants, who consume a wide variety of goods and services, increase the demand for labor across the range of occupations.

Tax Payments

If immigrants paid relatively little in taxes they might still burden natives, despite using fewer welfare services. But data on family earnings, which allow us to estimate tax payments, show that this is not at all the case.

Immigrants pay more than their share of taxes. Within three to five years, immigrant-family earnings reach and pass those of the average American family. The tax and welfare data together indicate that, on balance, an immigrant family enriches natives by contributing an average of $1,300 or more per year (in 1975 dollars) to the public coffers during its stay in the U.S. Evaluating the future stream of these contributions as one would a dam or harbor, the present value of an immigrant family—discounted at the risk-free interest rate of 3 percent—adds up to almost two years' earnings for a native family head. This means that the economic activities of an average immigrant family reduce the taxes of a native head of household enough to advance his or her possible date of retirement by two years.

Curiously, contemporary welfare-state policies render immigration more beneficial to natives than it was in earlier times when welfare was mainly voluntary. There are two main reasons why today's immigrants make net contributions to the public coffers. First, far from being tired, huddled masses, immigrants tend to come when they are young, strong, and vibrant, at the start of their work lives. For example, perhaps 46 percent of immigrants are in the prime labor-force ages of twenty to thirty-nine, compared with perhaps 26 percent of natives. And only 4 percent of immigrants are aged sixty or over, compared with about 15 percent of natives. Second, many immigrants are well educated and have well-paying skills that produce hefty tax contributions.

Because immigrants arrive in the early prime of their work lives, they ward off a major looming threat to U.S. economic well-being. This threat is the graying of the population, which means that each working native has an increasing burden of retired dependents to support. In 1900, there were five and one-half people aged twenty-five to fifty-four for each person aged sixty and above, whereas the Census Bureau projects that in the year 2000 the ratio will shrink to two and one-half to one—resulting in a burden that will be more than twice as heavy on workers.

Being predominantly youthful adults, immigrants mitigate this looming problem of more retired natives being supported by fewer workers. Indeed, immigration is the only practical way to alleviate the burden of increasing dependency that native workers would otherwise feel.

In the public sphere this means that immigrants immediately lessen the Social Security burden upon native workers. (The same holds for the defense burden, of course.) And if there is a single factor currently complicating the government's economic policies, it is the size of Social Security payments and other assistance to the aged. Immigration—and the resulting increase in tax payments by immigrants—provides the only way to reduce the federal budget deficit without making painful cuts in valued services.

Boosting Productivity

Most important in the long run is the boost that immigrants give to productivity. Though hard to pin down statistically, the beneficial impact of immigration upon productivity is likely to

dwarf all other effects after these additional workers and consumers have been in the country a few years. Some of the productivity increase comes from immigrants working in industries and
laboratories that are at the forefront of world technology. We
benefit along with others from the contribution to world productivity in, say, genetic engineering that immigrants could not make
in their home countries. More immigrants mean more workers,
who will think up productivity-enhancing ideas. As Soichiro Honda (of motorcycle and auto fame) said: "Where 100 people think,
there are 100 powers; if 1,000 people think, there are 1,000
powers."

It is well to remember that the development of the atomic
bomb hinged on the participation of such immigrants as Enrico
Fermi, John von Neumann, and Stan Ulam, among many others.
Contemporary newspaper stories continue this historical saga,
noting the disproportionate numbers of Vietnamese and other
Asian immigrant youths who achieve distinction in competitions
such as the Westinghouse Science Talent Search. Ben Wattenberg
and Karl Zinsmeister of the American Enterprise Institute write
that among the forty 1988 finalists, "22 were foreign-born or
children of foreign-born parents: from Taiwan, China, Korea,
India, Guyana, Poland, Trinidad, Canada, Peru, Iran, Vietnam,
and Honduras." They also note that one-fourth of recent valedictorians and salutatorians in San Diego have been Vietnamese, and
that thirteen of the seventeen public high school valedictorians in
Boston in 1989 were foreign born. Sometimes it seems as if such
names as Wang Computers and Steve Chen dominate our most
vigorous industry.

The Bottom Line

An economist always owes the reader a cost-benefit assessment for policy analysis. So I combined the most important elements pertaining to legal immigrants with a simple macroeconomic model, making reasonable assumptions where necessary. The net effect is slightly negative for the early years, but four
or five years later the net effect turns positive and large. And
when we tote up future costs and benefits, the rate of "investment" return from immigrants to the citizen public is about 20
percent per annum—a good return for any portfolio.

Does all this seem to be a far-out minority view? In 1990 the
American Immigration Institute surveyed prominent economists—all the ex-presidents of the American Economic Associa-

tion, and then-members of the Council of Economic Advisers—about immigration. Economists ought to understand the economic effects of immigration better than others, so their views are of special interest. More than four-fifths of the respondents said that immigration has a very favorable impact on economic growth; none said that its impact is unfavorable. Almost three-fourths said that illegals have a positive economic impact. And almost all agree that recent immigrants have had the same kind of impact as immigrants in the past.

The Real Reasons for Opposition

I began by citing various reasons for our failure to take in more immigrants, despite the clear-cut benefits of doing so. The first is ignorance of the benefits described above. Second is the opposition by special interests, such as organized labor (which wants to restrict competition for jobs) and ethnic groups (whose members often fear that immigration will cause their proportion of the population to decrease). The third reason is well-organized opposition to immigration and a total lack of organized support for it.

FAIR, for example, has a large budget—it amassed $2,000,000 in revenues in 1989—and a large staff. It supports letter-writing campaigns to newspapers and legislators, gets its representatives onto television and radio, and is in the rolodex of every journalist who writes on the subject. Several other organizations play a similar role. On the other side, until recently no organization advocated more immigration generally. Now at least there is the fledgling American Immigration Institute; and the de Tocqueville Institute did excellent work on immigration in 1989 and 1990, before taking on other issues.

The fourth check to immigration is nativism or racism, a motive that often lies beneath the surface of the opposition's arguments.

Rita Simon of American University, who has studied the history of public opinion toward immigrants, has found that the arguments against immigration have remained eerily identical. In the first half of the nineteenth century, Irish immigrants in New York and Boston were seen as the unassimilable possessors of all bad qualities. One newspaper wrote: "America has become the sewer into which the pollutions of European jails are emptied." Another asked: "Have we not a right to protect ourselves against the ravenous dregs of anarchy and crime, the tainted swarms of pauperism and vice Europe shakes on our shores from her diseased robes?"

The 1884 platform of the Democratic party stated its opposition to the "importation of foreign labor or the admission of servile races unfitted by habit, training, religion or kindred for absorption into the great body of our people or for the citizenship which our laws confer."

Francis Walker, Commissioner General of the Immigration Service, wrote in 1896:

The question today is . . . protecting the American rate of wages, the American standard of living, and the quality of American citizenship from degradation through the tumultuous access of vast throngs of ignorant and brutalized peasantry from the countries of Eastern and Southern Europe.

In the 1920s, the *Saturday Evening Post* also directed fear and hatred at the "new immigrants" from Southern and Eastern Europe: "More than a third of them cannot read and write; generally speaking they have been very difficult to assimilate. . . . They have been hot beds of dissent, unrest, sedition and anarchy."

Although statements like these are no longer acceptable in public, many people still privately sympathize with such views. One can see the traces in nativist code words that accuse immigrants of "disturbing national homogeneity" and "changing our national culture."

Improving Our Policies

In addition to admitting more immigrants into the United States, we should also consider instituting other desirable changes in policy. Specifically, we must go further to increase the benefits that accrue to the United States from the inflow of highly educated people with high productive potential—especially people with technical skills. To its credit, the 1990 legislation will increase the flow of talented people by increasing the proportion of immigrants who are admitted because of their economic characteristics rather than their familial ties to U.S. citizens. This was worth doing to reduce nepotistic "family connections" admissions, and to treat meritorious applicants without such connections more fairly.

The new system does not greatly increase the flow of highly

skilled people, however. An additional 100,000 or so immigrants will be admitted under the new provisions for economic selection; only 40,000 will be skilled people, the other 60,000 being their dependents. The overall increase in numbers admitted will yield perhaps another 30,000 highly skilled people. This is still only a small—though a most valuable—increment to our economy.

The 1990 legislation also contains a beneficial provision allowing entry to people who will invest a million dollars and create employment for ten Americans. Although this provision will not be as profitable for natives as an outright sale of the opportunity to immigrate, as permitted by some other countries, it does move in the right direction. But the new law does not go far enough; it permits entry to a maximum of only 10,000 persons per year under this provision—a piddling number by any standard.

Another policy that the U.S. might employ is simply to give permanent-resident visas to foreigners studying in the U.S. Many foreign students already find ways to remain under the present rules—about half of them students of engineering and science. And even more foreign graduates would remain if they could, which would push up our rate of progress even more.

Furthermore, if young foreigners knew that they could remain in the United States after completing their education here, more would choose to study here. This would provide multiple benefits to the United States. Given assurance that they could remain, these students could pay more realistic tuition rates than are now charged, which would benefit U.S. universities. And these increased rates would enable universities to expand their programs to serve both foreign and native students better. Best of all would be the increased number of highly competent scientific and managerial workers who would be part of the American work force.

In addition, a larger number of students requires a larger number of professors. And a larger number of openings for professors, especially in such fields as engineering and science, would attract more of the world's best scientists from abroad. This would enhance the process that has brought so many foreigners who subsequently won Nobel prizes to the U.S.—to the advantage as well as the honor of this country.

Political Advantages

Political power and economic well-being are intimately related; a nation's international standing is heavily influenced by its economic situation. And today the future of any country—especially of a major country that is in the vanguard with respect to production and living standards—depends entirely on its progress in knowledge, skill, and productivity. This is more true now than in the past, because technology changes more rapidly than in earlier times. Even a single invention can speedily alter a country's economic or military future—consider, for example, the atom bomb or the computer—as no invention could in the past, even the invention of the gun. That's why immigration safely, cheaply, and surely provides the U.S. with perhaps the greatest opportunity that a country has ever had to surpass its political rivals.

And the best way for the U.S. to boost its rate of technological advance, and to raise its standard of living, is simply to take in more immigrants. To that end, I would suggest that the number of visas be increased by half a million per year for three years. If no major problems arise with that total (and there is no reason to expect a problem, since even another one or two million immigrants a year would still give us an admissions rate lower than we successfully coped with in earlier times, when assimilation was more difficult), then we should boost the number by another half-million, and so on, until unexpected problems arise.

Immigration policy presents the U.S. with an opportunity like the one that faced the Brooklyn Dodgers in 1947, before blacks played baseball on any major-league team. Signing Jackie Robinson and then Roy Campanella, at the price of antagonizing some players and club owners, put the Dodgers way ahead of the pack. In the case of immigration, unlike baseball, no other "team" can duplicate our feat, because immigrants mainly want to come here. All we need is the vision, guts, and ambition of Dodger general manager Branch Rickey. (A bit of his religious zeal mixed in would do no harm.)

Can we see our national interest clearly enough to reject unfounded beliefs that some groups will lose jobs to immigrants, and to surmount the racism that remains in our society? Or will we pay a heavy price in slower growth and lessened efficiency for maintaining our prejudices and pandering to the supposed interests of groups—organized labor, environmentalists, and others—whose misguided wishes will not benefit even them in the long run?

INDIVIDUALIST AMERICA AND
TODAY'S IMMIGRANTS

There is much to admire in James Fallows's *More Like Us: Making America Great Again,* based on his reportage from Japan, where he lived with his family for several years. It is definitely not a book about Japan, trade deficits, industrial policy, or protectionism. Instead it is a rumination on America's unique qualities, which the author has come to appreciate from abroad.

In Fallows's view, America's greatness derives from the competitive individualism and antitraditionalism that are consonant with the "creative destruction" (he borrows the phrase from Schumpeter) of our capitalist economy. For Fallows the essence of our "abnormal" society is its "vision of people always in motion, able to make something different of themselves, ready for second chances until the day they die." It is precisely this quality that Fallows argues is now endangered by "class-bound roles" that lessen social mobility and undermine the creative forces of change set in motion by capitalism. He singles out for criticism the emergence of intelligence testing and academic credentialism, which he argues are better suited to a static Confucian society than to ours. In today's competitive world economy, Fallows fears that we are losing sight of what makes us unique; he therefore urges that we be "more like us." Toward that goal, he advocates a variety of policies including workfare programs, education vouchers, trimmed entitlements, and generous immigration levels.

Yet this book is not about programs and taxes, but about values and particularly culture—a concept that Fallows takes very seriously. Virtually banned from public-policy debate, cultural explanations of social, political, and economic phenomena have become the exclusive province of conservatives. So it is refreshing to encounter a writer with a decidedly liberal perspective who can wield the concept with some subtlety.

Article by Peter Skerry, director of Washington programs for the UCLA Center for American Politics and Public Policy, from *The Public Interest* No. 102:104–18 Winter '91. Copyright © 1991 by National Affairs, Inc. Reprinted with permission.

At the same time, Fallows avoids the predictable liberal fascination with European social-democratic values, and strives to understand our own homegrown ones. There is no hint here of intellectual slumming, however—of the deracinated intellectual who has found his way home, or merely switched to a popular-front mode, to revel in all that he once reviled. We have instead a rare commodity: a Washington-based journalist willing, in a non-election year, to venture beyond the Beltway for more than a weekend in West Virginia. Indeed, there is about James Fallows an openness and humility toward his subject that is notable and quite engaging. He even manages to compare Japan to America quite unfavorably without a trace of venom or nastiness.

Yet despite such appealing aspects, Fallows's effort is fundamentally flawed. Not surprisingly, a book entitled *More Like Us* hinges on the author's conception of who we are; and Fallows ultimately stumbles on his misreading of the American experience.

Fallows's theme is that "Japan is strong because of its groups; America, because of its individuals." More specifically, he argues that the genius of America has been to set individuals free from the bonds of tradition, thereby permitting them to adapt to, and take advantage of, the disorder and social change unleashed by capitalism.

Paradigmatic for Fallows in this regard is one Buddy Ginn, a middle-aged jack-of-all-trades whom he met in a Texas oilfield in 1982. Several years earlier, Ginn had grown discontented with life in the small Indiana town in which he had been born and raised. Though married with children, he pulled up stakes one day and took off for Texas with $500 in cash and a pregnant girlfriend. Between the two of them, they left behind two spouses, one ex-spouse, and several children. But of most interest to Fallows is the fact that Ginn, through sheer grit and determination, worked his way up through the oil-well maintenance business; got wiped out by the price drop in the early 1980s; and then, at the age of forty-two, started over in a training program that had him digging ditches for $7 an hour.

At about the same time he met up with Ginn, Fallows encountered a Vietnamese refugee in Southern California named Nguyen Dong. The first of a fourteen-member Saigon household to arrive here, Nguyen showed his many relatives how their pooled resources could be put to best use in the United States. Nguyen and his family were hardly uneducated peasants, but they arrived without connections or wealth. Nguyen started off working for $2.10 an hour in a waterbed factory in El Segundo. Within a decade of his arrival, however, he had emerged as the young patriarch of an immigrant clan whose members owned two houses, a furniture store, and a Beverly Hills beauty salon.

Fallows offers these two vignettes as examples of the "reinvented lives" permitted by America's remarkably open social and economic system. Yet a moment's reflection reveals that they present more contrasts than similarities. Buddy Ginn's story sounds depressingly familiar, an example of the extreme individualism that now allows American parents casually to abandon their family responsibilities. If Ginn were black, Fallows might well lament the continued unraveling of black family ties. Instead, Ginn's story exemplifies for Fallows how America offers second, third, and more chances to those willing to scratch and scramble. Fallows cannot be accused of ignoring the negative aspects of capitalism's "creative destruction," but he does not seem to understand that Ginn's life stands in stark contrast to Nguyen's.

Indeed, it seems safe to say that Buddy Ginn's evasion of familial responsibility would horrify Nguyen Dong. For Nguyen's story involves not escape from his family, but years of struggle and sacrifice to reunite his many siblings, who were scattered about the world after the fall of Saigon. As Fallows himself quotes Nguyen, "The way of living in our country is so different. We have a tradition of sticking together."

Like that of many other Asian refugees, the story of Nguyen's family underscores the fact that much of the entrepreneurial activity of which Fallows approves has been pursued not by individuals but by families—particularly immigrant families who have not yet adopted our individualistic ways. And although there is plenty of evidence to support this point in his own account, Fallows ignores it as he lumps the Nguyens' story with Buddy Ginn's as examples of "starting over in America."

He also ignores the related point that strong families like the Nguyens tend to produce the individuals who are most capable of taking the chances necessary to succeed in capitalist societies. Strong families can certainly offer sustenance, psychological as well as financial, for individual risk taking. Fallows includes but fails to acknowledge this point when he recounts how Mr. Nguyen had to talk his fainthearted brother into risking his savings in a furniture store.

This blind spot is particularly striking in light of Fallows's personal history. Illustrating his point about the opportunities that America provides to those willing to "reinvent themselves," he devotes an entire chapter to how, in the summer of 1955, his family left Philadelphia and drove cross-country to start a new life in Redlands, California. Despite the relocation, what emerges from that account is the image of a family with a solid sense of its past. Fallows notes that his father's forebears arrived in Pennsylvania from Lancashire, England, in the nineteenth century, and that his paternal great-grandfather, Josiah Fallows, was a railroad engineer who died saving a trainload of passengers from a collision. Of this "family hero," Fallows writes, "I grew up seeing his picture, which looked like a twin of my father's with a nineteenth-century handlebar mustache added on, in a big, old-fashioned oval frame hanging in my father's study at home." Fallows seems not to appreciate that families with pictures of revered ancestors hanging on the walls are more likely to produce individuals capable of taking advantage of the opportunities available to them in America. One wonders whether Buddy Ginn's children left behind in Indiana have fared as well.

Any reservations harbored by Fallows about the unfettered individualism personified by Ginn emerge only briefly at the end of the book. Having extolled American individualism for more than two hundred pages, Fallows suddenly acknowledges (on the penultimate page) that it has necessarily been counterbalanced by our sense of fair play and commitment to a uniform set of rules. He then intones: "The individual side of this balance has received nearly all the political and cultural attention in the last ten years. The pendulum is ready to swing the other way." Fallows goes on to quote Senator Paul Simon approvingly: "Americans instinctively know that we are one nation, one family, and when anyone in that family hurts, all of us hurt. There really is a yearning across this land for leadership that appeals to the noble in us rather than to the greed in us."

This passage is the closest Fallows comes to outright polemic. He offers no explanation of the difference between what he and Senator Simon call "greed" and the entrepreneurial pluck celebrated throughout his book. Was it greed or pluck that caused Buddy Ginn to abandon his family and move to Texas? How about the ceaseless striving of the Vietnamese refugees in Southern California? In both cases Fallows sees pluck. Yet he offers no criterion by which the aspirations of blue-collar whites or recent immigrants can be judged as more noble than those of other

Americans—though he does suggest that supporting Reagan is somehow ignoble.

Fallows similarly fails to address the possibility that today's individualism is qualitatively different from that of earlier generations of Americans. Indeed, despite his focus on culture, Fallows has a static view that lacks any appreciation of how values change over time. Take, for example, Fallows's recounting of a joke told by former Prime Minister Takeshita to his countrymen: on account of the weak dollar, American sailors could no longer afford Japanese bar girls; their only consolation was to stay on base and give each other AIDS. Fallows offers this story as an example of Japanese condescension toward foreigners in general and Americans in particular. It apparently does not occur to him that the Japanese tell this joke because they, like many Americans, believe that our individualism has reached decadent extremes.

Nevertheless, Fallows understands that this nation of individualists requires something to hold it together. For that he turns to the Cuomo-esque conceit of "the nation as family." In this formulation, "the nation" could accurately be replaced by "the state." In either case, the result is an oxymoron. But this is what happens when contemporary liberals, having reduced society to an agglomeration of rights-claiming individuals enmeshed in a matrix of rules and regulations, seek to sustain their cold, legalistic leviathan with the warm blood of organic social institutions.

Of course, it's not quite fair to tar Fallows, a neoliberal, with this brush. But it is striking that he never reconciles his invocation of the nation as family with his opening declaration that Japan is not like America precisely because "Japan . . . works like a family, in which people are definitely not equal but instinctively recognize shared interests and pull together for the common good."

No wonder Fallows is left ruminating on William James's search for a moral equivalent to war, recalling how World War II brought us together as a nation, and pondering the hapless effort of Jimmy Carter (for whom Fallows wrote speeches) to find in the energy crisis a source of national cohesion. In a book subtitled "Making America Great Again," such thoughts call to mind the fate of turn-of-the-century Progressives who, similarly dismayed by what they regarded as a lack of community, ended up supporting Woodrow Wilson's war to make the world safe for democracy as a means of unifying the nation. As that episode teaches, such utopianism leads to despair and disillusionment. It can also lead to a contempt for the lives of ordinary Americans that is fundamentally at odds with the decency and humility of a James Fallows.

Yet Fallows must be placed among those liberals whose hostility to existing sources of community and social cohesion leaves them dependent on the musings of the philosopher-governor on the Hudson. In a chapter entitled "State Societies," Fallows writes disparagingly of the way of life that he found in the shadows of silent steel mills in South Chicago in the early 1980s: "The life of the steel communities was dominated by big, unwieldy institutions: the church, the schools, the army, the union, the mill, the Chicago political machine. Despite their many differences, they all taught one lesson: people should know their place."

While many would hold up such institutions as bastions of racism, sexism, and other unenlightened views, Fallows eschews such inquisitional liberalism. Instead he concerns himself with how these institutions inhibit individual mobility. But this is also a limited, skewed perspective. For one can certainly criticize the imprudent policies of the steelworkers' union while at the same time acknowledging the role it once played in advancing the interests of its members. Although the other institutions cited by Fallows have their flaws, they also have helped alleviate grinding poverty and promote individual and collective mobility. An obvious example is the record of parochial schools at educating underprivileged children—a record still impressive today, as these same schools continue to attract large numbers of non-Catholic, inner-city blacks. Surely it is not enough to describe the "dense, tightly connected society" of South Chicago in exclusively negative terms.

Fallows also overlooks the critical role played by these "unwieldy institutions" in helping millions of immigrants become Americans. Here again, his notion that "our openness encourages Americans to adapt as individuals rather than as a group" obscures the many ways in which group and organizational ties, in addition to family ties, have helped individuals adapt to change and take advantage of opportunities in our dynamic economy and society.

The workings of American pluralism are further obscured by Fallows's notion that "the act of immigration" is tantamount to "choosing to become an American." On the contrary, our history demonstrates that the decision to immigrate has never been more than the first step on a journey that didn't always end in becoming an American. On the one hand, the pain and ambivalence of that journey meant that many immigrants resisted becoming Americans by neglecting to learn English or refusing citizenship, or, in many cases, by migrating back to their homeland. Many others made no conscious decision; it was gradually made for them in the course of the day-to-day struggle to earn a living and raise a family. Contrary to Fallows's understanding, immigration to the United States has for the most part not been a discrete event but a process.

Moreover, immigrants did not so much choose as learn to become Americans. And for most immigrants, and their American-born children, this lesson has meant learning to become individuals. This is no easy task for those who, like the Vietnamese refugees discussed earlier, are enmeshed in extended-family ties. In the past, the struggle to loosen these bonds were typically aided by churches, schools, unions, and political machines—the very institutions that Fallows scorns. These institutions provided critical public arenas in which immigrants learned to expand their horizons beyond the narrow confines of family and friends. It was in such institutions that villagers from Sicily or Silesia learned to think of themselves as Italians or Poles, workers or Democrats. Moreover, such identities were way stations on the road to becoming Americans—hence the paradox that immigrants to America learned to become individuals through participating in groups.

Viewed by the Progressives and other contemporary reformers, these group ties smacked of a benighted and parochial self-interest that was deeply offensive to valued notions of liberal individualism and republican virtue. In the same vein, Fallows regards such ties as the lingering residue of the past, foisted on immigrants by backward institutions. But surely such relationships substantially reflected immigrant tastes and values. They certainly represented an important means by which immigrants and their children coped with wrenching and frightening change.

And cope they did. The genius of American institutions—at least up to now—has been to strike a balance, by affording immigrants the support of familiar habits and relationships while allowing them the freedom to leave these behind in the quest for advancement in a radically new social and economic environment. Indeed, this pattern of individuals freely associating with and dissociating from loosely defined groups is what distinguishes America from Japan, where group membership is officially and rigidly defined. Surely it is the difference between pluralism and corporatism that distinguishes America from Japan, rather than that between individualism and group identity, which Fallows emphasizes.

Of course, those ties offering immigrants comfort and support could stifle individual initiative and enterprise. This was surely true of those left behind in the South Chicago neighborhoods that Fallows visited. Yet to focus on these alone is to ignore the many others for whom such neighborhoods were springboards to something better. Nevertheless, Fallows's animus against such communities is so strong that he contradicts his near-libertarian emphasis on the primacy of individual choice and ends up depicting their residents as passive victims.

Fallows's misunderstanding of ethnic pluralism in America reflects in part his preoccupation with social class. Fallows is concerned that class barriers, like the "unwieldy institutions" of South Chicago, retard individual mobility. There is some plausibility to his argument that credentialism threatens to hinder social mobility by fostering the creation of rigid professional guilds that are sheltered from the challenges of the competitive economy and closed to the entry of the non-college-educated. Yet the real problem with Fallows's preoccupation with class is that it causes him to ignore the racial and ethnic cleavages that have, of course, been much more troublesome in our history. For example, drawing on his undergraduate experience at Harvard in the late 1960s, Fallows writes persuasively of class dynamics in Boston. But he completely ignores the racial tensions brewing there at that time, soon to erupt over busing.

The implications of Fallows's misreading of the American experience emerge most fully when he turns to immigration, which he describes as "the classic form of starting over in America." Misconstruing our current policy's emphasis on family reunification as merely "humanitarian," he fails to see that it is informed by the belief that stable, intact families promote the economic and social well-being of immigrants. Nevertheless, his support for current levels of immigration (in the range of 600,000 to 800,000 legal immigrants and refugees a year) is reasonable. So is his argument for reorienting our policy away from family preference and toward independent, so-called "new seed" immigrants, especially those with needed skills.

Still, Fallows's overall view of immigration is much too sanguine and insufficiently attentive to potential problems. Perhaps, as he argues, the effects of immigration on the American economy as a whole are positive. But he glosses over specific impacts on critical groups. For example, he cites an important study from the Urban Institute to support his argument, but he neglects to mention its finding that Mexican Americans in Southern California have been undercut in the labor market by immigrants. Relying on the same study, he notes that black employment levels in Southern California have not suffered from immigration, but he overlooks evidence that black wage levels have been affected. Fallows does acknowledge that *illegal* immigrants may have undercut working-class blacks and whites, but he claims that this problem was solved by the employer sanctions written into the Immigration Reform and Control Act of 1986. Even casual observers, however, realize that at most sanctions have only moderated the influx of illegals, not stopped it. Finally, Fallows, like most enthusiasts for immigration, pays no attention whatsoever to other arenas in which immigrants and blacks may compete economically—for example, in the housing market.

Even if Fallows were correct in saying that the negative effects of immigration on blacks are minimal, survey data typically reveal that blacks themselves are not convinced. And at some point, black perceptions of the effects of immigration must be taken as political, if not economic, facts. Nowhere does Fallows mention the decade-long record of violence between blacks and Hispanics in Miami. Nor does he have anything to say about the political competition between blacks and the steadily increasing number of Hispanics, particularly as we approach redistricting.

Moreover, such tensions are only exacerbated by affirmative action. Having granted Hispanics, and Asians, the same extraordinary benefits that we afford blacks, we now find the relatively stable black population pitted against growing immigrant communities. Blacks in Southern California have certainly begun to realize this, yet Fallows has nothing to say about it.

Indeed, it is astonishing that a book asserting that America's unique virtue is its "belief that everyone is playing by the same set of rules" never even mentions affirmative action. Fallows rightly laments the racial discrimination that historically subjected blacks to a different set of rules. Yet not once does he acknowledge the fact that affirmative action (whether one approves of it or not) also constitutes a major departure from the rules.

To be sure, Fallows recognizes some of the problems that result from the present influx of immigrants: "The main resistance to immigration at the moment is not economic but cultural." Yet his characterization of that resistance as "fear of the other," like his use of the words "ethnic, racial, and emotional," indicates that in this instance "cultural" really means psychological. Fallows admits no rational basis for concerns about cultural coherence, given today's context of language rights, bilingual education, and multiculturalism—all topics that he scarcely mentions.

In essence, Fallows argues that if the present influx is to work out successfully, then we Americans must acknowledge and live up to our unique history by tolerating diversity. Thus he once again abandons his emphasis on individual choice by choosing to view immigrants as passive victims of intolerance. Completely, and conveniently, overlooked is the irony that, in this antitraditional society, immigrants themselves are frequently the main source of both traditionalism and intolerance—clinging to both as they struggle to cope with drastic change.

One has only to think back to the 1989 events in the Bensonhurst section of Brooklyn, where the son of Italian immigrants, himself the bearer of an Italian passport, was charged with the murder of a black youth who ventured into his "urban village." It would not be difficult to envision a similar scenario in Los Angeles, with a black youth appearing at the wrong time in a Mexican neighborhood.

Immigrants play a central role in what Fallows refers to as "the reopening of America." Yet aside from dismissing the notion that they compete against blacks, Fallows has virtually nothing to say about Hispanics—the largest and fastest growing immigrant group. Indeed, as his focus on the Nguyen family indicates, when Fallows talks about immigrants, he tends to have Asians in mind.

It is ironic that Fallows's defense of American individualism depends in no small measure on Asian immigrants, who typically arrive here not only with some education and resources, but also with strong family and group values of a sort that most definitely teach them, in Fallows's formulation, "to know their place." Indeed, it is arguable that Asian immigrants thrive in contemporary America precisely because their group values render them resistant to mainstream tendencies deemphasizing or even denigrating achievement. In any event, Asians certainly perform well in our credential-oriented meritocratic system, which Fallows describes, with some irony, as "Confucian."

Similarly, he ignores the significant differences between Asian and Hispanic immigrants. Like Asians, Hispanics also have strong

family values. Yet with less education and less urban or cosmopol-
itan backgrounds, they have a more difficult time making it in
America. Hispanics certainly experience greater tension between
family loyalty and individual achievement than do Asians. And
the preponderance of Hispanics among illegal immigrants will
further complicate the group's efforts to assimilate.

While many of these disagreements with James Fallows reflect
my disaffection with his liberalism, when it comes to immigration
my criticisms could also be directed against conservatives who
share his enthusiasm for the present influx. Although they start
from different assumptions, Fallows and pro-immigration conservatives share many of the same blind spots.

For example, both Fallows and conservatives tend to focus on
Asian successes, while ignoring problems evident not only among
Hispanics, but also among Asians—such as gang activity and welfare dependency among Vietnamese in California. And like Fallows, conservatives underplay or completely ignore tensions between blacks and immigrants, whether Asian or Hispanic. Finally,
while conservatives vehemently oppose affirmative action, like
Fallows they ignore the ways in which two decades of such policies
have shaped the political behavior of Asian and especially Hispanic immigrants, both of whom now qualify for affirmative-
action benefits.

Similarly, Fallows and conservatives share a preoccupation
with values and culture that leads them to ignore the enormous
institutional changes that this nation has experienced since it last
faced a comparable wave of immigrants. As his subtitle, "Making
America Great Again," suggests, Fallows does sense a change for
the worse. Indeed, he laments the demise of the public school
system and the pre-Vietnam War draft, which he depicts as institutions that "encouraged the sense that most Americans were
part of a single, broad common culture."

Yet he never squares his nostalgia with his condemnation of
the effect of the schools and the army on South Chicago's residents. Nor, with his static view of culture, does he consider that
the decline of such institutions owes much to the recrudescence of
the individualism that he regards as an unqualified virtue. He
does not come to terms with the fact that the America he ad-
mires—the strong, united nation brought together by World War
II or the exuberant, confident society of his postwar childhood—
was one in which those "unwieldy institutions," where people
were "taught to know their place," played an important, if not

dominant, role. Thus, to the extent that he acknowledges such institutional change, Fallows neither understands its cultural origins nor faces up to its implications for his argument.

Conservatives, on the other hand, are concerned precisely with the changes in values that Fallows ignores. Indeed, conservatives welcome today's immigrants precisely because they regard their "traditional values" as reinforcing threatened notions of respect for family, religion, and hard work.

But are such values, however admirable in and of themselves, enough to sustain the healthy adaptation of immigrants in today's America—much less to reform the rest of us? Our history suggests that poor and uneducated immigrants have generally done best when their traditional values, and the intense primary-group ties in which they are embedded, encounter strong mediating institutions. Yet today such institutions are greatly weakened or virtually extinct, especially in the heavily impacted Southwest. Judging by the significant defections of Hispanic immigrants to Protestant fundamentalist sects, even the Catholic Church is functioning less effectively as a mediating institution than it once did.

Our political system has similarly changed. Gone are the ad hoc, informal ways that big-city politicians used to insinuate themselves into the warp and woof of immigrant communities. Today's politics is not only more professionalized, it is also less corrupt. But the world of media consultants, campaign-finance lawyers, and polling experts is that much further removed from the life of today's immigrants. Without the institutional means of bridging the widened gap between the face-to-face relationships that predominate in immigrant communities and the formalized procedures and bureaucratic structures of the political system, it has become more difficult for immigrants to organize for political ends.

The resulting vacuum will not go unfilled, however. Aside from protest efforts, the obvious, and most prevalent, response has been affirmative-action programs—either to increase employment or to encourage voting. Unlike machine politics, though, such programs do nothing to mediate between ethnic-group ties and larger organizational goals. Indeed, affirmative action rigidifies and institutionalizes ethnic (or racial) ties and identity. Moreover, it does so on the basis of group rights.

Without the institutional supports enjoyed by earlier immigrants, how will today's newcomers bridge the gap between their family-centered folkways and the formalized, bureaucratized

structures of contemporary American society? It is curious that
conservatives, so attuned to the societal developments contributing to the demise of mediating institutions, have not themselves
posed this question. This oversight can be traced to the demands
of post-1960s polemics. Particularly in the public-policy debate,
the liberal assault on cultural explanations of social problems has
led conservatives to insist all the more strenuously on the importance of values. Chief among these have been "family values,"
which have gradually become a surrogate for an array of favored
conservative cultural themes. Family values came to the fore as an
obvious response to the individualist and liberationist tendencies
of contemporary liberalism, but also as common ground on which
traditionalist, communitarian, libertarian, populist, and free-
market conservatives could all stand together.

This consensus around conservative values found its purest
expression in the romance of the entrepreneurial family. Indeed,
the image of a hard-working immigrant family running a restaurant reassured traditionalist and communitarian conservatives,
while gratifying libertarians and free-marketeers who instinctively saw in such efforts an alternative to the more typical paths of
immigrant economic advancement—through trade unions and
politics.

Yet as an implicit model guiding immigration policy, the entrepreneurial family is misleading; most immigrants will not be
entrepreneurs. To assume otherwise is to explain away the economic and cultural reality of day-to-day life in immigrant communities, at least as presently constituted. But even when immigrant
families do succeed in establishing businesses, their efforts are not
always consistent with the mobility of individual family members.
A telling example arises in a recent book about the renowned East
Los Angeles calculus teacher, Jaime Escalante. In *Escalante: The
Best Teacher in America,* Jay Mathews relates the story of Leticia
Rodriguez, the third of seven children of a couple who met in
Mexico, came to the United States as cooks, and eventually started
their own small restaurant west of downtown Los Angeles—an
apparent American success story. Yet when Leticia's trigonometry
interfered with her responsibilities at the family's restaurant, her
parents decided that she had to drop Escalante's demanding class.
It was only after Escalante visited the restaurant and made noises
about child-labor laws that the parents relented.

What conservatives have lost sight of is that family values are
perhaps necessary, but certainly not a sufficient, condition for a

healthy society. The point was made cogently by Edward Banfield in *The Moral Basis of a Backward Society.* Writing of life in a peasant village in Southern Italy in the 1950s, Banfield coined the term "amoral familism" to depict a milieu in which bonds of reciprocity and trust did not extend beyond nuclear families and, hence, in which there was little or no sense of the public good.

When he turned his attention to politics in American cities, Banfield identified similar, though not identical, tendencies in the "private-regarding" values of immigrant voters. But unlike Southern Italy, where, among other factors, the remote institutions of a highly centralized political system offered few arenas in which the narrow bonds of family could be broadened, the decentralized structure of American politics provided many such opportunities. In many cases, the result was literally the corruption of the political process. Yet at the same time the horizons of European peasants were expanded beyond the confines of family and village, and new attachments to the wider society, however imperfect, were forged. Indeed, where strong machines developed, newly formed neighborhood and ethnic ties were used to build a city-wide organization to which many different ethnic and interest groups adhered.

This brief analysis underscores not only that family values do not by themselves adequately predict immigrant success, but also that values generally must be examined in the institutional context within which they are guides to action. Today's immigrants display many of the same values that characterized their predecessors, but the institutional means of reorienting these values toward those of the wider society have been transformed.

Moreover, the foregoing discussion indicates that elites of very different persuasions are using immigration to reassure themselves that America is still vital in this period of enormous and unsettling change. One can hear the implicit refrain with regard to the assimilation of all these newcomers: "We've done it before, and we can do it again."

But the American public is not so sure, and its understandable anxieties and questions about the largest immigrant wave since the record high levels at the turn of the century are largely ignored by the elites—or attended to by nativists and demagogues. The irony here is that the questions most often asked are easily, and affirmatively, answered. For the available evidence indicates that, yes, these immigrants will learn English, listen to heavy-metal music, and follow the Dodgers: in sum, they will become typical Americans. This doesn't mean there won't be problems and tensions, but by and large there is every reason to believe—assuming no drastic downturn in the economy or increase in present levels of immigration—that these immigrants will "assimilate" as others have before them.

The critical question, though, is not whether but how—on what terms—these immigrants will assimilate. They will be good consumers. But will they be equally good producers? They will learn English. But will they also demand, as some already have, special rights for Spanish? They will be loyal Americans. But will they see themselves as individual citizens, or as members of ethnically or racially defined claimant groups?

These are the questions that immigration advocates have yet to address. In one way or another, they all subscribe to James Fallows's view that immigrants will help us to find ourselves—to be "more like us." The problem is that "us" is a large and multifaceted nation with changing values and institutions. Immigration proponents must recognize this and take a more clear-eyed look at the fit between what immigrants bring to us and what we have to sustain them. The recently enacted legislation designed to encourage immigrants with marketable skills indicates that one part of this process is underway. Now it is time to take up the other part, by considering the effects that dramatic changes in our culture, and especially our political institutions, will have on the manner in which record numbers of newcomers become part of American society. It is true that "to make America great again," we must maintain the spirit of competitive individualism. But if our history is any guide, we must remember that individualism leads to greatness only when it is nurtured—and tempered—by the appropriate institutions.

BIBLIOGRAPHY

An asterisk (*) preceding a reference indicates that the material or part of it has been reprinted in this book.

BOOKS AND PAMPHLETS

Aleinikoff, T. Alexander. Immigration, process and policy. West. '91.

Anastos, Phillip & French, Chris. Illegals: seeking the American dream. Rozzoli. '91.

Anzovin, Steven, ed. The problem of immigration. H. W. Wilson. '85.

Auster, Lawrence. The path to national suicide: an essay on immigration and multiculturalism. American Immigration Control Foundation. '90.

Bailey, Thomas. Immigrant and native workers: contrasts and competition. Westview. '89.

Baker, Susan Gonzalez. The cautious welcome: the legalization programs of the Immigration Reform and Control Act. Urban Institute. '90.

Bean, Frank D. Opening and closing the doors: evaluating immigration reform and control. University Press of America. '89.

_____, et al., eds. Mexican and Central American population and U.S. immigration policy. Center for Mexican American Studies. '89.

Bode, Janet. New kids on the block: oral histories of immigrant teens. Watts. '89.

Bogen, Elizabeth. Immigration in New York. Greenwood. '87.

Borjas, George J. International differences in the labor market performances of immigrants. Upjohn Institute for Employment Research. '88.

_____. Friends or strangers: the impact of immigrants on the U.S. economy. Basic Books. '90.

Boswell, Richard A. Immigration and nationality law. Carolina Academy Press. '91.

Brubaker, William R. Immigration and the politics of citizenship in Europe and North America. University Press of America. '89.

Buss, Fran & Cubias, Daisy. Journey of the sparrows. Lodestar. '91.

Caplan, Nathan & Whitmore, John. The boat people and achievement in America: a study of family life, hard work, and cultural values. University of Michigan. '89.

Catalano, Julie. The Mexican Americans. Chelsea House. '88.

Chan, Sucheng, ed. Entry denied: exclusion of the Chinese community in America, 1882–1943. Temple University Press. '91.

Chierici, Rose-Marie Cassagnol. Demele, "making it": migration and adaptation among Haitian boat people in the United States. AMS Press. '91.

Chiswick, Barry R. Illegal aliens: their employment and employers. Upjohn Institute for Employment Research. '88.

Cockcroft, James D. Outlaws in the promised land: Mexican immigrant workers and America's future. Grove. '86.

Congressional Requesters Report. Soviet refugees: processing and admittance to the United States. General Accounting Office. '90.

Conover, Ted. Coyotes: a journey through the secret world of America's illegal aliens. Vintage. '87.

Cordasco, Francesco. The new American immigration: evolving patterns of legal and illegal emigration: a bibliography. Garland. '87.

———. Dictionary of American immigration history. Scarecrow Press. '90.

Davis, Marilyn P. Mexican voices/American dreams: an oral history of Mexican immigration to the United States. Henry Holt. '90.

Daniels, Roger. Coming to America: a history of immigration and ethnicity in American life. HarperCollins. '90.

Danilov, Dan P. Immigration to the U.S.A. ISC Press. '89.

DeFreitas, Gregory. Inequality at work: Hispanics in the U.S. labor force. Oxford University Press. '91.

Deutsch, Howard D. Employer's complete guide to immigration: new law, new questions, new answers. Prentice-Hall. '87.

Didion, Joan. Miami. Simon & Schuster. '87.

Dinnerstein, Leonard. Ethnic Americans: a history of immigration. Harper & Row. '88.

D'Innocenza, Michael & Sirefman, Josef, eds. Immigration and Ethnicity. Greenwood. '91.

Dowty, Alan. Closed borders: the contemporary assault on freedom of movement. Yale University Press. '89.

Dudley, William, ed. Immigration: opposing viewpoints. Greenhaven. '90.

Eagleburger, Lawrence S. Proposed FY 1991 refugee admission levels. U.S. Department of State, Bureau of Public Affairs. '90.

Ferris, Elizabeth. The Central American refugees. Praeger. '87.

Fitzpatrick, Joseph P. Puerto Rican Americans: the meaning of migration to the mainland. Prentice-Hall. '87.

Foner, Nancy. New immigrants in New York. Columbia University Press. '87.

Fragomen, Austin T. Coping with the new immigrant law. Practising Law Institute. '87.

Freeman, James M. Hearts of sorrow: Vietnamese-American lives. Stanford University Press. '89.

Gibney, Mark, ed. Open borders? closed societies?: the ethical and political issues. Greenwood. '88.

Haines, David W., ed. Refugees vs. immigrants: Cambodians, Laotians, and Vietnamese in America. Rowman. '89.

Harwood, Edwin. In liberty's shadow: illegal aliens and immigration law enforcement. Hoover Institution Press. '86.

Hauser, Pierre N. Illegal aliens. Chelsea House. '90.

Heer, David M. Undocumented Mexicans in the United States. Cambridge University Press. '90.

Helweg, Arthur Wesley. An immigrant success story: East Indians in America. University of Pennsylvania Press. '90.

Hewett, Joan. Hector lives in the United States now: the story of a Mexican-American child. Lippincott. '90.

Holtzman, Wayne H. & Bornemann, Thomas H., eds. Mental health of immigrants and refugees. Hogg Foundation. '90.

Hoskin, Marilyn. New immigrants and democratic societies. Greenwood. '91.

House Committee on the Judiciary, Report to the Chairman, Subcommittee on Immigration, Refugees, and International Law. Refugee program: the orderly departure program from Vietnam. U.S. General Accounting Office. '90.

Hubbard, Jim. American refugees. University of Minnesota. '91.

Immigration and Naturalization Service. Citizenship education and naturalization information. U.S. Government Printing Office. '87.

Immigration and Naturalization Service. The President's comprehensive triennial report on immigration. U.S. Government Printing Office. '89.

Jasso, Guillermina. The new chosen people: migrants in the United States. Russell Sage. '90.

Jensen, Leif. The new immigration: implications for poverty and public assistance utilization. Greenwald. '89.

Kalergis, Mary Motley. Home of the brave: contemporary American immigrants. E. P. Dutton. '89.

Kivisto, Peter & Blanck, Dag. American immigrants and their generations. University of Illinois Press. '90.

Lacey, Dan. The essential immigrants. Hippocrene. '90.

Lambertson, David F. U.S.-Vietnam relations and emigration. U.S. Department of State, Bureau of Public Affairs. '90.

Larzelere, Alex. The 1980 Cuban boatlift. National Defense University Press. '88.

Legomsky, Stephen. Immigration and the judiciary: law and politics in Britain and America. Oxford University Press. '87.

LeMay, Michael C. From open door to Dutch door: an analysis of U.S. immigration policy since 1820. Praeger. '87.

Levine, Barry B. The Caribbean exodus. Praeger. '87.

Liptak, Dolores Ann. Immigrants and their church. Macmillan. '89.

Loescher, Gil. Calculated kindness; refugees and America's half-open door, 1945 to the present. Free Press. '86.

Mangiafico, Luciano. Contemporary American immigrants: patterns of Filipino, Korean and Chinese settlement in the United States. Praeger. '88.

Martin, David A. Major issues in immigration law. Federal Judicial Center. '87.

Masud-piloto, Felix. With open arms: the political dynamics of the migration from revolutionary Cuba. Rowman & Littlefield. '87.

Moore, Jonathan. Update on immigration and refugee issues. U.S. Department of State, Bureau of Public Affairs. '89.

Morales, Julio. Puerto Rican poverty and migration. Praeger. '86.

Nathan, Debbie. Women and other aliens: essays from the U.S.-Mexico border. Cinco Puntos Press. '91.

Palmer, Ransford W. In search of a better life: perspectives on migration from the Caribbean. Praeger. '90.

Parmet, Robert D. Labor and immigration in industrial America. Krieger. '87.

Perez, Ramon. Diary of an undocumented immigrant. Westview. '91.

Portes, Alejandro. Immigrant America: a portrait. University of California. '90.

Pozo, Susan, ed. Essays on legal and illegal immigration. Upjohn Institute for Employment Research. '86.

Pozzetta, George, ed. Contemporary immigration and American society. Garland. '91.

———. Education and the immigrant. Garland. '91.

———. Ethnic communities: formation and transformation. Garland. '91.

Richmond, Anthony H. Immigration and ethnic conflict. St. Martin's Press. '88.

Rieff, David. Going to Miami: exiles, tourists, and refugees in the new America. Penguin. '88.

Rivera-Batiz, Francisco, et al. U.S. immigration policy reform in the 1980s: a preliminary assessment. Praeger. '91.

Rolph, Elisabeth & Robyn, Abby E. A window on immigration reform: implementing the Immigration Reform and Control Act in Los Angeles. Urban Institute Press. '90.

Serow, William J., ed. Handbook on international migration. Greenwood. '90.

Siegal, Mark A., et al., eds. Immigration and illegal aliens: burden or blessing? Information Plus. '89.

Simcox, David, ed. U.S. immigration in the 1980s: reappraisal and reform. Westview. '88.

Sloan, Irving J. Law of immigration and entry to the United States. Oceana. '87.

Stepick, Alex. Haitian refugees in the United States. Minority Rights Group. '86.

Suarez-Orozco. Marcelo. Central American refugees and U.S. high schools: a psychosexual study of motivation and achievement. Stanford University Press. '89.

Tomsho, Robert. The American sanctuary movement. Texas Monthly Press. '87.

Tucker, Robert W., et al., eds. Immigration and U.S. foreign policy. Westview. '90.

U.S. Department of Justice, Immigration, and Naturalization. United States immigration laws: general information. U.S. Government Printing Office. '89.

U.S. Department of State. Soviet emigration: U.S. policy. U.S. Department of State, Bureau of Public Affairs. '89.

Vance, Mary A. Alien labor: a bibliography. Vance bibliographies. '87.

Waxman, Chaim. American alive: portrait of an innovative migration movement. Wayne State University Press. '89.

Winnick, Louis. New people in old neighborhoods: the role of new immigrants in rejuvenating New York communities. Russell Sage. '90.

Yans-McLaughlin, Virginia, ed. Immigration reconsidered: history, sociology, and politics. Oxford University Press. '90.

Zucker, Norman & Zucker, Naomi. The guarded gate: the reality of American refugee policy. Harcourt Brace Jovanovich. '87.

ADDITIONAL PERIODICAL ARTICLES WITH ABSTRACTS

For those who wish to read more widely on the subject of immigration, this section contains abstracts of additional articles

that bear on the topic. Readers who require a comprehensive list
of materials are advised to consult the *Reader's Guide to Periodical
Literature* and other Wilson indexes.

California indicts the immigration law. *America* 162:163–4 F 24 '90

The California Fair Employment and Housing Commission has issued a
report that is highly critical of the 1986 Immigration Law. The law sought
to regularize the status of undocumented aliens who had come to the
United States before 1982 and to stem further illegal immigration by
penalizing employers who hire undocumented workers. When the law
was passed, many people feared that its employer penalties would lead to
discrimination against any qualified job applicant who looks or sounds
foreign, and the California report concludes that this fear was justified.
The report also asserts that the Immigration and Naturalization Service
(INS) has failed to adequately educate the public about the details of the
law's employer sanctions and antidiscrimination provisions. One of the
report's most important recommendations is that a moratorium on enforcement of employer sanctions be established until the INS can do a
better job of educating the public.

Business becomes an enforcer. Hazel Bradford and Tim Smart. *Business Week* 36–7 My 16 '88

Starting June 1, the Immigration and Naturalization Service will step up
enforcement of the Immigration Reform and Control Act of 1986. The
INS must still act cautiously on the tough new legislation, which punishes
employers of illegal workers with jail and fines of up to $10,000 per
worker. INS efforts will be hampered by a proliferation of phony citizenship papers and a shrinking labor pool that makes it tempting to hire
illegals. Employers are worried about the 1986 law's antidiscrimination
provisions, which threaten sanctions against those who refuse to consider
hiring noncitizens even as the law punishes those who hire illegals. Despite these problems, the INS's record indicates that sanctions probably
can be effective.

Hong Kong's best and brightest: ours for the asking. Gary Stanley Becker. *Business Week* 20 O 17 '88

The United States should change its immigration policies to encourage
Hong Kong's skilled emigrants to move to the United States rather than to
other countries. Since Britain's 1983 decision to turn Hong Kong over to
China in 1997, the rate of emigration from Hong Kong by skilled workers
has risen markedly. Unfortunately, computer programmers, engineers,
English teachers, researchers, middle managers, and others whose skills

would be welcome in the United States are being kept away by U.S. immigration policies, which are much stricter than those of Australia and Canada. To take advantage of the Hong Kong brain drain, the United States should significantly raise the number of skilled immigrants that it accepts from Hong Kong.

Refugees find little refuge in U.S. Dan Moul. *Christianity Today* 33:40–1 Ap 21 '89

A new Immigration and Naturalization Service (INS) policy is limiting Central American refugees' chances for receiving asylum in the United States. Refugees seeking political asylum must demonstrate well-founded fear of persecution or life endangerment in their home country. Under the new policy, which calls for a one-day adjudication at the point of entry, more than 90 percent of asylum applicants have been rejected. Those who are turned down or awaiting appeal are not eligible for work permits. Churches and humanitarian agencies are working to feed, clothe, and house refugees who are unable to support themselves as a result of the new policy.

A fortress America? Mexican immigration. Sol W. Sanders. *Current* (Washington, D.C.) 284:22–8 Jl/Ag '86

Reprinted from the Winter 1986 issue of Strategic Review. There is clear evidence to suggest that a continued influx of Mexican immigrants into the United States will have serious socioeconomic consequences. Conditions in Mexico that contribute to the problem include a rapid rise in population over the past few decades, high unemployment, and poor living conditions in urban areas. Historical factors and the U.S. economy's dependence on cheap immigrant labor also play a role. If Mexico experiences a major upheaval, like the rebellion of 1910–1924, and if the political situation in Central America continues to deteriorate, the number of Mexican immigrants will increase accordingly. Although some claim that U.S. fears are exaggerated, immigration trends indicate that the situation will only become worse until the United States addresses the problem.

Along the Tortilla Curtain. Pete Hamill. *Esquire* 113:39–41 F '90.

Millions of aliens will continue to enter the United States illegally over the Mexican border each year unless the U.S. economy collapses or the Mexican economy expands dramatically. No one is certain how many aliens cross the 1,950-mile border annually. In 1988, more than 900,000 people were stopped, arrested, and sent back to Mexico. Because so many people depart for America, Mexico is experiencing a skill drain. Skilled aliens are more likely to stay permanently in the United States than are migrant agricultural workers.

Any happy returns? Pete Hamill. *Esquire* 114:33–4 Jl '90

The Miami suburb of Sweetwater, Florida, has been a Nicaraguan strong-
hold since the early 1980s, when massive numbers of Nicaraguans began
immigrating to the United States following the Sandinista revolution.
Now that the Sandinistas are out of power, however, few of Sweetwater's
Nicaraguan residents plan to return to their native country. According to
one man, the majority of Nicaraguan immigrants left home because of
poverty, not politics. Having found the better life that they sought in the
United States, they have no reason to go back.

The anti-Malthus. Eric Hardy. *Forbes* 146:110+ D 10 '90

Author Ben J. Wattenberg is optimistic about America's future. Far from
being worried by forecasts of increased populations eating up ever-scarcer
resources, he believes that the relatively high and increasing U.S. fertility
rate and the continued attractiveness of America for smart, hardworking,
ambitious immigrants signal good fortune for the country. He notes that
competitors such as Japan and Germany have low fertility rates. He believes that the United States will be the undisputed world leader in every
important economic and military category by the end of this century.

Train 'em here, keep 'em here. Susan Lee. *Forbes* 147:110–14+
My 27 '91

The foreign students who flock to American schools for an advanced
scientific and engineering education are a valuable resource. America is
not producing enough knowledge workers, so it must rely on foreign
engineers and scientists to fill spots in some fields. Even with these imports, shortages are beginning to develop, and international competition
for the relatively few people who possess advanced scientific skills is heating up. Clearly, America needs to keep more of its foreign graduate
students, but its immigration policy undermines this effort. This policy
has long been dominated by family rather than economic considerations,
so not enough of the immigrants America accepts are skilled. Immigration laws also put obstacles in the way of both potential immigrants and
the businesses that want to hire them. To boost its economic competitiveness, America needs to change its immigration policies.

No sanctuary. Tristan Reader. *The Nation* 249:193 Ag 21–28 '89

The Bush administration has declared war on Central American refugees. Under a new Immigration and Naturalization Service (INS) plan to
stem the flow of frivolous asylum claims, asylum applicants are given brief
hearings and then summarily detained if their requests are denied, as
most are. Two new reports reveal that INS detention facilities in southern

Texas are overcrowded, unsanitary, and inhumane and that refugees are systematically denied due process. About 80 percent of the refugees do not have legal counsel, and the conditions of detention restrict their access to evidence that would prove that their fear of persecution is well founded. The House of Representatives should consider legislation that would give refugee status to all people who are fleeing war zones.

Fast track, si. Edwin Rubenstein. *National Review* 43:16 Je 24 '91

A free-trade agreement with Mexico—an occurrence that seems nearly inevitable now that President Bush has secured fast track trading authority—will be beneficial to both countries. Labor leaders have claimed that corporate profits will be increased at the expense of U.S. employment, but the agreement would actually be the latest in a series of trade moves to increase employment on both sides of the border. Since 1985, Mexico has lowered its tariffs from an average of 30 percent to 10 percent, allowing U.S. exports into the country to rise from $11.9 billion in 1986 to $28.4 billion in 1990. Because every $1 billion of exports creates an additional 22,800 jobs, the expansion of trade with Mexico has brought 376,000 jobs that otherwise wouldn't exist. Restrictive quotas, however, still govern many crucial areas of trade. If they were lifted, even more U.S. jobs would be created. Increased opportunity in Mexico would also help stem illegal immigration.

Insult to injury. Jerome E. Groopman. *The New Republic* 204:13–14 Je 24 '91

The Bush administration's recent decision to renege on altering the immigration law that bars HIV-infected foreigners from entering the United States without a special waiver owes more to homophobia and xenophobia than to the ethics of public health. The measure appears to be directed against homosexuals; there is no effort to extend the regulation to other, less stigmatized conditions, such as hepatitis and HTLV. This decision does a disservice to those infected with the HIV and to those involved in the medical struggle against AIDS. It also damages the reputation of the United States abroad. Last year, the organizers of the International AIDS Conference decided that the conference would not take place in a nation that discriminates against people with HIV. Harvard University has decided that it will serve as host of the conference in 1992 only if the law is repealed.

Texas pitches a tent city. Eloise Salholz. *Newsweek* 113:27 Mr 6 '89

In an attempt to curb an influx of Central American refugees into the United States, the Immigration and Naturalization Service (INS) has instituted new procedures for processing immigrants. Previously, applicants for political asylum were released while their claims were processed, then called back to immigration hearings weeks later. More than three-quarters of the applicants never showed up at their hearings, preferring to slip into the United States illegally. Most applications are now processed on the day they are filed. Those whose applications are rejected must await deportation in a detention center unless they can post bond. The number of aliens requesting asylum has dropped significantly since the new policy was instituted.

The great British brain drain. Donna Foote. *Newsweek* 114:60 Jl 17 '89

British scholars and scientists are fleeing Britain for the United States because the Thatcher government has not been increasing their pay to keep up with the cost of living. The academics are attracted by the comfortable housing, high salaries, and reduced work load in the United States. American universities welcome the influx and in some cases actively recruit British professors. The British education minister acknowledged the problem but asserts that professors will have to accept the country's economic realities.

Will the contras' next home be Miami? *Newsweek* 114:29 Ag 21 '89

The presidents of five Central American countries recently voted to evict the Nicaraguan contras from their bases in southern Honduras, but finding a new home for the U.S.-backed rebels may prove difficult. In Miami, which has an estimated 150,000 Nicaraguan exiles, city fathers fear a huge influx of refugees. The Bush administration wants to continue giving aid to the contras at least through February, when the Sandinistas have promised elections.

The new brain trust. Barbara Lovenheim. *New York* 24:26–33 Jl 22 '91

New York City's new breed of Russian emigres are talented, tough, proud, and determined to succeed in America. Since 1979, the New York metropolitan area's Russian population has doubled to 120,000, and if current trends continue, by the mid 1990s more than 200,000 Russian Jews will have arrived in New York since the early 1970s. They will compose the largest wave of Russian immigration to the United States since around the turn of the century. Many of the Russians who arrive in New York are happy to leave the Soviet system, although they experience extreme culture shock. The language barrier can be difficult to overcome, and highly skilled men in particular are susceptible to conflicts, anxieties, and depression brought on by the job market. It is too soon to predict what will happen to this new wave of immigrants or how they will affect New York's urban culture.

. . . and a sweep in Utah. Ron Dionne. *The Progressive* 50:18 Ag '86

In Wendover, a small casino town on the Utah-Nevada state line, local law enforcement agencies acting on behalf of the Immigration and Naturalization Service arrested 127 Hispanics in a raid that the INS claims was directed against an armed gang of illegal aliens. According to an attorney for the 71 plaintiffs in a lawsuit against the INS and other officials, the police jailed small children, deported a four-year-old boy without notifying his parents, assaulted a woman, kicked in doors, shouted racist obscenities, and demanded identification from people solely because they appeared to be Hispanic.

AIDS and the INS. Marc Ramirez. *The Progressive* 54:30–3 My '90

A misguided federal policy requires certain immigrants, including illegal aliens who are applying for amnesty under the Immigration Reform and Control Act, to undergo testing for HIV, the virus that can cause AIDS. HIV infection is on the list of dangerous contagious diseases that can be used to deny U.S. residency. According to immigration attorneys, many HIV-infected aliens do not know that the Immigration and Naturalization Service (INS) can grant waivers to people denied residency for medical reasons. Part of the problem is that many physicians and INS interviewers are unaware of the possibility of a waiver. The federal policy requiring AIDS testing has, in effect, created an underground society of people who are not receiving the treatment and counseling they need to avoid spreading the virus. The program, therefore, harms not only the immigrants but also the public health of the United States.

No American dream for Soviet emigres. Constance Holden. *Science* 248:1068–70 Je 1 '90

Despite a looming shortage of scientific manpower in the United States, many Soviet emigres with advanced degrees in science and engineering are having difficulty finding employment. The United States received 36,732 Russian Jewish refugees in 1989, and even more are expected in 1990. Many worked as scientists and engineers in the Soviet Union, but only a few have found comparable positions at U.S. universities. Barriers to their employment include educational credentials that are difficult to evaluate, lack of experience with up-to-date equipment, narrow specialization, lack of familiarity with U.S. culture, and age. Informal groups have been established to help Soviet Jews in their job searches, but the impact of these groups has been small.

Immigration challenge. *Society* 24:2 My/Je '87

According to a new report from the American Council of Life Insurance, titled New Immigrants/New Minorities, the number of Asian immigrants to the United States is expected to increase nearly sixfold to 17.3 million and the number of Hispanic immigrants should reach 36 million by the year 2030. This influx will present new challenges for the nation's schools, political parties, and economy.

Letting their people go. Bruce W. Nelan. *Time* 134:51 O 9 '89

After demanding for years that the Soviet Union loosen its emigration laws, Washington has issued rules that will severely restrict the number of Soviets allowed to enter the country. U.S. officials estimate that some 300,000 Soviet citizens will file applications for visas during the next 12 months, but Washington's annual quota will permit only 50,000 of these to receive refugee visas and another 30,000 to obtain parole status, meaning that they may come to America but are not eligible for financial assistance. The situation is embarrassing for the United States, but it is a boon for Israel, which hopes to receive an influx of refugees to balance its rapidly growing Arab population.

Hatred, fear and vigilance. Ricardo Chavira. *Time* 136:12+ N 19 '90

The continuing flood of illegal aliens across the Mexican border has fueled a wave of anti-immigrant activism in San Diego. In protest of what they see as a criminal invasion of America, hundreds of southern Californians park along the San Diego-Tijuana border and illuminate a narrow stretch of boundary with headlights and hand-held spotlights. These demonstrators reject the conventional wisdom that the illegal immigrants are benign job seekers who do work that Americans shun and that generally benefits the U.S. economy. The protests coincide with a surge in ethnic tensions and racially motivated crimes both in the local area and across the country. Armed robbers and overzealous U.S. Border Patrol agents have beaten and shot countless immigrants at the frontier. Latino activists argue that the situation in San Diego should get the same kind of high-profile attention that has been given to racial killings in New York City's Bensonhurst section and anti-Semitic incidents in France.

Browns vs. blacks. Alex Prud'homme. *Time* 138:14–16 Jl 29 '91

Once solidly united in a drive for equality, blacks and Hispanics are becoming increasingly divided. Hispanics are demanding a larger slice of the economic and political pie, and blacks fear that Latino gains will come at their expense. The major points of contention between the two largest minority groups in the United States are immigration, politics, and jobs.

U.S. immigration policy favors Cuban immigrants, who are treated as political refugees from Castro's regime, while almost all Haitian immigrants are categorized as economic refugees and sent back to Haiti. Attempts at long lasting political coalitions between blacks and Hispanics in most large cities have been difficult to sustain. Finally, many blacks fear that Hispanic immigrants will take away their jobs because they will often work for less than the minimum wage.

Fact sheet: US expands orderly departure for Vietnamese refugees. *US Department of State Dispatch* 2:225 Ap 1 '91

On April 1, the United States is scheduled to begin expanding the Orderly Departure Program (ODP) for Vietnamese immigrants and public interest parolees, refugees, and Amerasian immigrants. U.S. officials will increase the number of monthly interviews from 7,500 to 10,000, and monthly departures will increase from 6,000 persons to 8,000 persons during the summer. This expansion is expected to promote legal emigration as a safe and predictable alternative to boat departures, clear the present backlog of current immigrant visa cases, reduce the time it takes for eligible applicants to be interviewed and sent on their way, accelerate the resettlement of former reeducation detainees, conclude interviews with Amerasians by mid 1992, and give applicants an understanding of how soon ODP will consider their cases.

US response to the recent Haitian exodus. Robert Gelbard. *US Department of State Dispatch* 2:864–5 N 25 '91

In a November 20 statement before the subcommittee on international law, immigration, and refugees, the deputy assistant secretary for inter-American affairs discusses the U.S. response to the recent exodus of Haitian boat people: A regional solution was first sought in response to the flow of Haitian boat people, but after nearly 2 weeks of intense diplomacy, there has not been a sufficient number of responses from countries willing to accept the fleeing Haitians. Consequently, it was decided on November 18 to repatriate those Haitians on Coast Guard vessels, to bring to the United States those Haitians who appear to qualify for asylum, and to bring those at the naval base at Guantanamo to regional countries for temporary safehaven. A court order that has suspended repatriation efforts is expected to encourage Haitians to continue to go to sea in small, dangerous boats, which could lead to loss of life.

A fresh Irish wave laps U.S. shores. Brian Duffy and Robin Knight. *U.S. News & World Report* 102:15 Mr 2 '87

A new wave of highly skilled and well-educated Irish citizens is leaving its economically troubled homeland for the promise of prosperity in the

United States. In January of this year alone, the U.S. embassy in Dublin
approved 250,000 visa applications, compared to 40,000 for all of 1985.
Because the United States accepts only 515 Irish immigrants annually,
many come on tourist visas and never leave. There may be more than
200,000 Irish illegals in the United States. The alarming rate of emigration is a response to Ireland's desperate economic situation. Unemployment today stands at nearly 20 percent, while economic growth has stalled
at below 2 percent. Those who have jobs must endure both high prices
and high taxes.

End of the road for littlest illegals. Peter Dworkin. *U.S. News &
World Report* 102:23 Ap 13 '87

An Immigration and Naturalization Service policy that has held 200 minors at a time under lock and key for weeks or even months is generating
increasing controversy. The INS policy requires that the alien minors be
released only to parents or court-appointed guardians. For parents who
are illegal aliens themselves, this means coming out of hiding to claim
their children and subjecting themselves to deportation hearings. Children who have no parents must wait for long periods to be appointed a
permanent guardian. Homesick or discouraged by the bureaucratic red
tape, many give up and agree to be deported. The American Civil Liber-
ties Union and other groups have sued to halt the practice.

The sanctuary movement. Alan Nelson. *Vital Speeches of the Day*
52:439–42 My 1 '86

In an address delivered to the Commonwealth Club in San Francisco,
California, the commissioner of the U.S. Immigration and Naturalization
Service discusses the sanctuary movement's illegal importation of aliens:
The sanctuary movement is primarily a political protest that exploits well-
intentioned people's humanitarian instincts. The United States has the
most liberal immigration and refugee assistance policies in the world.
The Refugee Act of 1980 provides a legal method for aliens to establish
their refugee status. Sanctuary groups insist that illegal Central American
aliens who are returned to their homelands are frequently persecuted,
but statistics belie their claims. The general public does not support sanctuary resolutions. The smuggling and sponsorship of illegal aliens in the
United States erodes public respect for the law and may spur the passage
of restrictive immigration laws.